Management for a
Small Planet
Second Edition

To the seventh generation

Only if we have a beautiful world
can we have a beautiful mind and a beautiful soul.

—Father Thomas Berry

Management
for a
Small Planet
Second Edition

Strategic Decision Making
and the
Environment

W. Edward Stead
Jean Garner Stead

SAGE Publications
International Educational and Professional Publisher
Thousand Oaks London New Delhi

For information address:

SAGE Publications, Inc.
2455 Teller Road
Thousand Oaks, California 91320
E-mail: order@sagepub.com

SAGE Publications Ltd.
6 Bonhill Street
London EC2A 4PU
United Kingdom

SAGE Publications India Pvt. Ltd.
M-32 Market
Greater Kailash I
New Delhi 110 048 India

Printed in the United States of America

Library of Congress Cataloging-in-Publication Data

Stead, W. Edward.
   Management for a small planet: Strategic decision making and the
environment / authors, W. Edward Stead, Jean Garner Stead.—2nd ed.
      p.   cm.
   Includes bibliographical references and index.
   ISBN 0-7619-0293-7 (recycled paper).—ISBN 0-7619-0294-5 (pbk.:
recycled paper)
   1. Economic development—Environmental aspects. 2. Natural
resources—Management. 3. Strategic planning. 4. Industrial
management—Environmental aspects. I. Stead, Jean Garner.
II. Title.
HD75.6.S74   1996
333.7—dc20   95-50214

96 97 98 99 00 01 10 9 8 7 6 5 4 3 2 1

Sage Typesetter: Andrea D. Swanson
Sage Cover Deisgner: Candice Harman

Book printed on recycled paper.

Contents

Preface

Since the first edition of *Management for a Small Planet* was published in 1992, tremendous progress has been made in the search for sustainable strategic management systems in business organizations. On the practice side, organizations, which have historically been major contributors to environmental problems, now seem primed to become major parts of finding solutions to these problems. Pollution prevention, TQEM, design for environment, and so forth are becoming ingrained within the strategic cores of organizations around the world. Industry standards, such as Responsible Care, the ICC Business Charter for Sustainable Development, and ISO 14,000, are making excellence in environmental management a requirement for doing business in the global economy. Organizations from many of the world's developed nations, such as the United States, are making serious efforts to transfer their environmental best practices into developing nations where they have operations. Through all of this, improved environmental performance is finding its way to the plus side of the economic scorecard, helping organizations to improve both their operational efficiency and their competitiveness in the marketplace.

On the academic side, environmental management is becoming a legitimate research issue and curriculum path in business schools across the globe. Probably the most exciting and challenging part of preparing this second edition has been the journey we have taken through the incredible explosion of literature related to improved environmental performance in business organizations. Further, many schools, such as the University of Michigan, the University of Washington, and the University of Tennessee, have developed graduate curricula in environmental management, and others, such as Georgetown and Michigan, have held important conferences on environmental management research and practice. The Management Institute for the Environment and Business (MEB) is making great strides in its efforts to integrate the natural environment into business school curricula, and the Greening of Industry Network has been successful in bringing academics and practitioners together in a forum of communication and learning. The academic legitimacy of including Nature into management research and education was officially recognized by the Academy of Management in 1994, when it approved the formation of the Organizations and the Natural Environment (ONE) Interest Group.

There is a dark cloud within the silver lining of improved environmental management, however. The Earth hasn't gotten any larger since the first edition of *Management for a Small Planet* was published. It is still about 25,000 miles in circumference, about two thirds of that salt water. Yet humans have added another 270 million of their species to the planet during that time. The fastest population growth rates are occurring in the developing nations, where economic activity is also expanding the fastest. The developed nations are contributing their share to this issue as well. For example, the population of the United States, the world's third-largest country and largest per capita resource user, is rising at a rate of about 4 million people per year. If this rise continues, U.S. population growth will offset any resource savings achieved by improved environmental efficiency in business organizations, and it will severely challenge the ability of the United States to continue to provide sufficient jobs and social services for its citizens. Of course, the basic answer to achieving a sustainable global population level is to reduce birthrates, but reducing birthrates is a very complex issue with multiple, interdependent dimensions. Improved education, sufficient health care, economic and political security, and social, gender, and racial equity are some of the key factors related to reducing birthrates.

Thus, we believe that the most compelling piece in the sustainability puzzle in the coming decade may very well be finding ways to effectively factor worldwide birthrate reduction into the environmental management formula. This is indeed a tall order, but there do seem to be some natural links between long-term business success and the above-mentioned factors related to reducing birthrates. Educated, healthy, just, equitable, economically successful, politically stable societies are the ideal environments for successful business. They certainly provide the highest percentage of citizens who can meaningfully participate in the economy, both as productive members of organizations and as consumers of organizational products.

However, the entire system of economic activity will have to evolve to a different level of planetary awareness and involvement if business is to actually become a meaningful catalyst for the types of changes necessary to achieve reduced birthrates. Improved environmental management practices such as the ones discussed above are certainly important components of such efforts, but it is our sense that business organizations are going to have to be willing to go even further. We believe that achieving a sustainable balance between the economic system and the ecosystem will ultimately mean an evolution to an economy that is truly integrated into the global community. This means that organizations are going have to go beyond doing things differently; they are going to have to begin viewing things differently. They are going to have to see themselves not only as economic entities but also as integral parts of the communities in which they function, from the local community to the sovereign nation to the "society of the planet."

Many people have contributed in so many different ways to the completion of this book. Our deepest thanks to Marion Garner for all her support. She makes so many things possible for us. As in the first edition, we sincerely thank Herman Daly of the University of Maryland and Ed Gray of Loyola Marymount University, who provided us with the foundation knowledge and motivation we needed to pursue our research and teaching dreams. Also, as in the first edition, we would like to thank Glen Riecken, chairperson of East Tennessee State University's Management and Marketing Department, and Allan Spritzer, dean of East Tennessee State University's College of Business. These gentlemen have continued to provide the academic environment and support we have needed to pursue our environmental management research and teaching interests, even when these interests lead us in interesting and often unusual directions.

We also extend our most heartfelt gratitude to our friends and colleagues in the Organizations and the Natural Environment Interest Group (ONE) and the Social Issues in Management Division (SIM) of the Academy of Management, the International Association of Business and Society (IABS), and the Center of Process Studies at the Claremont School of Theology, Claremont, California. Our associations with these people have not only contributed tremendously to our professional development, they have also enriched our lives.

We offer special thanks to three scholars and friends who spent their valuable time reviewing the completed manuscript of this second edition for us—Mark Starik of the George Washington University, Gordon Rands of Pennsylvania State University, and Gary Throop of Clarkson University. Their academic qualifications, their deep personal commitments to understanding and changing the relationships between organizations and the natural environment, and their honest friendships with us are all reasons why we value their comments so highly.

As was true with the first edition, this second edition has greatly benefited from the outstanding editorial efforts of both Amanda Moss Cowran and Rick Watson. Their professional, timely assistance was invaluable to the quality, readability, and logic of this book. To Amy Wilcox Lawson, our outstanding graduate assistant and coauthor, go our deepest thanks for finding, retrieving, analyzing, and/or summarizing a significant portion of the new information that has been incorporated into this edition; her contributions to our survey research on sustainability strategy implementation are especially appreciated. And we also thank Richard Lawson for his excellent and always timely graphic art work.

The person we most want to thank in this second edition is our daughter, Garner Lee Stead, who will be 16 years old when this book comes out. We thank her, as we did in the first edition, for being our friend and teacher as well as our child. We also thank her for enduring us while we revised this book. Researching it and writing it have consumed a great deal of our time and energy, much of which rightfully belonged to Garner Lee. That time and energy were gifts from her to us that we will never be able to repay. If we have any regret about writing this book, this is it. Finally, we thank Garner Lee for being our personal contact with posterity. She is our link to the next generation, and her children will be our link to the next. Thus, it is through Garner Lee that we can visualize and commit ourselves to the "seventh generation," those children of the future to whom we owe our consideration in all of our decisions.

Prologue: Killing the Bird

One day, Gaia and the Green Man were walking in the deepest part of the forest when they saw a young boy pursuing a wondrous bird. They followed the boy, watching him stalk the bird with stealth that defied the boy's age. The bird truly had the most beautiful song that Gaia and the Green Man had ever heard, and they knew that it was the song that was attracting the boy as well. Finally, the boy set a trap, captured the bird, and took it to his home. Gaia and the Green Man watched as the boy caged and fed the bird just so that he could hear its beautiful song every morning. They also watched as the boy's father scolded the boy for spending so much money to care for the bird, saying that feeding the bird only for its song was not worth it. Well, late one night, while the boy was sleeping, the father took the bird to the top of the mountain and strangled it. However, as soon as the bird died, the father dropped dead on the very spot with the bird. The man had killed the bird, and with the bird he had killed the song, and with the song he had killed himself. (This story is adapted from an old Pygmy myth, as told in Campbell, 1988.)

Gaia and the Green Man immediately understood what had happened, and they both began to weep. The bird, like Nature, had value well beyond its economic worth. Just as the boy used his superior brain and technology to control the bird for his own purposes, humankind has used the same tools to control Nature for its own ends. Just as the father made an economic decision to destroy the bird and its beautiful song, humankind consistently destroys the natural beauty and resources of the Earth for short-term economic benefits. And just as the death of the bird meant the death of the father, humankind risks its own survival by destroying the natural environment that supports it.

As they wept, Gaia and the Green Man remembered the words of Rachel Carson in *Silent Spring* (1962): "There was a strange stillness. The birds . . . where had they gone?" (p. 2).

PART I

When Business Meets a Small Planet

What is a small planet, and what happens when business interacts with it? In this section, we attempt to answer this question. We introduce many of the ideas that we will develop throughout the book, including the dimensions and problems of a small planet, the fundamental reasons why economic activity is currently at odds with ecological sustainability, and the role of strategic managers in all of this. Then we examine the ecological problems that are occurring as the planet gets smaller and smaller. Finally, we examine several scientific principles that help to explain the interactions between business and the small planet Earth.

Chapter 1

It's Time for a Change

Humankind has reached a point in its history where it needs to reassess where it is going and how it will get there. For the past 350 years, humans have built their hopes and dreams on the concept of unlimited economic wealth. The desire for economic growth has been raised to mythic proportions that rival any religion in human history. As Joseph Campbell (1988) says, you can tell which institution a society considers most important by the relative height of its buildings. In medieval times, the churches were the tallest buildings. After the Renaissance, the tallest buildings were the seats of government. Today, the tallest buildings are the centers of economic activity. Personal and societal welfare are measured almost solely by the amount of growth experienced in the economy. More production and consumption are good. Less production and consumption are bad. It's as simple as that.

Yet as society continues at breakneck speed to produce-consume, produce-consume, produce-consume, it does so with the knowledge that eventually the very resources that support human life on this planet will be exhausted. If humans continue to foul the air and water, degrade the land, and exploit natural beauty, the human species is in danger of disappearing. It will kill its bird, it will kill its song, and it will kill itself. Father Thomas Berry (1988) says this:

> The mythic drive [for economic growth] continues to control our world even though much is known about the Earth, its limited resources, the interdependence of life systems, the delicate balance of the ecosystems, including the consequences of disturbing atmospheric conditions, of contaminating the air, soil, waterways, and seas. The drive continues despite the limited quantities of fossil fuels in the Earth and the inherent danger of chemicals discharged into natural surroundings. Although all of this has been known for generations, neither the study nor commercial-industrial practice of economics has shown any capacity to break free from the mythic commitment to progress, or any awareness that we are in reality creating wasteworld rather than wonderworld. (p. 76)

Now is the time to break free from the mythic drive for economic growth. Humans need a new economic myth based on what Joseph Campbell (1988) calls the *society of the planet*, an interconnected world community that functions in harmony with Nature. The environmental crisis is rapidly reaching epic proportions. Recent environmental issues include the depletion of the upper ozone layer, the devastation of lakes and mountaintops by acid pollution, the potential for rising global temperatures, the death and destruction caused by toxic spills and dumps, the massive deforestation of the world's rain forests for commercial purposes, the harm caused by numerous oil spills, the degradation of the oceans, and the destruction of wildlife habitats for human development. These problems have made it clear that strategic decision makers in business organizations need to reorient their choices to account for the limits of the ecosystem. Managers who make strategic decisions concerning what products to produce, how to produce them, how to sell them, and so on are in need of new approaches and frameworks that incorporate assumptions and values that are in concordance with the limits of human survival on the planet.

Purpose of the Book

The purpose of this book is to prepare managers to make strategic decisions that are both economically successful and sensitive to the Earth's natural environment. More specifically, the book is designed to (a) provide managers with a basic understanding of environmental science and environmental issues as they relate to business activity; (b) provide managers with an understanding of sustainability, including its biophysical, ethical, cognitive, and economic dimensions; and (c) provide managers with strategic decision-making frameworks and tools that will aid them in their search for long-term economic success within the limits of the ecosystem.

A Basic Model of Business and the Ecosystem

What role do the strategic decisions made by individuals in business organizations play in protecting or destroying the ecosystem? This question can best be addressed by realizing that the Earth is a living system; as such, it can survive only by achieving a sustainable balance within its various subsystems. Achieving a sustainable balance means maintaining levels of resource use, industrial activity, agriculture, population growth, and so on that can be sustained for generations to come.

The most basic living subsystems on Earth are composed of the individual organisms that inhabit it, and the most dominant of the planet's individual organisms is humankind. Because of this dominance, the decisions made by human beings are major forces influencing the ultimate state of the planet. Ornstein and Ehrlich (1989) point out that the ability of human beings to make the correct choices about how they interact with the planet depends on the accuracy of the mental processes they use to make those choices. What people perceive and how they perceive it determines how they react to it. For example, if a person perceives time in terms of a human life span, then 100 years seems to be a long time. Using such a time horizon means that 5- or 10-year periods are considered long-term planning. What if time is perceived in terms of the age of the Earth, though? In that case, a 100-year life span amounts to only about 1/45,000,000 of the total 4.5 billion years of the Earth's existence. Such a perception makes 5- or 10-year periods anything but long-term horizons. Obviously, these widely varying perceptions of the same 100 years can lead individuals to make vastly different decisions about how they use the Earth's resources.

Humans make choices in a variety of contexts, and normally those choices are made in some collective sense. Decisions are made in the context of families, business organizations, educational institutions, government agencies, interest groups, and religious denominations, to name but a few. As Etzioni (1988) points out, there is often divergence and conflict among these collectives, leading to tension within the individual members because of their varying commitments, desires, and values. In the economic realm, individuals are members of organizations that produce goods and services; they are members of the collective of consumers who purchase and use these goods and services; they are investors in the financial performance potential of business organizations; and they are often members of interest groups that monitor the actions of business organizations. Decisions are made in all of these contexts even though each may require different perceptions, assumptions, values, and ethics.

Of course, these collectives do not exist in isolation. Together they make up what is referred to as the economy, the subsystem that encompasses all global business activities. This economic subsystem is normally depicted as a closed circular flow between production and consumption. According to neoclassical economics, the costs and benefits of economic activities can be confined within this circular flow model, for all practical purposes assuming away factors outside the model as simply insignificant externalities.

This may have been acceptable earlier in human history, but current circumstances, such as rapid population growth and environmental problems resulting from global economic activity, dictate that humankind can no longer ignore these factors.

Human beings simply cannot afford to assume away the limits of the planet and the greater community and society in which economic activity takes place. As Fritjof Capra (1982) states,

> Economists generally fail to recognize that the economy is merely one aspect of a whole ecological and social fabric; a living system composed of human beings in continual interaction with one another and with their natural resources, most of which are, in turn, living organisms. (p. 188)

It seems only logical to acknowledge that global economic activity must function within the natural and social boundaries of the planet. It certainly has no place else to function. The Earth is the ultimate source of economic capital since it is the only source of natural resources that are converted to goods and services in the economic subsystem. As Daly (1977, 1991b) and others have pointed out repeatedly, the circular flow of economic activity can be sustained over the long run only if business recognizes that economic activity must function within the limits of the Earth's biophysical processes. Socially, the economic decisions made by individuals and organizations occur in the context of norms, values, emotions, and morals emitted by the larger society. Yet Etzioni (1988) contends that these factors are ignored in economic theory.

In sum (as depicted in Figure 1.1), individual organisms form the most elementary subsystems of the planet, and human beings are the most dominant individual species. Human beings are a collective species that participates in economic activities by making decisions as consumers, members of business organizations, and so forth. These decisions are based on individual perceptions of reality and involve the application of values, beliefs, assumptions, and ethics. Taken as a whole, these business organizations and consumer patterns compose the circular-flow economic subsystem of production and consumption. However, this economic subsystem is Earthbound, and thus can function only within the greater society and ecosystem. Collectively, then, human values, beliefs, assumptions, and ethics guide the production-consumption cycle. Thus, if the

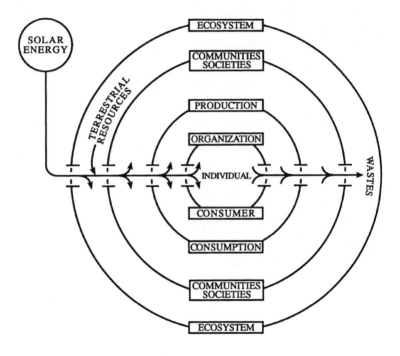

Figure 1.1. A Basic Model of Business and the Ecosystem

human species wants to maintain a sustainable balance of the Earth's subsystems over the long run, economic values and assumptions that are consistent with the limits of the Earth need to be adopted.

The Earth Is a Small Planet

Humans have historically perceived the Earth as a large, expansive space with unlimited resources that can support humankind's activities regardless of the scale and nature of these activities. Nothing could be further from the truth. The planet is small, and its capacity to support successive generations of humans is both limited and potentially threatened. Let's examine why the Earth is a small planet and getting smaller.

Unprecedented Population Growth in the Industrial Age

On the outer edges of a spinning cluster of stars and other heavenly bodies called the Milky Way galaxy lies a blue-green planet known as the Earth. The Earth has evolved from a hot, gaseous ball to a planet rich with the ingredients of life—breathable air, fresh water, abundant minerals, and so on—in approximately 4.5 billion years. Life began on Earth as single-celled algae (prokaryotes) some 3.8 billion years ago, and today there are between 10 million and 80 million species living on the planet. The evolutionary processes of the Earth have resulted in an incredible ecological balance among plant life, animal life, and the organic materials that support both (Ryan, 1992; Tobias, 1990). For example, an atmosphere has evolved that contains 21% oxygen. If this percentage were slightly lower, larger species (such as human beings) would not have enough oxygen to survive. If this percentage were slightly higher, the toxic effects of the gas would also threaten human survival (Lovelock, 1988).

For the past 350,000 years or so, the Earth has been inhabited by a species known as *homo sapiens*—humankind. The uniqueness of this species can be recognized in its name. The word *sapiens* comes from the Latin verb *sapere*, which means to be wise. Thus, this is the intelligent species, "the one with the brains" as one TV commercial put it. The human brain is so powerful that it can design and build machines able to store and process millions of times the amount of information the brain itself can handle. Frederick Taylor saw the perfect worker as an extension of the machine; on the contrary, the machines that humans create are extensions of themselves.

Before 1650, people employed their machines in very limited ways, using wheels for wagons and grain mills, for example. Most of the population was engaged in agriculture, a 10,000-year-old activity, and most people spent their time simply trying to survive. Life was very hard and tenuous, and thus, population growth was slow. There were 250 million people on Earth when Christ was born, and only 500 million people on Earth in 1650—it took over a millennium and a half for the population to double (Ehrlich & Ehrlich, 1990). Then came the Industrial Revolution with its powerful fossil fuel energy sources, mass production techniques, and modern transportation and communication systems. In only 350 years, humankind moved away from older forms of society whose primary activities were hunting, raising livestock, planting, gathering, and milling to the modern industrial society of today.

During that time, survival has become much easier and more secure. Modern farming techniques have made it possible to raise more food than humans can consume (although the prospects for the future are not so bright). High-speed communications and transportation have made it possible to speak with almost anyone in the world in a matter of seconds and carry on a face-to-face conversation with them in a matter of hours. Modern medicine has transformed deadly illnesses of the past century into minor irritations today; the human species' ability to survive has greatly improved, resulting in an unprecedented growth in the number of people on the planet. The population, which had previously taken some 1,650 years to double, doubled again to 1 billion by 1850. From 1850 to 1987 the population multiplied fivefold to 5 billion. The planet now houses 5.64 billion people, and it is estimated that this figure will come close to 10 billion by the year 2050 (Sachs, 1995).

The Earth isn't getting any bigger. This beautiful blue marble is still only 25,000 miles in circumference, three-quarters water, and much of the rest uninhabitable mountain and desert land. The Earth's natural resources are being depleted and wastes are being generated at rates unheard of in human history. Tropical forests are being cleared at an annual rate equivalent to twice the size of Austria (Acharya, 1995); water tables are being drawn down to dangerous levels throughout the world, especially in Northern Africa and the Middle East (Gardner, 1995); and soil erosion is exceeding soil replenishment rates by about 25 billion tons a year (Wilken, 1995).

The cycle of the lemmings of arctic Norway provides food for thought. Lemmings breed voraciously and eat voraciously in the grasslands of the Norwegian fjords. Early in the cycle there is plenty of food for all of them; their wastes actually fertilize the Earth, resulting in increased vegetation for them to eat. However, approximately every 4 years they overpopulate and ravage their territory. In a frenzy, they seek food elsewhere. They eventually plunge into the water of the fjord in an attempt to get to another place where food will be available. Most drown or die of exhaustion. A few survive, though, and the cycle begins again (Tobias, 1990).

From this can be gleaned the first key factor that makes the Earth a small planet. A small planet is one that is responsible for supporting a rapidly growing human population, all of whom at one level or another are seeking the improved lifestyles promised by the Industrial Revolution. By 2050, this planet may have over 10 billion people who want to own their own cars, live in their own houses, and have their own refrigerators, TVs, VCRs, stereos, computers, and robots. In other words, the planet is in a mathematical bind. Like the lemmings, humankind is doing everything possible to squeeze more and more from less and less.

The Earth Is a Closed System

All of this would be well and good if it were not for the fact that the life-giving and life-supporting processes of the Earth operate in what is essentially a closed ecosystem. According to the laws of thermodynamics, the amount of energy in the universe is constant (the conservation law), but when energy is transformed from one form to another, it always loses some of its concentration, order, and usefulness (the entropy law). The more open a system is (that is, the more it can exchange energy, information, and wastes with its environment), the more renewing it can be, and thus, the less entropy it suffers. This is because an open system is able to import sufficient amounts of energy from its environment to replenish what it loses when it transforms its own energy, and it can expel the waste products that result from this transformation back into the environment. However, the more closed a system is, the less renewing it can be because it can neither import sufficient quantities of energy to replace its depleted resources, nor can it dispose of its wastes. Thus, the more closed a system is, the more entropy it suffers.

Open and closed are relative terms. As a system, the Earth has only one significant energy input from its environment—solar flow, the sun. Through photosynthesis, solar energy provides the Earth with the power to feed all of its species; it also provides the basic energy for water and wind cycles. The remainder of the planet's energy is tied directly to terrestrial resources and processes—oil, coal, wood, water, natural gas, wind, and uranium. Further, the Earth must absorb the wastes generated when energy is converted into something useful. These wastes must be buried in the ground, dumped in the water, or spewed into the air. For all but the past 350 years of the 4.5-billion-year history of the Earth, these mechanisms provided a more than adequate amount of openness to meet the needs of life on the planet. Father Thomas Berry (1988) says,

> In the natural world there exists an amazing richness of life expression in the ever-renewing cycle of the seasons. There is a minimum of entropy. The inflow of energy and the outflow are such that the process is sustainable over an indefinite period of time. (p. 71)

It has only been during the Industrial Age that humankind has been using the Earth's resources and discharging wastes at rates faster than renewal can take place. This means that the balance the planet once enjoyed has in 350 years—a split second of eternity—almost disappeared. The Earth has embarked on an experiment unprecedented in its long history. As humankind is beginning to discover, the results of this experiment may be disastrous. Again quoting Father Berry (1988),

> So long as the human process is integral with the processes of nature, the human economy is sustainable in the future. The difficulty comes when the industrial mode of our economy dis-

rupts the natural processes. . . . In such a situation the productivity of the natural world and its life systems is diminished. (p. 71)

Therefore, the second key factor in defining the Earth as a small planet is this: Its natural resources are being expended faster than it can renew them. The population of the planet has engaged willingly in an unprecedented economic experiment, using an ecosystem that has evolved in a beautiful symphonic balance for 4.5 billion years. Although it has been known for years that the results for the human species may be nothing short of disastrous if civilization fails to adjust its rates of economic activity to the evolutionary processes of Nature, the experiment continues at full throttle. Many believe that humans can save themselves from these problems with new technologies; however, this promise remains unfulfilled. Real change will require new values and new ways of thinking.

In sum then, the Earth is a small planet—one that is limited in the life-supporting resources needed to support an exponentially increasing population base with ever-increasing economic demands. Such a dilemma puts short-term economic gratification in direct conflict with long-term survival of the species.

The Need for New Economic Models

What alternatives are available to deal with this dilemma? One solution is to leave it up to Nature to solve the problems herself. The Earth will likely be able to renew itself over time, no matter what happens. The problem with this solution is that the Earth renews itself at evolutionary speeds, and the current destruction is occurring at revolutionary speeds. Oil, top soil, and other terrestrial sources will be gone in a matter of decades, and the land, air, and water cannot clean themselves as fast as they are being fouled. Relying on nature to take care of environmental ills will mean waiting thousands of years while the Earth heals itself. Further, Nature will use mechanisms such as war, starvation, natural disaster, and disease as her means for restoring ecological balance. This is not much of a legacy for our children; more positive steps are needed.

Positive steps can certainly be taken in the form of population control. If population growth trends could be significantly reversed over the next 100 years (Kendall & Pimentel, 1994), the environmental problems would be much easier to solve. However, achieving ecological balance by focusing solely on population control will not be enough. The fire of runaway economic activity also needs extinguishing if humankind is to balance itself with the planet's ecosystem.

The facts clearly point to economic activity as a prime source of the Earth's current environmental ills. As discussed earlier, population has exploded in the Industrial Age (a fact predicted by Malthus in the 18th century). Further, while trade has multiplied 800 times in the Industrial Age and production has multiplied 100 times in the past century, energy use has risen 80 times per person, water use has risen 36 times per person, the amount of methane in the air has doubled, and the amount of carbon dioxide in the air has increased by 25% (Clark, 1989).

The lion's share of the responsibility for changing economic activity lies with rich nations such as the United States. More than 50% of the Earth's energy is consumed by the 15% of the population who are the richest (Clark, 1989). The amount of energy that goes into feeding the average American for 1 day (all of the oil, gas, chemicals, etc.) adds up to about 250,000 calories (Tobias, 1990). The average American consumes 70 times the water of the average Ghanian (Maurits la Riviere, 1989). The world's developed nations consume 12 times the energy, 10 times the steel, and 15 times the paper used by the rest of the world (Robertson, 1990).

Further, the ideals on which economic activity are based are born and grow within these large, successful industrial societies. These nations serve as the economic role models for the struggling, developing nations of the world; the free enterprise systems of successful industrial societies are seen as the most direct path to economic prosperity. This is appropriate: No economic institution in a capitalistic democracy can survive if it doesn't properly serve the interests of its stakeholders, the constituents on whom it relies for economic survival. Thus, a corporation operating in a free enterprise system has to respond to pressures from its customers, investors, employees, and so on. If these stakeholders demand that corporations be more environmentally responsible, then the corporations will have to comply in order to survive. Halal (1986) makes an excellent case that a "new capitalism" is arising from such pressures.

There is no more logical place to begin economic reform than within the discipline of economics itself. Economic theory forms the foundation of the other business disciplines, which have evolved within the basic closed circular-flow model of economic activity. That is, all the business disciplines have historically dealt with either the production of goods and services, the consumption of goods and services, or the exchange of money that links production and consumption together (see Figure 1.1). Therefore, making changes in how business is practiced requires making changes in current economic theory.

Calls for changes in economic theory are certainly nothing new. Economists have been proposing new theoretical frameworks that incorporate the Earth's limits for several years. Kenneth Boulding's famous essay, "The Economics of the Coming Spaceship Earth," was published in 1966; Nicholas Georgescu-Roegen's *The Entropy Law and the Economic Process* was published in 1971; E. F. Schumacher's *Small Is Beautiful: Economics As If People Mattered* was published in 1973; and Herman Daly's *Steady State Economics* was first published in 1977. More recently, Herman Daly's and John Cobb's *For the Common Good* was first published in 1989, and Robert Costanza's edited volume, *Ecological Economics*, which includes the thoughts of Costanza, Daly, and several other ecological economists, was published in 1991.

Calls for changes in economic theory have come from outside the discipline as well. Sociologist and management scholar, Amitai Etzioni, in his 1988 book, *The Moral Dimension: Toward a New Economics*, questions the basic foundations of neoclassical economics and cautions against applying it to management decisions without considering moral and social factors. In his 1986 book, *The New Capitalism*, management scholar William Halal contends that a trend is emerging toward a human economy that is based on smart growth. Physicist Fritjof Capra, in *The Turning Point* (1982), points out that economic theory is at an impasse because of the unrealistic assumptions it makes about the natural environment and the values that people hold. Paul Hawken (1993b), cofounder of Smith & Hawken and other successful businesses, calls for "a system of commerce . . . [that integrates] economic, biologic, and human systems" in *The Ecology of Commerce* (p. xiv).

At the heart of these criticisms is the current economic assumption that unlimited economic growth is possible forever. These scholars have developed convincing arguments contending that unlimited economic growth is a fairy tale with the potential for a nightmare ecological ending. For example, Schumacher (1973) says that the unlimited growth assumption leads to business practices that rapidly deplete the planet's resources, destroy the Earth's natural beauty, create mindless tasks for workers, and breed violence through greed and envy. Daly and Cobb (1989, 1994) and Etzioni (1988) argue that a great deal of the excessive egoism found in business practices can be tied directly to the unlimited growth assumption. All of these scholars believe that economic thought needs to be changed so that the economic system is not viewed as an entity in and of itself but as a subsystem of the larger social system and ecosystem (see Figure 1.1).

Influencing Strategic Decision Makers

As would be expected, the unrealistic assumption of unlimited economic growth has led to many strategic decisions in business organizations that have resulted in environmental harm. After all, the people who most often apply economic concepts are managers making strategic decisions in business organizations. This is the group that makes most of the decisions that have the potential to affect the balance of nature. Thus, it is within this group that changes in thinking about the relationship between economic activity and ecological sustainability are most critical.

It is important that managers understand that the economic models they adopt play a key role in shaping the values they apply to making decisions. Even though traditional economic theories ignore values in all but the most shallow and abstract ways (Daly & Cobb, 1989, 1994; Etzioni, 1988), the role of values in making complex strategic choices is well established in other areas of business, such as organizational cognition, strategic management, human resource management, and consumer behavior. Values have been clearly shown to influence not only the decisions strategic managers finally make but also the alternatives and data they choose to consider. Freeman and Gilbert (1988) say, in explaining the role of values in strategic decision making,

> The whole point of corporate strategy is to act intentionally in the name of some collective, the corporation. The alternative to corporate strategy is to act randomly or according to the dictates of an outsider. It follows that acting strategically is a matter of acting according to certain values. The values that support a corporate strategy are the most important purposes that we are able to admit to ourselves, or to discover by questioning others. (pp. 51-52)

Values are the key ingredients people use to judge right and wrong. Thus a person's ethical system is, in fact, the sum total of the values he or she holds dear. Further, corporations have ethical systems that are primarily composed of the dominant values of the key strategic decision makers in the firm (Goodpaster & Matthews, 1982). This means that ethical considerations are an inherent part of corporate strategic decision-making processes (Hosmer, 1994), whether their influence is hidden and implicit or open and explicit. Thus, it stands to reason that ethical reasoning should be incorporated as an explicit element in strategic decision-making processes (Freeman & Gilbert, 1988).

Effectively incorporating the Earth into strategic decision-making processes means extending the firm's ethical reasoning to the planet. Aldo Leopold (1949) says that humans will never be able to properly care for their natural environment until human ethical systems are broadened to include Nature.

Paul Shrivastava (1995a) suggests that this can be done in business organizations through a shift to what he calls the "ecocentric management paradigm," which "places Nature at the center of management and organizational concerns" (p. 127). Shrivastava (1995a) says that the ecocentric paradigm has two basic elements: (a) the development of industrial ecosystems made up of networks of ecologically interdependent firms and (b) the adoption of ecocentric management principles that allow for ecologically sensitive organizational structures and practices.

Plan of the Book

This book is divided into three parts. In Chapter 2 of this introductory section, we provide a summary of the environmental issues faced by the planet. We examine how the conversion of natural resources into economic outputs in order to satisfy the economic desires of an ever-increasing population base has led to problems such as global warming, ozone depletion, water pollution and depletion, deforestation, oil and mineral depletion, and land degradation. In Chapter 3, we present several scientific frameworks, including living systems theory, Gaia theory, thermodynamics, and industrial metabolism, designed to help managers understand the biophysical dimensions of doing business on planet Earth.

In Part II, we examine several frameworks that we believe are relevant to the central concept of this book—sustainability. In Chapter 4, we attempt to define sustainability, focusing on its biophysical, its socioeconomic, and its moral dimensions. In Chapter 5, we discuss complex human decision-making processes. Since strategic decisions represent the most complex and multidimensional decisions made by business managers, we attempt to provide managers with a clear picture of how their values and thought processes influence their strategic choices, and we attempt to provide managers with cognitive models that will allow them to include Nature in these values and thought processes. In Chapter 6, we discuss some of the basic fallacies of modern economic thought, and we present some of the ideas being forwarded about new, more environmentally sensitive economic models. In Chapter 7, we present a system of values for a small planet, composed of a core value of sustainability and six instrumental values, which we believe provides a solid ethical framework within which strategic managers can make choices that are compatible with both economic success and ecosystem protection.

The final part of the book focuses on how business managers can adapt their strategic decision-making approaches to include a small-planet way of thinking and acting. In Chapter 8, we present support for the idea that the Earth is a stakeholder of significant power and influence in organizations. We focus on defining the Earth as a stakeholder, and we examine in some depth the many green representatives of the Earth in the immediate business environment, including regulators, investors, consumers, employees, lenders and insurers, interest groups, and industry standard setters. In Chapter 9, we present several concepts, including ecocentric management, enterprise strategy, sustainability strategies, industrial ecosystems, learning organizations, and fundamental change efforts. When tied together, we believe that these concepts provide sound philosophical, ethical, strategic, operational, and structural dimensions for what we refer to as *sustainable strategic management*. In Chapter 10, we examine some of the specifics of managing in more ecologically sensitive ways. We discuss tools and processes of effective environmental management systems that can make it possible for organizations to be environmentally sensitive while adding value to their activities throughout the closed-loop value chain. In the concluding chapter, Chapter 11, we address the question of what is really necessary for humankind to find a sustainable balance between business and the ecosystem. We discuss some of the fallacies related to the belief that a neat win-win relationship between business and the Earth will always be possible; we present many of the barriers that have to be conquered as humankind searches for sustainability; and we conclude by discussing our belief that achieving sustainability will require a new human myth based on the *society of the planet*.

Chapter 2

The Issue Wheel

Gaia said to William, "Economic disaster is closing in on your species from all sides. Gas and oil will soon be in short supply. The reserves of precious metals and coal are being exhausted. Tropical rain forests are vanishing, while topsoil is eroding away. The human population is increasing by billions. The atmosphere is becoming denser with carbon dioxide. Your fossil fuel emissions are accumulating in the upper atmosphere, trapping the sun's radiation and thus warming up the entire planet. That might work for hothouse orchids, but not for human beings. Meanwhile, the problems associated with hundreds of millions of people stuck without the basic energy needs are rapidly escalating." (Tobias, 1990, p. 198)

This passage from Michael Tobias's *Voice of the Planet* succinctly summarizes the burdens that humankind is putting on the Earth. According to Gladwin (1993), it is generally agreed that the environmental burdens of humankind's activities can be assessed by analyzing the interactions among population growth, the level of human affluence (as measured by the growth in per capita gross national product [GNP]), and the impact of technology on the natural environment (as measured by the environmental impact of technology for each unit of GNP). Using this formula of Population × Amount of Economic Growth × Means of Economic Growth, humankind's ability to maintain today's levels of environmental degradation in 2050 will require dramatic reductions (more than 80%) in the technological impacts of GNP growth. This is because the human population is expected to double over that period and per capita GNP is expected to continue to increase (Gladwin, 1993). This will require that the developed nations of the world create lifetyles and technologies that essentially have no impact on the natural environment. Although a great deal of technological improvements can be expected over that time, they cannot be expected to achieve the kinds of technological-impact reductions necessary to support the expected population and economic growth trends (Daly, 1977, 1991a; Daly & Cobb, 1989, 1994). Thus, it appears that effectively dealing with the planet's environmental ills will mean stemming both population and economic growth rates.

Thus, like a wheel, the environmental issues faced today seem to begin at a central source and radiate out into the larger ecosystem. As depicted in the issue wheel (Figure 2.1), unlimited economic growth and population growth are acting together to create rapidly increasing production and consumption. As humankind incessantly produces and consumes in order to meet the demands of the exponentially growing number of people, it continues to deplete its resources and foul its nest with its own wastes and pollutants. The resulting problems include environmental catastrophe, poor air and water quality, loss of species, climate change, land degradation, deforestation, wetlands loss, and a lower quality of life, now and for posterity. In this chapter, we will try to present readers with a coherent summary of existing and potential environmental problems in a way that will elucidate the nature of these problems, the contribution of business activity to these problems, and the complexity of the interrelationships among these problems.

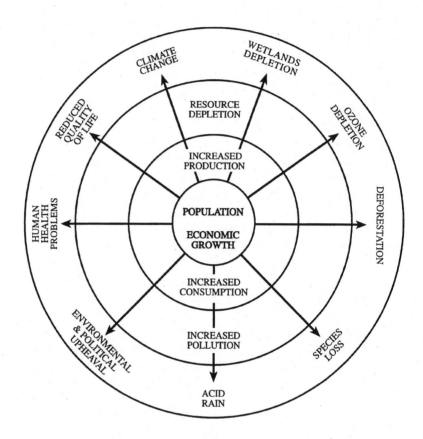

Figure 2.1. The Issue Wheel

Population and the Growth Mentality at the Hub

We demonstrated in Chapter 1 that the Earth's population is growing at a phenomenal rate, with estimates ranging as high as 10 billion by the year 2050. Well-known environmentalist Garrett Hardin (1968) spoke to this problem over 20 years ago in his classic article, "The Tragedy of the Commons," in which he graphically describes the dire consequences to the human species that may result from unlimited population growth. He demonstrates that an exponentially growing population will eventually use and degrade the natural environment to the point that scarcity of the Earth's limited life-supporting resources (which he calls the *commons*) will finally begin to affect humankind's ability to survive as a species.

An important point concerning population growth is to realize that overpopulation is not just a problem of space. A letter to the editor of the Johnson City, Tennessee, *Press* blasted environmentalists as nothing but doomsayers. The writer based his argument on the fact that all the people in the world could fit into Carter County, Tennessee. He was right, of course. Everyone on Earth can fit in a space of 1,000 square miles with 5 square feet for each person. The problem, however, is not lack of space, but the fact that it takes a vast quantity of natural resources to keep everyone alive and to absorb all of their wastes (Ehrlich & Ehrlich, 1990; Kendall & Pimentel, 1994; Ornstein & Ehrlich, 1989). Thus, overpopulation occurs "when [an area] can't be maintained without rapidly depleting nonrenewable resources . . . and without degrading the capacity of the environment to support the population" (Ehrlich & Ehrlich, 1990, pp. 38-39).

This point is critical because it is often assumed that overpopulation is solely a problem in developing nations. In fact, developed nations such as the United States, Western European countries, and Japan are overpopulated not only because of increasing numbers of people but also because they are more expensive for Nature to support. For example, the United States gained 1.2 million people in 1992, and each U.S. citizen consumed twice the grain sustainable at a worldwide level (Brown, 1994; Douglis, 1993). Albert Gore told the President's Council on Sustainable Development that each U.S. citizen has 30 times the environmental impact of someone born in India (Douglis, 1993). It was recently reported that by the year 2020, population growth in the Chesapeake Bay watershed of the United States (which includes parts of Maryland, Virginia, and Pennsylvania, as well as Washington, D.C.) may offset the environmental improvements the area is currently experiencing because of better sewage treatment and pollution control (LeBlanc, 1991).

Ehrlich and Ehrlich (1990) give an excellent example of overpopulation problems in developed nations with what they call the "Netherlands Fallacy." They point out that the Netherlands (a densely populated developed nation) has been portrayed as an example of a country that is not overpopulated. However, the Netherlands imports massive tonnages of various foodstuffs and 100% of its iron, tin, bauxite, copper, and many other minerals; further, it extracts most of its fresh water from the Rhine River, which flows in from countries to the north. Until productive natural gas fields were discovered in the 1970s, the Netherlands also imported all of its energy; these gas fields will be exhausted soon, and the Netherlands will again be 100% dependent on energy imports. Ehrlich and Ehrlich (1990) say, "The Netherlands can support 1031 people per square mile only because the rest of the world does not" (p. 39).

Although overpopulation is an issue in all corners of the globe, population growth is occurring fastest in developing nations in Latin America, Asia, and Africa, where approximately 75% of the Earth's people live (Commoner, 1990; United Nations Population Fund, 1994). The developing nations are doubling their populations about every 29 years, while the developed nations are doubling their populations about every 120 years. This gap is likely to widen in the foreseeable future because the age of the population in the developing countries is much younger than in the developed nations. Over 40% of the population of developing nations is under 15, meaning that they have most of their reproductive years ahead of them (Ehrlich & Ehrlich, 1990). That is why 90% of the world's population increases in the next century are expected in the developing world (Toufexis, 1989).

The next factor in the hub of the issue wheel is unlimited economic growth. As we discussed briefly in the last chapter and will discuss in more depth later in the book, economic growth is not sustainable forever because of the limits of the planet. Yet the potential for unlimited economic growth is a key belief that pervades current free-market economic systems; the myth that everyone can have all the material wealth he or she wants forever is still a dominant element in the economic paradigm. Peter Senge (1990) says, "For most American business people the best rate of growth is fast, faster, fastest. Yet virtually all natural systems, from ecosystems to animals to organizations, have intrinsically optimal rates of growth. The optimal rate is far less than the fastest possible growth" (p. 62).

When economic theory was first developed by Adam Smith and others in the early days of the Industrial Revolution, unlimited growth was a relatively harmless assumption because very few people in very few nations were actually involved in significant economic activity; it certainly seemed like there was plenty for everyone. However, rapid population growth and the increased number of nations involved in high levels of economic activity since that time have changed the situation drastically. If there are 10 billion people in 2050, and most of them are living in growth-oriented economic systems (which could certainly occur if current economic, political, and population trends continue), the planet will not be able to manage the stress without making significant changes in the way business is practiced. The Earth does not have the natural capital (fossil fuels, groundwater, clean air, forests, etc.) to absorb an exponential increase in humankind's assault.

For example, in the developing nations, economic growth has accelerated significantly during the 1990s, and there has been a resulting decline in the percentage of people living below the poverty line. Although this trend sounds positive, it is being offset by the rapid population growth in these countries. Although the percentages of people living in poverty may be declining, the absolute number of people living in poverty in these countries continues to increase. There are currently 1.1 billion people in the developing world living on the equivalent of about 1 U.S. dollar per day. Besides the incredible human misery indicated by such numbers, environmental stresses on the land, water, atmosphere, resources, and wildlife habitats are enormous (United Nations Population Fund, 1994). Humankind is now faced squarely with the need to evaluate what kind of economic growth and how much economic growth it wants.

Resource Depletion and Pollution Radiating From the Hub

We discussed previously the fact that the Earth is a relatively closed system with little ability to import inputs or export outputs beyond its boundaries. Thus, the increased production and consumption associated with a growing population in a growth-oriented society flies directly in the face of ecological balance. Resources are being depleted at increasingly rapid rates, and the environment is being degraded by an overflow of pollutants and waste products. Frosch and Gallopoulos (1989) estimate that if humans in 2030 consume at the same rate the average U.S. citizen consumes today, "Critical natural resources would last less than a decade. On the waste side of the ledger . . . [humankind] would generate 400 billion tons of solid waste every year—enough to bury greater Los Angeles 100 meters deep" (p. 144). In this section we examine the problems of resource depletion and pollution more closely (see Figure 2.1).

Depleting Resources

Resources are so important because, ultimately, they are the only capital humans have. They are the basic source of material wealth, financial wealth, and psychological wealth. The news on how well humans are protecting their natural capital is not good. Per capita decreases are expected in a variety of worldwide renewable resources, including fish and agricultural land (Postel, 1994). Commenting on this, Ornstein and Ehrlich (1989) say,

> Humanity is living largely on its "capital." . . . The capital that we inherited included fossil fuels, high grade mineral ores, rich agricultural soils, groundwater stored up during the ice ages, and above all, the millions of species that inhabit the Earth along with us. Our total inheritance took billions of years to assemble; it is

being squandered in decades. . . . We are a nouveau riche species struggling to become nouveau broke. (pp. 45-46)

One of the planet's most precious resources, forests, are disappearing at an astonishing rate. This is especially true in the tropics (Acharya, 1995; Brown, 1993; Postel, 1994), where 154 million hectares were cleared from 1980 to 1990, leaving only 1.75 billion hectares remaining worldwide (Acharya, 1995). Only 1 tree is being planted for every 10 cut in the tropics (McNeill, 1989). Albert Gore is fond of pointing out that all of the world's military forces would be aimed at a giant alien monster from outer space if it were tromping down the rain forests at a rate of one football field per second (approximately 45,000 square feet). Yet that is the rate at which these forests are disappearing. Ethiopia's forest cover declined from 30% of its land to 1% of its land in 40 years. India's forest cover has declined from over 50% to around 14% since 1900. In Brazil, where Chico Mendes died protecting what he called the "lungs of the planet," 20 million acres are being cut annually (McNeill, 1989). Indonesia is second in deforestation to Brazil, cutting 12,000 square kilometers per year (Petrick & Quinn, 1994). With these forests go the habitats of most of the Earth's species, the water and watersheds for billions of people, the ability of the planet to combat global warming, and much of the oxygen needed to breathe (Acharya, 1995; Durning, 1994).

Economic activities are the primary culprit in this problem. The forests are being harvested and shipped to nations such as Japan and the United States where they are converted into wood for furniture, homes, chopsticks, and so on. Forest clearing is also occurring in order to convert the land for farming and raising livestock. The economic life span of a cleared tropical forest is incredibly short; farming can be conducted for only 3 to 5 years and grazing for only 5 to 10 years (Brown, 1993). Lester Brown (1993) says, "Clearing tropical forests is, in effect, the conversion of a highly productive ecosystem into a wasteland in exchange for short-term economic gain" (p. 6).

Wetlands are another land resource that is rapidly disappearing. Between one quarter and one half of the world's coastal and

inland wetlands have been the victims of construction, channeling, draining, pollution, or some combination of these (Corson,
1994). Over the past 20 years in the United States, 11 million of
the 100 million acres of wetlands (mostly in Florida and Louisiana) have disappeared. Wetlands are vital ecosystems that help
to stem floods and erosion, replenish groundwater aquifers,
and facilitate the settling or removal of inorganic matter and
organic microbes (Kolluru, 1994). Further, wetlands, like tropical forests, are rich in biodiversity (Gore, 1992; Kolluru, 1994).
Most of the endangered species in the United States depend on
the wetlands for their survival (Kolluru, 1994).

Nonrenewable fossil fuels are also being exhausted at incredible rates, and this trend is likely to increase in the years to
come as the economies in Central and Eastern Europe and
developing nations continue to expand (Brown, 1995a). Oil
consumption is an especially complicated issue. As current
sources of oil are exhausted, new sources are sought. These new
sources are invariably less accessible and more costly, both
economically and environmentally. The cost of oil production
has increased exponentially, doubling every 15 years (Commoner, 1990). Although there is currently an excess in the
amount of oil being produced worldwide, this is likely to reverse itself by the year 2000, when the world will need 5 to 8
million additional barrels of Middle Eastern oil per day to keep
up with demand (Flavin, 1995a). If substitutes for oil are not
found, massive shortages and price increases are likely to occur
beginning around 2020 (Commoner, 1990). If the economic
upheaval, human suffering, war, and environmental destruction associated with humankind's greed for oil in the last quarter of the 20th century are any indication of what may happen
when this occurs, then humankind has some serious problems
to face.

The reserves of topsoil and cropland are also being consumed at unsustainable rates. Topsoil and cropland loss are
interrelated, multidimensional problems that involve overcul-
tivation, salinization, wind, use of chemical fertilizers, and
urbanization (Brown, 1995b). It is estimated that 24 to 26 billion
tons more topsoil are depleted every year than are replenished

by Nature (Brown, 1993; Ehrlich & Ehrlich, 1990). This leads to nutrient loss and eventually cropland loss (Wilken, 1995). Cropland has not expanded over the past 15 years, and this trend is expected to continue. Given the rapid population growth, this means that humankind can expect a long-term decline in usable cropland per person (Brown, 1995b). Humans in general and the agricultural industry in particular face a real challenge in the next century—trying to feed twice the current population on less land with less environmental damage (Crosson & Rosenberg, 1989).

Agriculture is a major contributor to another resource problem as well—the loss of water. Water use has tripled globally since 1950 (Postel, 1993), and the amount of irrigated cropland has also risen dramatically in that period (Brown, 1992). The annual world water use rate is currently equivalent to eight times the flow of the Mississippi River (4,340 cubic kilometers) (Postel, 1993). Irrigation is primarily responsible for the rapid depletion of the Ogallala aquifer under the Great Plains of the United States as well as the aquifers under the San Joaquin Valley of California (Ehrlich & Ehrlich, 1990; Gore, 1992). Aquifer depletion is also occurring in other parts of the globe. For example, China faces water shortages by the year 2000 because of water table drops of 1 meter per year (Brown, 1992; Ehrlich & Ehrlich, 1990), and India is already reporting declining water tables and wells going dry (Brown, 1992). Twenty-six countries are now considered "water scarce," meaning that they have a per capita water supply of less than 725 gallons per day (Postel, 1993). Ten of these countries, all in the Middle East and North Africa, already consume water beyond renewable rates, and six other nations in those regions will exceed their renewable water use rates in the near future (Gardner, 1995).

Increasing Pollution

So there is little doubt that humankind is overspending its natural capital. But where does it go? The answer, of course, is that it goes into the air, water, and ground in the form of environmentally degrading pollution. These are human wastes:

Although human wastes are normally thought of in terms of personal biological processes, it is time to expand that term to account for the incredible amount of "stuff" emitted into the environment as a result of consumption and production processes.

Let's begin by examining air pollution. Fossil fuel burning, biomass burning (i.e., burning the rain forests to clear them for grazing land, or burning wood in stoves and fireplaces), agricultural activities, and declining forest cover are infusing massive quantities of toxins into the atmosphere every day (Faltermayer, 1989). During the Industrial Age, there has been an unprecedented increase in the presence of potentially dangerous trace gases in the atmosphere; trace gases are those that make up a very small proportion of the total atmospheric gases.

Examples of dangerous trace gases that are increasing in the atmosphere include sulfur and nitrogen compounds, which are being released into the air at more than twice the rates today than in 1950 (Kane, 1994). Sulfur dioxide (SO_2) has increased from .03 parts per billion to 50 parts per billion, nitrogen oxides (NO and NO_2) have increased from .001 parts per billion to 50 parts per billion, and nitrous oxide (NO_2) is expected to increase from 310 parts per billion to 350 parts per billion by the year 2030 (Graedel & Crutzen, 1989).

Methane (CH_4), another trace gas, is expected to increase from 1,700 parts per billion to 2,500 parts per billion by the year 2030 (Graedel & Crutzen, 1989). Various chlorofluorocarbons (CFCs) currently account for 3 parts per billion in the atmosphere, and this concentration will continue to grow for several years (Graedel & Crutzen, 1989; Ryan, 1995), although production of CFCs is currently dropping drastically worldwide (Ryan, 1995). Another trace gas, the hydroxyl radical (OH), presents a different problem. OH exists in concentrations of only .00001 parts per billion; however, it serves as a primary filtering agent for the atmosphere. Recent data indicate that OH may very well be decreasing; if this occurs, the atmosphere's ability to cleanse itself could be seriously affected (Graedel & Crutzen, 1989).

By far the most prominent trace gas in the atmosphere is carbon dioxide (CO_2) (at over 350,000 parts per billion); it is also the trace gas that is increasing most rapidly (Graedel & Crutzen,

1989; Lemonick, 1989; Roodman, 1995a). Each year about 6 billion tons of CO_2 are released into the atmosphere (Roodman, 1995a). The primary responsibility for CO_2 emissions lies with industrialized nations; for example, CO_2 in the United States is emitted at a rate of 5 tons per person per year, which is five times the world's per capita rate (Weiner, 1990). However, the fastest rise in CO_2 emissions is occurring in developing nations in Asia and Latin America (Roodman, 1995a). A great deal of the excessive increases in CO_2 in the atmosphere during the Industrial Age can be attributed to the reduction in the Earth's vegetation due to increasing population and economic growth. Since plants take CO_2 out of the air, declining vegetation means that the ecosystem has less ability to remove CO_2 (Commoner, 1990). Currently, the Earth's vegetation and oceans do not have the capacity to absorb the planet's CO_2 emissions (Roodman, 1995a).

Humankind is being no kinder to its water than it is to its air. Besides using water at irreplaceable rates in many corners of the globe, toxic chemicals and other waste products have been poured into the world's water supply as if it were a personal dump. The notion that people can put what they want into the waterways regardless of who is downstream has led to a major decline in the availability of safe drinking water throughout the world. Human and animal wastes, agricultural wastes, and industrial wastes are dumped into the Earth's aboveground and underground waterways (Maurits la Riviere, 1989). Almost half the waterways in the United States are polluted, which has led to often serious declines in edible fish and restrictions on recreational activities ("Twenty-Sixth Environmental Quality Index," 1994). The Mississippi River from Baton Rouge, Louisiana, to New Orleans, Louisiana, has been declared "cancer alley" because of the high levels of carcinogenic chemicals discharged into it by the hundreds of chemical plants along that stretch of the river. Toxins are injected into groundwater as well as surface water. The U.S. Geological Survey tested over 100,000 wells in the agricultural regions of the nation in the early 1980s, finding that there have been dangerous increases in nitrates (from fertilizers) as well as other toxic chemicals (Commoner, 1990). The oceans and seas don't seem to be faring much better, suffering from huge amounts of human discharge (Gore, 1992; Weber, 1994).

Even with these problems, the water resources in the developed countries have been steadily improving over the past 30 years, primarily because the public has let it be known that it would not tolerate unsafe water. The citizenry in developed countries has demonstrated loud public outrage over incidents such as the dumping of dioxin into the Pigeon River in Tennessee and North Carolina; the conflagration of the Cuyahoga River in Cleveland, Ohio; the massive dumping of metals, dyes, fertilizers, and herbicides into the Rhine River; and the dumping of mercury into the waters around Minimata, Japan. However, the public outcries for clean water are not as loud in the developing world, and the results have been disastrous. The overall concentration of dangerous pollutants in the world's waterways continues to increase at rapid rates. Water pollution has reached critical levels in many parts of the world, including India, Peru, and most of the countries in the former Soviet block (Gore, 1992).

The wastes that are not spewed into the air or poured into the water have been buried in the ground. On average, each U.S. citizen personally generates about a ton of solid waste per year; further, industrial solid wastes in the United States are generated at a rate of 1 ton per citizen per month (Gore, 1992). Most of these solid wastes go into the 5,000 or so municipal landfills still operating; in 1979 this number was 20,000, but 15,000 of them have since reached capacity and closed their doors (Gore, 1992; Langone, 1989). Finding new landfill locations has become a major political issue all over the country (Gore, 1992).

In addition to the landfill problem, there is the issue of disposing of hazardous wastes. The chemical industry is responsible for generating two thirds of all hazardous wastes. There are about 80,000 chemicals currently in use in significant amounts across the globe, and the vast majority of them have hazardous waste by-products that must be disposed of in some way. Besides chemicals, other significant hazardous wastes include heavy metals, petroleum-refining wastes, medical wastes, and nuclear wastes (Gore, 1992).

Although they don't come close to matching the amount of chemical wastes generated, nuclear wastes represent the most serious hazardous waste disposal problem facing humankind (Gore, 1992). Since 1965, the amount of nuclear wastes in the world awaiting burial has risen from 270 tons to 130,300 tons, and this number is rising by about 10.5 tons per year (Lenssen, 1995a). Many of these wastes will be dangerously toxic for thousands of years to come, and yet none of the 25 or so countries that produce nuclear wastes have come up with an acceptable solution for their disposal (Gore, 1992; Lenssen, 1995a). About 25% of all nuclear wastes have accumulated in the United States. Although these come from both power generation and weapons production, weapons-related nuclear wastes present the most pressing problem in the United States (Gore, 1992). The Department of Energy (DOE) has estimated that it will cost Americans $200 to $300 billion to safely bury the weapons-related nuclear wastes currently stored at 17 DOE facilities in 13 states, but others estimate that the figure will be three times that much (Murphy, 1994).

The Wheel of Misfortune

Thus, as can be seen from the above discussion, humankind is spending its natural resources more rapidly than they can be replenished, polluting air, water, and land in the process. In short, people are bankrupting themselves of the natural capital on which they depend for survival. Several environmental problems have resulted from these resource-depleting and polluting activities. Let's examine some of these environmental problems, which are portrayed on the outer rim of the issue wheel (Figure 2.1).

On August 7, 1978, President Jimmy Carter declared Love Canal, New York, the United States's first nonnatural disaster. Underneath an elementary school and a residential community with 239 homes, a toxic soup of some 200 chemicals had risen to the surface. This soup was the end result of a gaggle of mistakes made by Hooker Chemical Company, the City of Niagara Falls, New York, and many others over a period of 35 years (Hoffman, 1995). Love Canal quickly became the most famous symbol of environmental disaster in the world. Environmental disasters read like a list of nations, towns, and waterways on a perverted guided tour: Besides Love Canal, hundreds of oil wells were set ablaze in the Kuwaiti desert, and billions of gallons of oil were poured into the Persian Gulf by Iraqi soldiers during the Gulf War. There have been major oil spills at Monterey, California; Valdez, Alaska; Galveston Bay, Texas; and in the Shetland Islands. Chemical disasters have occurred at Times Beach, Missouri; Sacramento River, California; and Bhopal, India. Nuclear meltdowns have taken place at Three Mile Island, Pennsylvania, and Chernobyl in the former Soviet Union.

In addition to these man-made natural disasters, there have been numerous political confrontations associated with scarce resources, especially petroleum. The Arab oil embargo was imposed on nations who supported Israel in 1973, and the Gulf War was fought over Iraq's attempts to control the world's oil supply. But even though these environmental and political upheavals become major media events for a time, they are only the tip of the iceberg in terms of events causing environmental problems for the planet. For example, more motor oil is deposited into U.S. waterways every year than the oil that was spilled by the *Exxon Valdez* (Shrivastava, 1996). As Ornstein and Ehrlich (1989) point out, single spectacular events capture people's attention, but insidious long-term problems are often ignored.

One of these insidious problems is climate change. The increasing trace gases in the atmosphere mentioned earlier increase the Earth's potential for trapping heat near the surface and may result in rising temperatures now and into the future. CO_2 is by far the most prevalent and most important of the *greenhouse gases*, with others being carbon monoxide, methane, CFCs, and nitrous oxide (Roodman, 1995a). Experiments aboard the space shuttle *Endeavor* in the spring of 1994 found much higher

levels of greenhouse gases in the Earth's atmosphere than expected (reported on *CNN Prime News,* April 15, 1994).

Scientists have found that CO_2 levels and global temperatures have closely paralleled one another over the past 160,000
years, and they have found that both CO_2 levels and temperatures
have risen significantly since 1800. Also, the 10 warmest years
ever recorded have happened since 1980 (Roodman, 1995c).
Further, the area of the oceans with water temperatures exceeding 80 degrees Fahrenheit has increased by one sixth in the last
20 years, and the sea levels around the world are now believed
to be the highest in 5,000 years (E. Linden, 1994). Although there
is no debate over the fact that these signals may all indicate the
possibility of the *greenhouse effect,* there certainly is debate over
whether it will actually occur, to what degree it will occur, and
over what period of time. Will the average temperature rise 8
degrees or only 1 degree? Will it take 50 years or 150 years
(Schneider, 1989)? The most important question, however, may
be whether or not humankind can afford to wait and see. Is it
worth risking natural disasters such as increased hurricanes,
dramatic changes in the availability of farmland, the destruction of thousands of ecosystems, and the sinking of vast coastal
lands into the sea in order to have enough proof (E. Linden,
1994; Roodman, 1995c)?

Stratospheric (upper atmosphere) ozone (O_3) depletion is
another serious atmospheric condition. This depletion is primarily linked to one particular family of chemicals, CFCs, which
have been used since the late 1920s in air conditioning, refrigera-
tion, propellants, and solvents. The stratospheric ozone layer
protects the Earth from the ultraviolet radiation of the sun.
Without this protection, there is likely to be an increase in skin
cancer, a reduction in human immune system efficiency, and
potentially devastating effects on the food chain (Graedel &
Crutzen, 1989). The first hole in the ozone was discovered over
Antarctica in the late 1970s; by 1993, this hole had grown by 15%
(Ryan, 1994). The National Aeronautics and Space Administration (NASA) discovered an average worldwide decrease in
stratospheric ozone levels of about 3% from 1979 to 1991, but
the most serious losses are currently occurring in the temperate

zones of the northern hemisphere. In 1993, the ozone levels over North America, Europe, and Asia were about 14% below normal (Ryan, 1994).

There is some good news about stratospheric ozone depletion, however. Since the signing of the Montreal Protocol (discussed more thoroughly in Chapter 8), the production of CFCs has greatly declined. CFC production reached a record 1.25 million tons in 1988, but it has fallen to less than 300,000 tons since then, and it is hoped that it will be eliminated worldwide by 2005. Because of the 3- to 5-year time lag between the release of CFCs and their arrival into the stratosphere, the decline in production is not expected to result in reduced stratospheric ozone depletion until around 1998. However, assuming that production ceases as planned, the ozone levels in the upper atmosphere should be restored to 1979 levels by 2050 (Ryan, 1995).

Although ozone is necessary in the upper atmosphere, it causes smog when it exists in abundance in the lower atmosphere (Gore, 1992). Smog occurs when various trace gases react with solar radiation in the lower atmosphere "to produce reactive gases that can be destructive to living organisms" (Graedel & Crutzen, 1989, p. 61); thus, as fossil fuels are burned to power the economy, more smog is created. Ozone is the most prominent of these reactive gases; lower-atmosphere ozone levels have increased between 4 and 10 times in the past century. Smog has been related to eye and lung problems in human beings as well as to damage to foliage and agricultural crops (Graedel & Crutzen, 1989). Smog is a major problem in many large urban areas in the developed world, such as the Los Angeles basin, which exceeds U.S. air quality standards by a factor of 2.5 (Arnold & Long, 1994). Smog has also seriously reduced visibility in many national parks across the United States, such as the Great Smoky Mountains and the Grand Canyon. However, smog is an even more acute problem in heavily populated urban areas in the developing world, where 1.2 billion people are exposed to excessive lower-atmosphere air pollution (Steer & Wade-Gery, 1994).

Further, not all of these pollutants stay in the air. Certain trace gases have water-soluble molecules and thus mix with the moisture in the air to come back as *acid rain* (a term used to describe acidic snow, dew, and fog as well as rain). Nitrogen oxides and sulfur dioxide, released into the air because of the burning of fossil fuels for industrial activity, transportation, and so on, go through chemical reactions in the atmosphere and are converted into nitric acid and sulfuric acid. These acids mix readily with water molecules and plunge back to Earth in the form of precipitation. The result has been the acidification of lakes and streams, the decline in the diversity and the number of fish in certain regions, and the destruction of forests ("The Acid Rain Report," 1989; Graedel & Crutzen, 1989; Kane, 1994). States in the Northeastern United States, the Southern Appalachians, and the upper Midwestern United States have experienced serious problems of acidic pollution, as have Canada and many Central and Eastern European nations ("The Acid Rain Report," 1989; MacKenzie & ElAshry, 1989; "Vital Signs," 1991). Mt. Mitchell, North Carolina, the highest peak in the United States east of the Mississippi River, has lost many of its trees, and these effects are now being seen on lower peaks in North Carolina and Tennessee. However, there is some good news: After 40 years of steady increases, the sulfur and nitrogen emissions responsible for acid rain began to level off in the 1990s because of improved industrial technology, especially in the developed nations of the world. Unfortunately, low-quality coal powers 75% of China's economy, so these gains could easily be offset as China's economic machine continues to grow (Kane, 1995).

Many scientists believe that the worst problem resulting from polluting and resource-depleting activities is declining biodiversity. Noted biologist Edward O. Wilson (1989) says, "In one sense the loss of diversity is the most important process of environmental change . . . because it is the only process that is wholly irreversible" (p. 108). Of the between 10 million and 80 million species currently inhabiting the planet, only 1.4 million have been classified (Ryan, 1992). At least 140 species a day are being driven to extinction, and this trend is predicted to continue for years to come (Corson, 1994). Extinction is nothing new; 99% of the species that have inhabited the Earth are now extinct. However, the current rate is 1,000 times higher than at any other time in history (Easterbrook, 1989; Linden, 1989). For example, 6,600 of the 9,600 species of birds on the planet (70%) are either declining or are in danger of extinction (Youth, 1994). Most of the decline in biodiversity is occurring in the tropics, where between 60% and 90% of the Earth's species live (Acharya, 1995). Further, approximately 25% of pharmaceuticals are obtained from tropical plants (Linden, 1989), and most of the Earth's 75,000 plants with edible parts exist in the tropics (Wilson, 1989). Given all these facts, it seems that carelessly shepherding species into extinction without even discovering them, much less determining their usefulness, makes little sense.

There are also direct human health costs of the Earth's depletion and pollution problems. Over 20% of the planet's population is exposed to dangerous levels of air pollution (Brown, 1993; Steer & Wade-Gery, 1994); over 30% do not have safe drinking water; and over 50% do not have safe sanitation facilities, meaning that their drinking water is threatened (Gore, 1992; Steer & Wade-Gery, 1994). Some of the health costs of conditions such as these include cancer, birth defects, malnutrition, radiation poisoning, respiratory problems, chronic bronchitis, emphysema, dysentery, cholera, and typhoid. Further, these health costs are more often born by the poor in the developing world. For example, four of five common diseases in the developing world are waterborne, and they are killing about 25,000 people every day (Gore, 1992). Of the deaths in sub-Sahara Africa, 62% are related to poor drinking water and sanitation (Steer & Wade-Gery, 1994). In the *maquiladoras* of Mexico (industrial plants, many from the United States) that have concentrated in towns along the U.S. border, there are widespread reports of illness, birth defects, and ecological degradation (Gore, 1992; Selcraig, 1994). The New River of Northern Mexico and Southern California, into which many of the wastes from the *maquiladoras* are discharged, is considered the most polluted river in North America (Gore, 1992).

The human health costs of environmental degradation are also most often borne by laborers. For example, accidents with toxic substances and long-term exposure to them contribute significantly to the fact that workers in the oil, chemical, and nuclear industries in the United States have a life expectancy 10 years below that of the average American (Mazzocchi, 1990). Cancer in the workplace is a particularly insidious employee health problem related to pollution and wastes. Worker exposure to carcinogenic materials is a long-standing and well-documented problem (Stead & Stead, 1980, 1986). Asbestos was suspected of causing lung cancer as early as 1930 (Epstein, 1975). Chemicals such as arsenic, vinyl chloride, chromium, nickel, and benzene are often found in the workplace and have been identified as carcinogenic (Cole & Goldman, 1975). Epidemiologic evidence suggests that cancers of the lungs, liver, urinary bladder, skin, and hematopoietic and lymphatic systems are related to occupation (Swanson, 1988).

There is, however, widespread disagreement about the incidence levels of cancer caused by occupational factors. One reason is that the data are so incomplete. For example, there is no information available on the health effects of more than 80% of the chemicals produced and used in U.S. industry (Misch, 1994). Also, determining incidence levels of cancer is a complex and inexact process at best. The best available data show that about 4% of all cancer is directly caused by occupational exposure to carcinogens (6% for males and 2% for females) (Peto, 1985). However, when this figure is extended to include cases in which occupational carcinogens play a partial as well as a direct role in the chances of employees developing cancer (for example, when an industrial carcinogen reacts synergistically with tobacco smoke), then it is believed that between 20% and 38% of the total incidence of cancer is occupationally related (Bridbord, Decoufle, & Fraumeni, 1978). Regardless of whether the proportion is 4% or 38%, the numbers are significant since cancer accounts for hundreds of thousands of deaths each year.

If people were to ask themselves if economic growth improves their quality of life, their initial reaction would likely be that it does. But a closer look at this question reveals that unlimited material consumption is not all that it is cracked up to be. Abraham Maslow pointed out years ago that material growth does not necessarily bring personal fulfillment on the job or in life. People's personal happiness is based on meaningful social relationships and sufficient opportunities to grow personally and spiritually.

Both Wachtel (1989) and Durning (1992) make excellent cases that more does not necessarily mean better or happier. Wachtel (1989) points out that from 1958 until 1980, the proportion of air conditioners in the U.S. population rose 484%, freezer use rose 134%, clothes dryer use rose 356%, and dishwasher use rose 743%. (Remember this is proportionate use, meaning that the percentage of the population having access to these appliances rose by these astounding figures.) Durning (1992) says that the world has consumed more goods since 1950 than it did in all of history previous to that time. If it were ever going to be proven that increased material growth means more happiness, then this was the time to prove it. But guess what? People were *not* happier. In fact, people perceived that their quality of life declined during the period that Wachtel and Durning address. The 1970s are viewed as a time of stagflation, when growth rates were low and prices (especially energy prices) were high. President Reagan won a landslide election over President Carter in 1980 by asking, "Are you better off than you were four years ago?" Most Americans answered no and rushed to elect a new President—even though real income was actually up 6%.

Why? How can people feel worse off when they are economically better off? Wachtel (1989) says that such feelings are due to the growth mentality that causes high levels of psychological stress. Two cars were a luxury for the last generation, but they have become a necessity for the current generation. If parents bought their dream house in their 40s, their children feel that they should buy theirs in their 20s. On and on it goes until this penchant for material consumption knocks the wind out of human psychological well-being. Kanter and Mirvis (1989) have documented an American society that is cynical and disillusioned. Lester Milbrath (1990) calls growth "a false god," and Fritjof Capra (1975) warns that, just as a person traveling east will eventually end up in the West, the incessant accumulation of economic wealth will eventually lead to a poor quality of life.

Conclusions

Population and the unlimited growth mentality react together like two equally powerful tug-of-war teams matched on a dirt field with a muddy pond between them. They pull at each other with all of their might. As they continue the endless cycles of digging in, sliding to the edge of the pond, and pulling away; they destroy the dry ground under their feet until it slowly absorbs the water from the pond. Long before the end of the contest, each team is likely to be mired in grime and mud. As the pressing questions concerning how much population growth and economic growth humankind can afford are pondered, try to imagine a world in which 10 billion people on the planet enjoy the same growth-oriented lifestyle of the average U.S. citizen with all the ecological and psychological baggage that this entails. Then it becomes clear that, in fact, it may not be advisable for everyone to be as "well off" as the average U.S. citizen, even if it were possible. The Earth and its human inhabitants simply cannot afford it. Posterity cannot be risked for short-term economic gain. People are not any happier (and in fact they are less happy) in spite of increased economic wealth. The current economic activities are dangerously affecting the air that people breath, the water that people drink, the land that people live on, and the life conditions of other living species of the Earth. Donald Trump once told Larry King of CNN that business is all just a game. Well, if that is true, and no doubt many believe that it is, then some new rules for the game are sorely needed—rules that will protect planet Earth, the household of all living things.

Chapter 3

Management Happens on Earth

Strategic managers are frequently eyewitnesses to the environmental impacts of their decisions. Some of the first people on the scene at Three Mile Island and Valdez, Alaska, were executives. Warren Anderson, then CEO of Union Carbide, went directly to India after the accident at Bhopal, and he was arrested when he got there. Strategic managers see smokestacks, drain pipes, and emission statistics on a regular basis. All this exposure should make one fact obvious to these managers: They are Earthbound in practicing their profession.

The problem is that business managers are trained to focus on only one of the Earth's many subsystems—the economic subsystem (see Figure 1.1). However, the economic subsystem does not exist in isolation. Long-term economic well-being can exist only within an ecosystem that has sufficient energy and resources to support it. Thus, strategic managers interested in making decisions that are compatible with the long-term survival of the human species need a basic understanding of the living system called Earth. The purpose of this chapter is to provide such an understanding. We will examine the Earth as a living system, explore Gaia theory, discuss the relationships between the laws of thermodynamics and economic activity, and examine the economic system from a metabolic perspective.

The Earth Is a Living System

A basic mystery for humankind is defining *life* itself. It is like trying to solve a series of riddles with no answers. Where does it come from? Where does it go? Why can humans destroy it but not create it? Science, philosophy, and religion sprang from humankind's quest to solve these riddles, but so far they've generated more questions than answers. Dictionaries provide little insight; they define life as that which distinguishes the living from the dead. Our favorite definition of life comes from Michael Tobias (1990) who says, "Life is the energy that organizes matter into self-portraits" (p. 50).

Though people may not be able to define it, they know life when they see it. The difference between alive and not alive is fairly obvious in most cases. Since life can't be defined but is usually easy to recognize, scientific inquiries into its nature are typically restricted to delineating those characteristics that help to distinguish the living from the nonliving. For example, it is known that living things have boundaries (qualities that distinguish them from their environments); process matter, energy, and information; maintain individual identity; are made of living parts; and live in collectives with others of their kind (Lovelock, 1988).

What Is a Living System?

The term *living system* refers to something that exhibits the characteristics of life. A living system doesn't have to be alive in the biological sense, but it does have biological functions, such as birth, death, and reproduction. A living system is open, meaning it exchanges information, matter, and energy with its environment in order to counteract uncertainty and decay. It receives feedback from its environment, and that helps it balance inputs and outputs to maintain a dynamic equilibrium. A living system is morphogenetic, meaning that it can renew, reproduce, and/or regenerate itself. A living system has some purpose, goal, or final state that it seeks (Lovelock, 1979, 1988; Sheldrake, 1991; Van Gigch, 1978).

A living system is complex; it is composed of a finite number of component subsystems, each of which process information, matter, and energy. These component subsystems are highly interdependent and cannot be treated as isolated entities. A living system is an irreducible whole; its survival is threatened when its component subsystems break down. Further, a living system is synergistic, displaying certain properties that could never be anticipated by analyzing its component subsystems; it is different from the sum of its parts (Lovelock, 1979, 1988; Sheldrake, 1991; Van Gigch, 1978).

The component subsystems of living systems exist in nested hierarchies, with each subsystem contained in a larger system (Boulding, 1956; Schumacher, 1977; Sheldrake, 1991; Van Gigch, 1978). These hierarchies of subsystems exist at different levels of physical, social, and/or spiritual complexity. Dozens of authors have postulated various systems hierarchies (often called chains of being) (Wilber, 1985). Kenneth Boulding (1956) points out that these hierarchical arrangements help people to understand that there aren't just systems; there is a "system of systems" (p. 202). E. F. Schumacher (1977) elucidates this point further, saying that various systems can be understood only if their "level of being is fully taken into account" (p. 14). Living systems are, of course, of a higher order than nonliving systems. A number of hierarchies of living systems have been proposed. J. G. Miller says that cells are at the lowest level of living systems, followed by organs, organisms, groups, organizations, societies, and finally, supranational systems (cited in Van Gigch, 1978). Boulding (1956) also begins with cells but follows them with plants, animals, humans, social systems, and transcendental systems. Each level both includes and transcends the previous level. For example, animals include the basic properties of plants, but they are also more conscious of their environment and better able to react to it. Humans have the environmental consciousness of animals, but they are also self-aware; they can set goals for themselves and reflect on their experiences. Organizations are collectives of humans, but they have the potential to harmonize the conflicting goals of individual members into synergistic cooperative efforts that can achieve very ambitious outcomes (Schumacher, 1977; Van Gigch, 1978).

Earth: The System of Systems

The Earth is a living system that both encompasses and transcends the matter, plants, animals, people, and organizations that make it up. From its environment, it imports sunlight, which provides the energy for resource development and life itself. The planet's survival depends on the delicate interaction among the atmosphere, oceans, land masses, species, and other subsystems that compose it.

Figure 1.1 (Chapter 1) represents a hierarchy of living subsystems associated with economic activity. Individuals are basic components of business organizations, business organizations are basic components of economies, economies are basic components of societies, and societies are basic components of the Earth. Because of its supranational position, the Earth cannot be defined simply as the sum of the individuals, organizations, economies, and societies that compose it. Such a definition would imply that the purpose of the Earth is to serve the economic needs of its human citizens. Rather, the opposite is true; long-term human survival depends on the needs of the Earth superseding the needs of any of its subsystems. In Boulding's (1956, p. 202) terms, the Earth is the "system of systems" where economic activity is concerned.

Factors of Production: A Living-Systems Perspective

According to economic theory, the factors of production (land, labor, capital, and entrepreneurial activity) are at the heart of all business activity. Essentially, economic growth occurs when entrepreneurial activity, defined as individuals having an idea about how to earn a profit and taking the necessary financial risks to implement that idea, is applied in order to efficiently and effectively organize the other three factors of production in ways that bring the idea to fruition with reasonable financial returns. Because entrepreneurial activity requires control over the other factors of production in order to implement new ideas, it by definition occupies a superior position among the factors. Further, because the primary goal of entrepreneurial activity is profit, the worth of the factors of production tends to be measured solely in financial terms.

From a living-systems perspective, there are some problems with how the factors of production are viewed in current economic theory. First, in keeping with the idea that the Earth's subsystems should support one another, it should be assumed that the financial goals of entrepreneurial activity need to be compatible with, rather than superior to, the goals of labor and land. If this assumption is made, then entrepreneurial activity would more likely be carried out in ways that are in keeping with the long-term viability of the planet. Note that we are not suggesting that entrepreneurial activity is inherently destructive to the environment. On the contrary, the ideas produced through entrepreneurial activity can be the seeds of many new ways for ensuring the future survival of the planet while maintaining a viable economic system. The point here is that when entrepreneurial activity is assumed to be superior to the land on which it occurs as well as to the employees who carry it out, there is greater potential that both the Earth and the employees may suffer.

Second, from a living-systems perspective, there is a potential problem associated with using money as the only means for expressing the value of land and labor. The abstract, nonliving nature of money renders it void of the ethics necessary to account for living systems. Valuation based solely on money improperly equates human assets and land with the other nonliving assets of the firm, such as buildings and equipment. This exposes the land to the potential for undue exploitation, and it makes people potentially vulnerable to corporate actions that are taken purely for financial gain.

Events a few years ago at the Bristol, Tennessee, plant of the Unisys Corporation reveal what can happen when strategic decision makers view their employees and their land purely in financial terms and assume that entrepreneurial activity is superior to these other factors of production. When Burroughs and Sperry consolidated to form Unisys, executives announced unequivocally that Sperry's Bristol plant, which employed 1,600 workers at the time, would definitely remain open because it was profitable. Two weeks later these same executives announced that they had decided to close the plant for financial reasons. They never disputed the fact that the plant was profitable, but they indicated that closing it would allow them to increase profits by consolidating the plant's functions with Burroughs. Further, unbeknownst to the community, the firm had been illegally dumping toxic wastes on its property for years in order to avoid expensive disposal costs. These wastes were discovered leaching into the area's water supply after the plant was closed. Were the financial gains achieved by illegally dumping toxic wastes on the land and putting people out of work even though the plant was profitable really worth it? Viewing the Earth as a living system might have given the strategic managers at Unisys a little different perspective on their decisions.

A number of environmental scientists and economists have suggested that land could be more easily accounted for in living-systems terms if energy rather than money were used to express its value. H. T. Odum (1983) says that using energy to determine land value would allow humankind to account for land in terms of its potential to provide energy on a sustainable basis; this would encourage economic decisions that are compatible with the Earth's long-term survival. Herman Daly and John Cobb (1989, 1994) agree, saying that land "is itself an embodiment of solar energy, and transforms that energy into the vast multiplicity of living things that make it up" (p. 259).

Bioregionalism is one concept that has emerged as a way to place the economic development of land into a living-systems perspective. Bioregionalism involves dividing the planet into natural regions based on native vegetation, geology, and distinctive life forms. These bioregions would develop their own economic systems around their regional resources, and they would be responsible for processing their own wastes in ways most suited to the unique characteristics of the region. This self-reliance would encourage the regions to promote economic systems geared to long-term ecological sustainability (Sale, 1985). Though somewhat idealistic in today's world of nation states, bioregionalism offers an enlightening vision of how localities can take a living-systems approach to their economic activities.

In fact, the idea has begun to take root in a limited way. States have passed laws restricting the production and transportation of toxic substances within their borders, chambers of commerce and industrial development boards are recruiting "clean industries," and community action groups are regularly blocking polluting firms, new landfills, and so on from locating in their areas. Although such acts are often chided as being nothing more than selfish NIMBYism ("not in my backyard"), these activities indicate that people are starting to realize that the land is more than a factor of production; it is the foundation of the living community. As such, it is worth a great deal more than the economic activity it can generate for a few years.

Gaia Theory: A Metaphor for Future Survival

As we mentioned above, living systems are not necessarily living organisms even though they display such characteristics. However, British scientist James Lovelock (1979) has forwarded his *Gaia hypothesis*, the proposition that the Earth is actually a living superorganism. (Gaia is an ancient Greek name for Mother Earth.) Lovelock's thoughts about the Gaia hypothesis began to form while he was working at the Jet Propulsion Laboratory on the problem of how to detect life on other planets (Lovelock, 1988). In researching this problem, Lovelock developed his now famous computer models of *Daisyworld*, which clearly demonstrated that the key to achieving and maintaining the proper environmental balance necessary to support life on any planet is species diversity because it helps to regulate the climate. As diversity declines, the fluctuations in the weather become more severe. This implies that any massive perturbation within the environment will significantly disturb a planet's ability to regulate itself (Lovelock, 1988). He says, "Sparse life on a planet would be as unstable as half an animal" (Lovelock, 1991, p. 10).

Lovelock (1988) explains that the living Earth was actually born with the big bang of creation some 15 billion years ago, when the energy necessary for the formation of the universe was released. During the 4.5 billion years since Earth became a discernible hot, gaseous ball, it has changed dramatically in terms of chemical content, geological activity, and the evolution of life. The basic contention of the Gaia hypothesis is that these three have not changed separately but, rather, have coevolved on the planet. That is, the Earth's living organisms have continuously interacted with their natural environment to change and regulate chemical, atmospheric, and climatic processes in much the same way that a plant or animal self-regulates its internal state (Ayres, 1994; Lovelock, 1988). Thus, according to the Gaia hypothesis, the Earth can be accurately understood only from an interdisciplinary geological-biophysical perspective (Ayres, 1994; Joseph, 1990; Lovelock, 1979, 1988, 1991; Margulis & Hinkle, 1991). Lovelock (1988) says,

> Geologists have tried to persuade us that the Earth is just a ball of rock . . . and that life is merely an accident, a quiet passenger that happens to have hitched a ride on this rock ball. . . . Biologists have been no better. They have asserted that living organisms are so adaptable that they have been fit for any material changes . . . in Earth's history. But suppose that the Earth is alive. Then the evolution of organisms and the evolution of rocks need no longer be regarded as separate. . . . Instead, the evolution of the species and the evolution of their environment are tightly coupled together as a single and inseparable process. (pp. 11-12)

The Gaia hypothesis has also been fostered by biologist Lynn Margulis. Whereas Lovelock supported the Gaia hypothesis by looking for life in interplanetary space and in macro Earthly processes such as weather and geological activity, Margulis provided a microbiological perspective. She has pointed out that symbiosis (cooperative relationships between organisms from different species) is a universal phenomenon among the Earth's microbes. Over time, symbiotic relationships evolve to the point where the microbes cannot live alone. They form colonies of microbes of different functions—that is breathing microbes, eating microbes, and so on. These colonies evolve into cells, and the cells evolve into plants and animals. Margulis calls these colonies of microbes the "tissues of Gaia," and she says they have evolved in order to regulate their natural environment. Like Lovelock, she envisions the planet as a living, breathing organism composed of coevolving biological and physical processes. Her observations have convinced her that microbes not only adapt to their environment, they also modify their environment to their needs. Life and its environment have evolved as one, not as separate entities (Joseph, 1990; Margulis & Hinkle, 1991).

Although the concept is still often referred to as the Gaia hypothesis, Lovelock (1988) makes it clear that research support for the idea has moved it well beyond the hypothetical stage, and now it should be properly referred to as Gaia theory. Kirchner (1991) identifies five Gaia hypotheses, ranging from the least extreme to the most extreme:

1. Biological forces have a substantial influence over the physical world.
2. The relationship between the Earth's biological and physical forces is one of mutual influence.
3. Long-term stability of the Earth's physical processes is dependent on biological processes.
4. Biological processes are teleologic, controlling the physical environment for a purpose.
5. Maintaining a biologically optimal physical environment *is* Gaia's purpose.

Kirchner (1991) points out that testing the less extreme hypotheses has been and will continue to be fruitful but that testing the more extreme hypotheses will be quite difficult, if not impossible. Others point out that the scope of Gaia theory is so vast that, like Newtonian physics and Darwinian evolution, it will take centuries of research to explore (Kirchner, 1991). However, Lovelock (1991) counters that evolutionary science leaves room for only one reasonable conclusion concerning the purposive and purposeful dimensions of Gaia: "Living organisms must regulate their planet, otherwise the ineluctable forces of physical and chemical evolution would render it uninhabitable" (p. 10).

One of the most important messages from Gaia theory is that humankind's environmental sensitivity need not be altruistic. Although environmental debates are often couched in terms of "business needs to clean up its act in order to help save the planet," Gaia theory points to the fact that the planet can take care of itself; it is humankind and its way of life that are threatened. Lovelock (1979) says, "It may be that the white-hot rash of our technology will prove destructive for our own species, but the evidence for accepting that industrial activities . . . may endanger the life of Gaia as a whole is very weak indeed" (pp. 107-108).

Is Gaia real? Is the planet really a living organism? This question will take years of further scientific debate to answer. At this stage, many scientists support the idea and many don't. In a sense, however, it really doesn't matter whether the planet is literally a living organism or not. Environmental scientist Daniel Chiras (1991) says that Gaia theory "is an elegant metaphor that underscores a key principle of ecology: that all living things operate together" (Gallery 1). It is a metaphor that can help human beings to better understand their place in the overall ecological scheme. It brings the phrase, "system of systems" to life. If people were to perceive Earth as a living, breathing, evolving being that exists through a beautiful and intricate dance of forests, rivers, oceans, atmosphere, microbes, plants, and animals, their perspectives on human activities would likely change. Lovelock (1988) says, "In Gaia we are just another species. . . . Our future depends much more upon a right relationship with Gaia than with the never-ending drama of human interest" (p. 14).

Thermodynamics and Economic Activity

As mentioned, survival for living systems is based on their ability to exchange energy, wastes, and information with their environment. It is a process of constantly swimming upstream against time, seeking order in a sea of chaos. This process is subject to the laws of thermodynamics, a set of principles governing the movement and transformation of energy in the universe (Ehrlich, Ehrlich, & Holdren, 1977).

That's All There Is: The Conservation Law

The first law of thermodynamics, the conservation law, says that the amount of energy in the universe is constant. Energy cannot be created or destroyed; it can only be transformed from one state to another. Initially, energy is in a *potential* form. This potential energy can be released by transforming it into a usable form. For example, the potential energy in a waterfall is released when turbines transform it into electricity, and the potential energy in gasoline is released when it is burned to power an automobile. The amount of actual energy available for use is dependent on the temperature difference between its potential state and its usable state (hence the term, *thermodynamics*). Thus, the greater the temperature difference achieved during transformation, the faster the energy flows, and the more *power* is available. When there is no temperature difference, the energy is said to be *bound* (unavailable for use). Gasoline powers a car very well, because it burns at high temperatures. Water is useless to power a car because it doesn't burn at all (Ehrlich et al., 1977; Odum, 1983).

It Won't Last Forever: The Entropy Law

So since energy can't be lost, it will always be here for people to use, right? Wrong. The second law of thermodynamics says that every time energy is transformed from one state to another, some of its available energy to do work is lost. This process is called *entropy*. Entropy occurs when stored energy becomes cooler, less concentrated, and/or less ordered when it is applied to do work. When energy is no longer available to do work, when it has degraded to the point of being useless, it becomes a waste product. For example, if you move hot water from the water heater to the wash basin in order to wash the dishes, the heat will escape from the basin into the air, and as it escapes, the heat will become much less concentrated and useless for washing the dishes; the water vapor that escapes is wasted energy. Further, entropy is associated with the forward movement of time; things always get older, never younger.

Living systems have the potential for *negative entropy*. That means they can slow down, arrest, or reverse the entropic process. Life has become more ordered and complex since appearing on Earth as single-celled sea creatures. Living organisms can postpone death by taking in energy from food, water, and sunlight. Organizations can concentrate the ideas and efforts of individuals into powerful, goal-directed entities.

However, negative entropy for the living system is not free. It can be maintained only if certain conditions are present: (a) Living systems need a continuous energy source to power their battle against time; (b) they need sufficient information from their environment that they can interpret correctly; and (c) they need sufficient ability to respond to the environmental changes they sense (the more severe the changes, the more complex the response processes need to be). Further, although entropy can be arrested and reversed at the local level, like the eddies in rushing streams, larger systems such as organizations are virtually always entropic, creating energy costs for the planet (Georgescu-Roegen, 1971).

Whereas entropy is a certainty for the Earth, there is little certainty about the path or time it will take (Georgescu-Roegen, 1971). It will depend on how efficiently humankind uses its available energy and how well it responds to the changes in its environment. The Earth and its living subsystems can survive and increase in orderliness while there is power from the sun as long as people respond correctly to signals from the environment. Global warming, ozone depletion, acid rain, smog, cancer, and energy crises are just a few signals that indicate that changes need to be made in how humans interact with the planet. The more serious these problems get, the more difficult they will be to control. However, if people respond correctly, the species can survive and develop for eons to come.

Entropy and the Economy

Since economic activity occurs on Earth, it is subject to the entropy law. Georgescu-Roegen (1971) contends that since the entropy law is a natural law that clearly defines the physical limits of economic activity, it should form the foundation upon which economic theories are based. He says that the only way to account for the true value of natural resources, the intrinsic value of life, and the actual cost of pollution and overpopulation is to base economic theories on the entropy law. Expanding on this point, physicist Fritjof Capra (1982) says that the mechanical economic models of the past century assume away the ecological contexts in which economic activity occurs. This leads to a social science that is unable to deal with the dynamics of the natural environment. Assuming that economic activity is not subject to the entropy law leads directly to the fallacious assumption that unlimited economic expansion is possible. He says that "it should be by now abundantly clear that unlimited expansion in a finite environment can only lead to disaster" (p. 213).

Basically, an economy functions by using energy to convert materials from their natural state into usable products or services for consumption by human beings. There are three inputs necessary for economic activity: (a) matter inputs (raw materials), (b) energy inputs (the solar flow and terrestrial energy stocks used to power the transformation of matter into products), and (c) information inputs (the knowledge, ideas, values, and motives that human beings use to determine what to produce, what to buy, etc.). Because energy provides the power for economic activity, the interactions among these three variables are governed by the entropy law. In this regard, economic activity requires that energy be converted from a high-potential, low-entropy state to a low-potential, high-entropy state as it is applied to the production of products and services (Boulding, 1966; Georgescu-Roegen, 1971)

Energy use in the economy has risen dramatically during the Industrial Age. In 1860, the world used the energy equivalent of 10 million barrels of oil per day. Today, that figure exceeds 150 million barrels (Davis, 1990). Terrestrial energy sources are currently being used at a rate 100,000 times greater than they are being created in nature, and it is projected that energy requirements will increase 50% to 60% in the next 20 years because of increasing population and economic activity (Davis, 1990).

Money and energy flow in opposite directions through the economy. For example, the farmers' money goes to town in exchange for the fertilizer they need to power their crops; the manufacturers' money goes to the utility company in exchange for the power they need to produce their products. However, while money stays within the economic system, energy often exists outside the system. Sunlight, nonrenewable resources, and other sources of energy that power the economy do not enter the economic cycle until they are purchased and/or converted to fuel. Further, the wastes that occur as a result of converting energy into economic wealth are also considered external to the system. The entropy law makes it clear that the principle of balance, so important in economics, really should be applied to energy use just as it is to financial transactions (Odum & Odum, 1976).

However, the news doesn't have to be so bleak. Whereas the energy and matter used in economic activity are by definition subject to the entropy law, information can actually increase (display negative entropy) in free societies that stress relevant education. Societies that encourage the continuous, free expansion of knowledge and information can literally create order out of chaos, beauty out of degradation (Boulding, 1966; Ornstein & Ehrlich, 1989; Wheatley, 1992). Of course, even this is not energy free; storing, processing, and retrieving information is generally an energy-intensive activity.

Thus, it is possible in democratic, capitalistic economies to increase valuable information—that is, to develop new knowledge, new ideas, new values, and new technologies—that will benefit humankind in its search for a balance between the economy and Nature. Though the laws of thermodynamics ordain that energy transformation is a linear process that will ultimately produce disorder and wastes, it is possible for humankind to use its ever-expanding knowledge to effectively intervene in this process, either speeding it up or slowing it down as it chooses.

Industrial Metabolism

One of the most enlightening frameworks for understanding the environmental impacts of a high-entropy economy is *industrial metabolism*. Just as living organisms have metabolic processes for transforming the energy they import from their environment into life-maintaining processes, economies can also be viewed as metabolic because they extract large quantities of energy-rich matter from the environment and transform it into products for consumption (Ayres, 1989, 1994). Ayres (1994) defines industrial metabolism as "the whole integrated collection of physical processes that convert raw materials and energy, plus labor, into finished products and wastes" (p. 25).

Whereas the metabolic processes necessary to maintain life in the ecosystem are balanced and self-sustaining, metabolism in the economic system is grossly out of balance with its environment (Ayres, 1989, 1994). The U.S. economy uses approximately 7.5 tons of nonrenewable resources per person each year to produce goods and services. Only 6% of these resources remains in the system for any length of time (basically as durable goods). The remaining 94% of these materials are used to produce food, fuel, and throwaway products (e.g., bottles, cans, batteries, and lightbulbs) that pass through the economic system from extraction to production to consumption to waste very rapidly. These wastes are often toxic and harmful to the natural environment. The amount of waste from economic activities is greater than the combined tonnage of all the crops, timber, fuels, and minerals that remain in the economic system.

According to Ayres (1989), these wastes "tend to disappear from the market domain, where everything has a price, but not from the real world in which the economic system is embedded" (p. 27). The damage is done not within the economic system per se, but in the atmosphere, water, and gene pool that have no current economic value.

Where within this metabolic process does the entropy that comes from transforming energy and resources into economic wealth result in waste and pollution? Of course, the answer is at all points—extraction, production, and consumption. However, most of the loss comes at the point of consumption. Ayres (1989) says that consumption is "naturally dissipative" (p. 26). Most foods, fuels, paper, lubricants, solvents, fertilizers, pesticides, cosmetics, pharmaceuticals, and toxic heavy metals are discarded as wastes after a single use, as are thousands of other products. Many of these are very difficult and expensive to recycle, so not only do people use too many of them, but they are also not likely to use them again. Thus, one step that can be taken to reduce energy use is to focus on the consumption end of the metabolic process. This can be accomplished in several ways, such as reducing packaging materials, improving transportation systems, increasing recycling efforts, improving insulation technology, shifting to organic farming methods, and producing high-quality, durable products.

The basic message from the industrial metabolism framework is that the metabolic processes in the economy need to achieve the same type of balance that is possible in the ecosystem when it is absent of economic activity. Just as the ecosystem can sustain itself indefinitely by importing sunlight and using it to power a system that operates almost totally by recycling materials, economic systems also need to incorporate sustainable energy transformation processes (Ayres, 1989, 1994).

Conclusions

The evidence is clear: Management happens on Earth. The long-term survival of humankind on the Earth is directly tied to its ability to maintain a sustainable balance between energy inputs and wastes. The high-entropy, energy-intensive, waste-generating economic activities of the past 350 years have seriously destabilized this balance. Energy and materials are being used faster than they can be replenished, and mountains of wastes (often toxic) are being created in the process.

Together, systems theory, Gaia theory, thermodynamics, and industrial metabolism present a framework for viewing the Earth as a living, holistic entity with myriad interconnected subsystems that must function within the evolutionary time scales of the ecosystem. These concepts make it clear that humans must find ways to balance the economic subsystem with the Earth's evolutionary entropic and morphogenetic processes, or the planet will use its own mechanisms to restore that balance. Therefore, these concepts represent an overarching framework for defining and operating within the carrying capacity of the Earth, providing a solid scientific base for managing effectively on a small planet.

PART II

Frameworks for a Small Planet

As a subsystem of the planet, it is not possible for the economy to grow forever. If the economy is to operate within the biophysical limits of Nature, frameworks are necessary that will allow managers to engage in successful business activities within the sustainable limits of the Earth. In this part of the book, we develop such frameworks, centering it on the concept of sustainability. First, we discuss sustainability, which we believe provides the underlying principles for framing the ethical, socioeconomic, and biophysical dimensions within which organizations can balance their operations with Nature. Second, we present a discussion of how integrating sustainability into strategic decision-making processes means developing organizational value systems and thought processes that will allow managers to perceive the mutually causal, long-term interconnections between their organizations and the planet. Third, we discuss how integrating sustainability into the global economic system means redefining "progress" in order to reflect a concern for the full development and well-being of the individual, the greater good of the community, and the need to balance economic and ecological processes. Finally, we present a value system with sustainability at its core, designed to provide managers with an ethical framework within which ecologically sensitive, economically successful strategic decisions are possible.

Chapter 4

Searching for Enoughness

The search for frameworks that will allow for more ecologically sensitive business practices begins with a critical question: How much economic activity can the planet afford? Humankind must acknowledge the ecological limits of economic activity to avoid the kind of environmental degradation delineated in the previous chapters. Strategic management processes that effectively account for the natural environment should be couched in terms of these limits.

Exploring this question leads to an examination of *sustainability*, the central concept upon which this book is based. Sustainability is most often defined as the point at which humankind "meets the needs of the present without compromising the ability of the future generations to meet their own needs" (World Commission on Environment and Development [WCED], 1987, p. 8). Understanding sustainability means recognizing that it goes well beyond ecological concerns; it also encompasses a wealth of economic and social concerns (Gladwin, Kennelly, & Krause, 1995; Starik & Rands, 1995). According to Gladwin et al. (1995), the definition of sustainability has five essential components:

1. Inclusiveness of all humans and species, now and in the future
2. Connectivity between economic, social, and ecological goals
3. Equity in the distribution of resources and property rights both within and between generations
4. Prudence in assessing the potential for environmental catastrophe and devastation
5. Security for humans both now and in the future to have a safe, healthy, high-quality life

Thus, sustainability is a concept that is biophysical, socioeconomic, and moral. Biophysically, understanding sustainability means defining the amount of resource depletion, waste generation, and population growth that the planet can realistically absorb without threatening the atmospheric, geospheric, and biospheric processes that support human life on Earth. Socioeconomically, understanding sustainability means exploring ways to ensure worldwide social, economic, and environmental justice, and it means developing interconnected, community-based decision-making structures that will allow humans to coordinate their individual actions in ways that will not destroy the commons that support humankind. Morally, understanding sustainability means exploring difficult issues such as the value of future generations, the value of aesthetic beauty, and the value of the planet's other species. In this chapter, we explore the concept of sustainability in some depth, focusing more completely on these important aspects.

The Biophysical and Socioeconomic Dimensions of Sustainability

As the above definition demonstrates, the characterizations of sustainability have been intellectually and spiritually inspiring. No one can deny the worthiness of trying to bequeath to our children a world of natural splendor and diversity, economic opportunity, and social justice. Walley and Whitehead (1994) say that arguing any other way would be like "arguing against motherhood and Mother Earth" (p. 46). As inspiring and intellectually sound as these images are, they really tell us little about the complex and highly integrated biophysical and socioeconomic dimensions of sustainability.

Thus, identifying these dimensions means moving beyond the inspirational level to the operational level in explaining sustainability. This means finding a biophysical definition of *enoughness* (Daly, 1977, 1991a, 1991b; Schumacher, 1973). This will require undertaking the difficult task of identifying "the amount of consumption that can be continued indefinitely without degrading capital stocks, including natural capital stocks" (Costanza, Daly, & Bartholomew, 1991, p. 8). The depth and breadth of this task can be mind-boggling. Incorporating natural capital into the framework of economic efficiency means adding "soil and atmospheric structure, plant and animal biomass, etc." (Costanza et al., 1991, p. 8) into the already incredibly complex economic formula. It means achieving a balance between the depletion and renewal of aggregate resources as well as between the planetary waste-generation and waste-assimilation rates, and it means stabilizing human population on the planet (Page, 1991).

Intertwined with the biophysical requirements of sustainability are myriad socioeconomic dimensions. Milbrath (1989) and Schumacher (1979) note that achieving a sustainable balance for the planet would require sufficient goods and services, fulfilling work, and global economic justice for the population. Costanza et al. (1991) paint a similar picture, saying that achieving sustainability means achieving a dynamic equilibrium in which individuals and human culture can survive and flourish forever within the biophysical limits of a natural environment that functions at evolutionary speeds. Daly (1995, p. 14) further explains that achieving sustainability will require a shift in the measures of economic progress from the *growth mode* (measuring the quantitative increase in resource throughput) to the *development mode* (measuring the qualitative improvement in people's lives). Gladwin et al. (1995) make it clear that social, economic, and environmental equity both within and across generations is a critical component of sustainability.

So how can these conditions be achieved? What specific dimensions need to be considered within the biophysical and socioeconomic dimensions of sustainability? In what follows, we explore some biophysical and socioeconomic changes that we believe humankind needs to achieve in order to make progress toward sustainability.

Achieving Total Materials Recycling

A key requirement to the resource depletion and waste generation aspects of achieving sustainability is to bring industrial metabolism into kilter (Ayres, 1989, 1994). To do this, virtually total materials recycling will have to be achieved (Ayres, 1994). That is, the four segments of the materials flow cycle—the natural environment, raw materials and commodities, productive capital, and final products—must achieve a balance through processes such as recycling, remanufacturing, reconditioning, and so on. This balance will be achieved when extraction rates from the natural environment are sustainable over time and when consumer and production wastes exported into the natural environment are of the types and quantities that can be readily absorbed by Nature. Ayres (1994) says,

> A long-term (sustainable) steady-state industrial economy would necessarily be characterized by near-total recycling of intrinsically toxic or hazardous materials, as well as a significant degree of recycling of plastics, paper, and other materials whose disposal constitutes an environmental problem. Heavy metals are among the materials that would have to be almost totally recycled to satisfy the sustainable criterion. (p. 31)

Operating on the principle of total materials recycling means measuring the environmental efficiency of industrial processes in terms of materials recycling/reuse rather than in terms of materials availability, which has been the traditional measure (Ayres, 1994). Ayres (1994) suggests two specific measures to accomplish this. One he calls *distance*. This is the percentage of current metal supplies that come from virgin ores. Based on the assumption that metals recycling must approach 100% in order to achieve sustainability, this measure is designed to quantify the distance that humankind has to travel in order to achieve the levels of environmental efficiency necessary for a sustainable economy. The second measure is *materials productivity*. This is defined as "the economic output per unit of material input" (Ayres, 1994, p. 34). This figure can be used to measure the metabolic efficiency for the entire economy, individual segments of the economy, individual firms, and natural resources.

Creating a Sustainable Energy System

Very much interrelated with complete materials recycling is the need to make a transition to a sustainable worldwide energy system (Holdren, 1990; H. R. Linden, 1994). Although humans often perceive the contrary, the Earth has an abundance of energy (Holdren, 1990; H. R. Linden, 1994). The planet receives 15,000 times the total world terrestrial energy supply from direct solar radiation every day (Davis, 1990). As Holdren (1990) says, humankind isn't running out of energy, it is running out of "cheap oil and natural gas . . . , the environmental capacity to burn coal, and public tolerance for the risks of nuclear fission" (p. 157). Coal, oil, and natural gas currently compose over 88% of the worldwide energy use mix (Gibbons, Blair, & Gwin, 1989).

Two critical economic segments that must be targeted if humankind is to reduce fossil fuel consumption are transportation and electrical power. With regard to transportation, increasing gas mileage to 45 miles per gallon in cars and 35 miles per gallon in small trucks can save 2.8 million barrels of oil a day. Improved public transportation and better energy planning in communities can also help to reduce the energy used for transportation (Davis, 1990; "Positive Energy," 1991). With regard to reducing electrical power consumption, energy expert Amory Lovins (1989), research director of the Rocky Mountain Institute, has said that methods such as energy-efficient appliances and compact fluorescent lighting already exist that can help to significantly reduce electricity consumption from current levels. Recently, utility companies across the globe have conducted campaigns to reduce the consumption of electricity through the use of compact fluorescent lights (CFLs). CFLs are more expensive on the front end, but because they are four times more efficient and last 10 times longer than incandescent bulbs, their total cost is only half that of incandescents. The use of CFLs increased sixfold from 1990 to 1994, and the trend seems likely to continue (Roodman, 1995b).

Ultimately, however, developing a sustainable energy system will require going beyond finding more efficient ways to use fossil fuels. Achieving sustainability will require developing a worldwide mix of energy sources that is more renewable, less dissipative, and more ecologically sensitive than the fossil fuel-based system that is currently in use. The transition to such a system will be neither easy nor cheap (Holdren, 1990). It will require an investment in improved storage technologies for solar- and wind-generated power, improved solar electric-generating technologies, improved wind turbines, and improved liquid fuels (made from biomass such as corn) among other things (Weinberg & Williams, 1990). However, if the initial investments necessary for the transition to more sustainable energy sources are made, these technologies can become economically competitive within the next decade or so (Weinberg & Williams, 1990). The use of wind turbine power is already increasing very rapidly around the globe (Flavin, 1995b), as is the use of photovoltaic solar cells, whose price declined by 9% in 1994 (Lenssen, 1995b).

H. R. Linden (1994) believes that both the stocks of fossil fuels and the planet's ecological capacity to absorb them are sufficient to allow a smooth transition to more renewable, less dissipative sources if (a) there continue to be significant advances made in efficient extraction, conversion, transport, and end-use energy technologies and (b) there is a willingness on the part of industrialized nations to effectively transfer energy-efficient technologies to developing nations so that they can avoid the typical energy and ecological inefficiencies associated with the early stages of economic development.

Controlling an Exploding Population

If humankind can achieve complete materials recycling and a sustainable energy system, then two of Page's (1991) factors—reducing resource depletion and waste generation to sustainable levels—can, in theory, be achieved. However, without satisfying his third criterion, population stabilization, these criteria will remain just that—theoretically satisfied. There is no way to realistically reduce resource depletion and waste generation on an already overcrowded globe that is currently adding roughly 90 million people per year (Brown, 1994; Harrison, 1994; United Nations, 1994). There will be 7 billion people on Earth by 2010, an increase of almost 33%; research indicates that this increase will have serious impacts on the availability of resources such as fish, wood, and agricultural land (cropland, rangeland, and pastures) (Postel, 1994).

In 1994, the United Nations held its Conference on Population and Development in Cairo, Egypt. The entire tone of the conference was reflective of the wide range of political, cultural, religious, and economic interests that were represented at such an international gathering. Nevertheless, the *Programme of Action* that resulted from the conference "establishes common ground with full respect for various religious and ethical values and cultural backgrounds" (United Nations, 1994, p. 5). The *Programme of Action* established 16 principles and well over 100 objectives necessary for stabilizing population. These principles and objectives focus on the following: "sustainable development; education, especially for girls; gender equity and equality; infant, child, and maternal mortality reduction; and the provision for universal reproductive health services, including family planning and sexual health" (United Nations, 1994, p. 4).

Whereas the focus of the United Nations is on population stabilization, some believe that more than just stabilization is necessary. They believe that a serious decline in population is necessary if humankind is to achieve sustainability. Ecologists Henry Kendall and David Pimentel (1994), who modeled human population levels against the availability of fossil fuels, cropland, and water for irrigation, conclude that the planet already has 2.5 times the number of people it can sustain indefinitely. They say that a reduction to 2 billion over the next century is necessary. According to these authors, this will require humankind to maintain a birthrate of 1.5 children per family for the next 100 years.

So how can humankind achieve such fertility rates? As the United Nations conference made clear, birthrate reduction is achievable only if education, health care, women's rights, and economic opportunities are improved in regions where population growth is out of control. According to Shrivastava (1995b), organizations in developed nations should be willing to establish production facilities in rural areas of developing nati ɔns. These facilities can help stem population growth by improving standards of living in these areas.

Reconciling the Developed and Developing Worlds

As is clearly implied by the discussions on population throughout this book, a real key to achieving sustainability lies in creating more ecological, economic, and social equity between the developed and developing nations of the world (Gladwin et al., 1995). Agenda 21 of the United Nations Conference on Environment and Development (the Rio Earth Summit) explicitly tied together environmental degradation with patterns of poverty, consumption, migration, and health (de Larderel, 1994; United Nations, 1994).

The disparities between the developed and developing parts of the globe are widely reported. The 25% or so of the Earth's population that lives in the developed world (mostly in the Northern Hemisphere) controls 85% of the world's financial resources and consumes 80% of the natural resources extracted from the planet. The 75% of humankind that lives in the developing world (primarily in the Southern Hemisphere but also including indigenous peoples and other minorities all over the globe) get few benefits from the global economic system, having to live on scarce resources, often without their basic needs being met (de Larderel, 1994).

Commenting on the meaning of sustainability, Lisa Conte (1995), President of Shaman Pharmaceuticals, a firm specializing in developing and marketing new medicines derived from the native healing potions found in the tropics, says this: "The only way we can ensure economic prosperity and protect the environment is to work directly with the local and indigenous people who inhabit the biodiversity-rich areas of the planet" (p. 14). Herman Daly (1995) calls for a "North/South bargain" in which the developed nations of the world agree to reduce their consumption, and the developing nations agree to reduce their fertility rates. Shrivastava (1995b) calls for "technology-for-nature swaps," in which developed nations offer debt forgiveness and green technologies to developing nations in exchange for the rights to use the natural resources of the developing nations in sustainable ways.

Creating Community-Based Decision-Making Structures

One of the most poignant points made by Garret Hardin (1968) in "The Tragedy of the Commons" was that the Earth's common resources will continue to be used at unsustainable rates as long as the decision-making structures regarding their management are based solely on individuals making decisions for their own gain. Meadows, Meadows, and Randers (1992) clearly demonstrate this point by examining how overfishing throughout the world has been exacerbated when individual decision makers, those who catch the fish and those who eat them, are the primary ones to determine the extent to which the world's fishing grounds are depleted.

Thus, many believe that a key to achieving sustainability is to develop what Andrew King (1995) calls "community property management," interlocking, community-based decision-making structures that will protect the rights of individuals to make choices but that will also allow for coordination and involvement in decisions that affect the general environmental health of the community (Daly & Cobb, 1989, 1994; Etzioni, 1988; Schmidheiny, 1992; Starik & Rands, 1995). According to Schmidheiny (1992, p. 7), achieving sustainability will require "political and economic systems based on the effective participation of all members of society in decision making." These structures need to function at each level of the community, from the family to the global society, with each level integrated into the next (Etzioni, 1991). Without such community-based decision-making structures to coordinate humankind's management of the commons, sustainability is an unlikely goal. We will discuss these community-based concepts in more depth in Chapters 6, 7, and 10.

Reconciling Economic Activity and Evolutionary Processes

Another key biophysical requirement for achieving sustainability is developing a better sense of the relationship between the pace of economic activity and the pace of the Earth's processes. The fact is, the Earth's biophysical cycles operate at evolutionary speeds, while industrial activity has historically functioned at revolutionary speeds. Ayres (1994) says, "In the case of the industrial system, the time scales have been drastically shortened" (p. 28). According to Costanza et al. (1991), "Sustainability is a relationship between dynamic human economic systems and larger dynamic, but normally slower-changing ecological systems" (p. 8). Thus, sustainability can be achieved only if these two time scales can be reconciled. Costanza et al. recommend the construction of multiscale measures of time that focus on how these two time scales interact. Further, as we will discuss in depth in the next chapter, reconstructing time scales is a perceptual as well as a biophysical and economic issue (Ornstein & Ehrlich, 1989).

In sum, several critical biophysical and socioeconomic factors for achieving sustainability emerge from the above discussion:

1. Creating total materials recycling
2. Making a transition to a sustainable worldwide energy system
3. Stabilizing or reducing human population levels
4. Reconciling the differences between the developed and developing nations of the world

5. Creating community-based decision-making structures that allow for widespread coordinated involvement in decisions about the Earth's common resources
6. Changing the relationship between economic and evolutionary time scales

Of course, these are not independent factors that can be approached one at a time. Like all interactions between humankind and Nature, these factors are inevitably and intricately interconnected.

The Moral Dimensions of Sustainability

The complex, interconnected nature of the requirements of sustainability discussed above demonstrate not only the biophysical and socioeconomic realities of sustainability; they also characterize its moral realities. The central theme of environmental ethics is that humankind is not separate from Nature; rather, it is a part of Nature. Environmental ethics emphasizes that the vision of the planet must evolve beyond the traditional anthropocentric, bureaucratic image of dispassionate, objective, all-knowing, humans deciding how to use other humans, other species, and the planet's resources in more efficient ways in order to continuously increase their economic gain. One popular image of the planet in environmental ethics is that of a web. The strength of the web does not lie in the ability of a single strand to dominate the rest; the strength of the web lies in the ability of each strand to remain strong in and of itself and to develop mutually beneficial bonds with the other strands.

Thus, environmental ethics is based on the idea that human survival and quality of life cannot be assured if they are based on the unrealistic assumption that humankind can lord over Nature. Long-term, quality survival of the species can be assured only under the assumption that humankind must exist in concert with Nature, giving back to the planet what it takes, accounting for Nature's timetables, and not destroying the strands of Nature's web. In this regard, Buchholz (1993) says,

> Human beings are not the center of the universe, nor are they at the center of the Earth. They are but one species, albeit an important one, in a world populated by thousands of species. Humans could not survive without the existence of these species, whereas other plant and animal species could survive quite well without human interference. (p. 59)

A general theme in the environmental ethics literature is that the dominant ethic of the Industrial Revolution, based on the Cartesian, Newtonian view of a quantitative, clockwork universe in which humans are objective observers, is both inaccurate and inadequate for humankind's survival. Essentially, this ethic is based largely on the concepts of objectivity, rationality, dominance, and cause-effect. It does not adequately account for quality, aesthetics, and the mutual causality of Nature (Capra & Steindl-Rast, 1991; Carson, 1962; Leopold, 1949; Rosenthal & Buchholz, in press; Ruether, 1992; Schumacher, 1977). Rosenthal and Buchholz (in press) say that the exclusion of qualitative experience from modern ethics has "resulted in a quantitatively characterized universe, a mind-matter dualism, the alienation of humans and Nature, and a radical dehumanizing of Nature."

Rachel Carson (1962) exemplified the frustration with these fallacies of modern ethics and the natural disasters that have resulted from these fallacies in her landmark book, *Silent Spring*. In the concluding chapter, she admonishes humankind,

> We now stand where two roads diverge. . . . The road we have long been traveling is deceptively easy, a smooth superhighway on which we progress with great speed, but at the end lies disaster. The other fork of the road—the one "less traveled by"— offers our last, our only chance to reach a destination that assures the preservation of our Earth. (p. 277)

Her call was one of many for a new, Nature-friendly ethic. The deep ecology movement has been very visible in efforts to restructure humankind's ethical frameworks in order to include the planet. The term *deep ecology* is generally credited to Arne Naess (1973), and it is centered on a basic biocentric principle: Human behavior that degrades Nature is unethical. Naess (1985) outlined eight general principles that he says are consistent with this ethic. With these principles, Naess attempted to capture deep ecology ideology and to provide a blueprint for deep ecology action. These ideological principles may be summarized as follows:

1. Humankind and all nonhuman life have inherent aesthetic value that supersedes their economic utility.
2. Biodiversity and ecological richness also have inherent aesthetic value that supersedes their economic utility.
3. Humans should never interfere with natural processes except to meet vital needs.
4. The quality of life, not the quantity of things, is what is really important and worth preserving.
5. Humankind has interfered excessively with Nature.
6. Human population has grown out of control and must be decreased.
7. Government policies should be developed that focus on protecting the richness and interconnectedness of Nature.
8. Deep ecologists should be activists, working to implement the changes implied by these principles.

Capra and Steindl-Rast (1991) describe the transition of humankind to this new ethic as requiring five basic shifts in human thinking:

1. A shift from focusing on the parts to focusing on the whole in order to more realistically reflect humankind's position in Nature
2. A shift from focusing on structure to focusing on process in order to better understand that "the entire web of relationships is intrinsically dynamic" (p. 116)
3. A shift from objective science, which views humankind as a passive observer in the universe, to epistemic science, which views humankind as a participant in the creation of the universe
4. A shift in science from an architectural metaphor, in which knowledge is "built" within discreet scientific domains that focus on the differences between things, to a networking metaphor, in which knowledge emerges through cooperative processes that focus on the relationships among things
5. A shift from defining truth in terms of absolute dogma to defining truth in terms of approximations of interconnections, reflecting

the reality that truth is something humans seek, not something
they know

Aldo Leopold: The Voice of the Land

We abuse land because we regard it as a commodity belonging
to us. When we see land as a community to which we belong, we
may begin to use it with love and respect. . . . That land is a
community is the basic concept of ecology, but that land is to be
loved and respected is an extension of ethics. (Leopold, 1949,
pp. viii-ix)

The above quote is from the preface of Aldo Leopold's
(1949) *A Sand County Almanac,* considered by many to be a foundation document in environmental ethics. However, Leopold,
the renowned environmental scholar and spiritual leader of the
wildlife conservation movement in America, ties his ideas
about the role of ecology in human history back thousands of
years to the biblical teachings of Abraham, Ezekiel, and Isaiah.
He contends that humankind is in its current ecological predicament because it has ignored these teachings, focusing instead
on the human actors who conquered Nature and other humans
in the process of establishing the human community. He says,
"In human history, we have learned (I hope) that the conqueror
role is eventually self-defeating. . . . A land ethic changes the
role of Homo sapiens from conqueror of the land-community
to plain member and citizen of it" (p. 204).
    Although obviously familiar with the traditional philoso-
phies of ethics, Leopold forgoes this approach in developing his
land ethic, letting the land itself be the teacher of good and evil,
right and wrong. Thus, rather than presenting a dry circular
discourse on the role of land within traditional philosophical
frameworks, Leopold chose the wildlife, landscape, weather,
and waterways as teachers. In *A Sand County Almanac,* Leopold
provides clear instruction on the interconnectedness of Nature,
the role of land in economics and politics, and the fallacies of
the assumption that Nature is humankind's personal possession.

True to his training as an ecologist, Leopold chose the concept of community on which to rest the development of his *land ethic*. He says, "All ethics . . . rest on a single premise: that the individual is a member of a community of interdependent parts. His instincts prompt him to compete for his place in that community, but his ethics prompt him also to cooperate" (pp. 203-204).

He points out that the ethical standards of humankind have evolved through two stages. The evolution from stage to stage has been characterized by humankind's collective decision to redefine the concept of property. The first stage was a human-human ethic. This system of ethics extended ethical considerations to certain persons, such as spouses, friends, kin, and the economically and politically powerful, but withheld it from others. Under it, slavery and indentured servitude were tolerated, classifying these people as mere property not worthy of ethical consideration. The second stage widened the focus of ethics from human-human to human-society; Leopold cites democracy as a system that emerged out of this evolution. Under a human-society ethic, slavery is not tolerated; all people fall within the venue of ethical rights and responsibilities.

Leopold says that it is now time for the transition to the human-land stage of ethical evolution, in which the status of the land is raised from property to a full member of the human community. He says, "The land-relation is still strictly economic, entailing privilege but not obligations. The extension of ethics to this third element in the human environment is . . . an evolutionary possibility and an ecological necessity" (p. 203).

Leopold points out that humankind cannot completely evolve to a land ethic without a shift in human consciousness. He believes that conservation efforts in the late 1800s and early 1900s were failures because, although they stressed the need to educate the public about the natural environment, they ignored the need to change the public's basic perceptions about its relationship to Nature. Leopold stresses that "we can only be ethical in relation to something we can see, feel, understand, love, or otherwise have faith in" (p. 214). "A land ethic, then, reflects the existence of an ecological conscience" (p. 221).

Specifically, what Leopold believed was lacking in human-kind's collective perception of the land was an image of the interconnected nature of the planet's organisms and processes. He suggests an image based on the "biotic pyramid," which demonstrates the energy circuit connecting the sun to the soil, the soil to the plants, and so on up the layers of the food chain. This circuitry is totally interconnected, meaning that change in any part of the circuit requires that the other parts adjust them-selves. He says that creating an image based on the biotic pyramid can have three significant effects on human conscious-ness, which, in turn, can facilitate the evolution to a land ethic on the planet: (a) It will create an awareness that land is some-thing other than soil; (b) it will create an understanding that plants and animals keep open the energy circuits necessary for human existence; and (c) it will create an understanding that recent human changes to the pyramid are qualitatively differ-ent from those that occur in Nature, with more far-reaching results than anticipated.

E. F. Schumacher: Guiding the Perplexed

E. F. Schumacher was an erudite gentleman who was born in 1911 and died in 1977. He was a brilliant economist who attended Oxford and Columbia. Lord Keynes once deemed Schumacher the most worthy candidate to carry the mantle as the world's top economist after his own death. As is true for most people, Schumacher's ideas matured and changed as he matured and changed. He began life as an arrogant, atheistic intellectual who disdained formal education and religion be-cause he believed himself smarter than his teachers and minis-ters. He focused only on facts, believing that they explained everything. However, as he grew older he turned to Buddhism and eventually Catholicism. As his religious and social enlight-enment progressed, his ideas about economic systems became more spiritual than intellectual, and he found that the most important things in life were learned from common people and from the soil, not from the economic experts with all their facts and figures (Wood, 1984).

Like Leopold, Schumacher believed that humankind's ethical sphere needed to be broadened to encompass the entire planet and all of its species. Schumacher (1977) bases the tenets of his ethical system on the concept of *higher*. He uses the progression of Earth's inhabitants, minerals-plants-animals-humans, to demonstrate that reality is at once empirical and spiritual. He says that the difference between the lower-level minerals and higher-level plants is life, the difference between plants and higher-level animals is consciousness, and the difference between animals and higher-level humans is self-awareness. Thus, progression from lower to higher levels of understanding is a progression from outer to inner, from mechanistic to organic, from control to understanding, and from the head to the heart.

Schumacher (1977) was rather vocal in his criticisms of the influence of Cartesian philosophy on the ethics of the Industrial Age. Prior to the Cartesian influence, ethics were based on a firm belief that human happiness was achieved through a search for higher spiritual meaning and experience. However, this search was eroded by the philosophy of Descartes, who said, " 'We should never allow ourselves to be persuaded excepting by the evidence of our reason' " (quoted in Schumacher, 1977, pp. 8-9). Descartes believed that this ability to reason placed humankind in a position separate from and above the environment in which it existed. In Descartes's words, humans were to become the " 'masters and possessors of Nature' " (quoted in Schumacher, 1977, p. 9).

Schumacher (1977) says that only the lifeless, lower mineral level lends itself to the Cartesian idea of a quantifiable universe. The objective, quantitative nature of the ethics that emerged from a Cartesian world, in Schumacher's opinion, created a utilitarian society in which value is believed to be a quantifiable concept. With the Cartesian paradigm came the belief among most people that nothing can exist beyond that which can be observed and measured. With this came the ideas of Kant and others that humans don't really know what they want, what makes them happy, and what fulfills them because they don't have all of the facts. This led to the separation of spiritual life from secular life, which, in turn, resulted in the denigration of the value of spiritual experience and the glorification of material wealth.

Within the philosophies of Descartes, there is no room for including Nature in humankind's ethical sphere because the aesthetic value of the natural environment necessary for such inclusion is absent from the Cartesian system. Schumacher (1977) says, "[The visible world] cannot register the inwardness of things and such fundamental invisible powers as life, consciousness, and self-awareness" (p. 50). Understanding at these higher levels can be done only by moving beyond quantifiable information to a higher level of knowledge. He describes his position as follows:

> Man's happiness is to move higher, to develop his highest facilities, to gain knowledge of the highest things, and if possible, to "see God." If he moves lower, develops his lower faculties, . . . then he makes himself deeply unhappy, even to the point of despair. (p. 50)

Schumacher, considered a statistical genius early in his career, believed that lower-level, quantitative measures of reality are quite sufficient for the plethora of linear, *convergent* problems that humankind faces regularly. Through the application of linear mathematics and rational thinking, convergent problems can be approached from a variety of directions that yield reasonable, remarkably similar answers. Schumacher pointed to the modes of transportation that have developed over the centuries as examples of the power of applying quantitative analysis and rational thought to convergent problems.

However, he points out that problems related to higher-level, aesthetic values and ethics are not convergent in nature; rather, they are *divergent*. Unlike convergent problems, divergent problems defy solutions attained with rational, linear logic. The more straight-line logic applied to such problems, the more diametrically opposed and outrageous the solutions become. Schumacher used an excellent example to illustrate this point. He says that the cry of the French Revolution, "liberty, equality, fraternity," includes one of the most serious divergent issues faced by Western nations in their march toward democracy—balancing liberty and equality.

Liberty and equality are certainly desirable outcomes of any democratic society; however, they are diametrically opposed from a rational perspective. Straight linear analysis would argue that if freedom is a good thing, more freedom is a better thing, and complete freedom is the best thing of all. Unfortunately, following this logic to its extreme leads to an anarchic society in which the strong prevail over the weak, destroying the very democracy on which the liberty was founded in the first place. On the equality side, it can certainly be reasoned that more social equality provides more opportunity for the citizens to improve themselves, lifting the entire society in the process. Unfortunately, equality is often achieved through legislation and social control. The more that equality is legislated the more freedom is restricted, resulting in a controlled, Big Brother society, again destroying the democracy on which the equality was founded.

The problem here is that, at its heart, democracy is not a rational concept; it is a higher-level, spiritual, ethical concept. Rationally, democracy has its pros and cons like every other humanly crafted political system. As an ethic, however, democracy expresses more of the higher-level social values than the political systems it replaces, as Leopold also pointed out. Thus, there are no meaningful rational answers to the dichotomous relationship between liberty and equality. The answers lie in qualitatively transcending this dichotomy, rising above the rational level and seeking solutions on a higher, more inward level. This is, as Schumacher (1977) points out, the genius of the French slogan. Its anonymous author saw this dilemma and added "fraternity" to the formula. Fraternity, or brotherhood, is a higher-level value than liberty and equality. It has the potential to transcend the dichotomy through immeasurable, spiritual, ethical concepts such as love, fairness, rights, commitment, and respect for others. Thus, it is only by adding fraternity to the mix that democracy can flourish indefinitely. Liberty and equality can exist together over the long run only if they are bound in brotherhood, in love and respect for fellow human beings.

The divergent problem focused on most extensively in the writings of Schumacher (1973, 1977, 1979) is the dichotomous relationship between the economic system and the natural environment. He says that modern industrial society is living under three dangerous illusions: (a) Unlimited growth is possible in a finite world; (b) there are unlimited numbers of people willing to perform mindless work for modest wages; and (c) science can be used to solve social problems. To him, these Cartesian illusions are paths to resource depletion, environmental degradation, worker alienation, and violence. He coined the phrase, "small is beautiful" to symbolize his belief that humankind's solutions to these problems lie in transcending to a higher level of analysis that can properly account for the aesthetics of both the economy and the ecology.

Economist and futurist Barbara Ward said that E. F. Schumacher " 'belongs to that intensely creative minority who have changed the direction of human thought' " (quoted in McRobie, 1979, p. vii). Schumacher's friend George McRobie (1979) probably captures the essence of his contributions the best when he writes,

> Fritz Schumacher . . . [brought] his personality and creative energy, as well as his remarkable mind, to bear on what is certainly one of the most critical tasks that now confronts rich and poor societies alike: How to enable us to do creative and satisfying work, earn a decent living, live in a becoming way; and having done so, to leave the planet Earth in a condition at least no less capable of supporting life than that in which we found it. (p. xi)

Conclusions

"Meeting the needs of the present without compromising the future" (WCED, 1987): This is certainly an elegant thought, a worthy goal, and a powerful vision. However, if humankind is serious about making real progress toward this utopian future, then it is going to have to move beyond elegant slogans and make some hard progress toward creating total materials recycling, establishing a sustainable energy system, controlling exploding population, reconciling disparities between developed and developing peoples, and reconciling perceptual processes and measures to account for the Earth's evolutionary processes.

Leopold (1949), Schumacher (1973, 1977), and others provide important insights into the fact that these changes are not just biophysical and socioeconomic; they are also ethical. Together, they espouse a new environmental ethic that includes the entire biotic pyramid within the community of those who have rights. It means envisioning the Earth as a web with all of its strands healthy and in concert with one another. It means seeking more of a balance between the value that society ascribes to the "higher" (more inward, qualitative, unmeasurable, from the heart) things such as beauty, and the value it ascribes to the "lower" (outward, quantitative, measurable, from the head) things such as economic wealth. It means defining an ethical system that will transcend the ecology-economy dichotomy, paving the way for humankind's evolution to a "land ethic."

Of course, the actual process of transcending the ecology-economy dichotomy falls distinctly into the bailiwick of strategic managers in business organizations. They are the ones responsible for ensuring that organizations pursue the strategic avenues necessary for achieving economic success within the limits of the planet. We believe that the concept of sustainability is central to successfully formulating and implementing such strategic initiatives. Sustainability provides an excellent biophysical, socioeconomic, and ethical framework for strategic managers to use as they establish the ethical and operational dimensions of new organizational strategies, strategies that allow them to survive and prosper "without compromising the ability of future generations to meet their own needs" (WCED, 1987, p. 8).

Chapter 5

We Are How We Think

When executives at Quality Devices, Inc. (a manufacturer of kitchen utensils designed to appeal to gourmet cooks) decided to purchase Mountain Empire Furniture Company (MEF) in 1984, it seemed like a great opportunity. The Rocky Top, Tennessee, company produced fine wood furniture designed for trendy urban condominiums; this seemed like a "can't miss" proposition for Quality Devices. The urban professionals buying the condos were also the ones getting into gourmet cooking. This synergy between the two lines of business provided MEF with an excellent opportunity to concentrically diversify. With the urban real estate market soaring and the material tastes of the growing yuppie population seemingly insatiable, the high debt the firm assumed when it purchased MEF (financed with high-interest junk bonds) seemed well worth the risks.

Business at Mountain Empire Furniture was great through much of the 1980s. The executives used the money to expand MEF's product lines and output of existing products, extending its debt even further. Then things began to change. The real estate market went into a deep recession nationwide in the late 1980s (nearly a depression in many of the urban areas where MEF sold a high percentage of its products). Scandals on Wall

Street, the collapse of the savings and loan industry, and the paring of layers of middle management by organizations in restructuring efforts made many people begin to seriously question their free-spending, materialistic lifestyles. Environmentally conscious consumers began to balk at buying products that damaged the environment, including those made from tropical or old-growth wood such as MEF used in several of its products. MEF was still earning a profit, but servicing the firm's large debt kept it well below what the executives would have liked.

Then workers in the plant began complaining about respiratory problems that they said resulted from breathing the fumes from the laminating and finishing processes. Because of these complaints, MEF hired an independent environmental consultant to audit the firm's compliance with Occupational Safety and Health Administration (OSHA) and Environmental Protection Agency (EPA) regulations (although they had been inspected only once in their 8 years of operation). The consultant reported that the levels of toxic fumes in the plant would probably meet minimal government standards. However, he also told them that data indicated that exposure at the levels present in the MEF plant over long periods of time might increase workers' risks of contracting lung cancer and other respiratory diseases, especially for those who smoked tobacco products. Most disturbing, however, was the consultant's discovery during his audit that MEF's previous owners had buried at least 50 barrels of toxic chemicals in a dump on the firm's property 10 years before Quality Devices bought it.

Sitting around a mahogany conference table, seven MEF executives discuss these issues. What will they decide to do? In this fictitious scenario,[1] the managers at Mountain Empire Furniture Company are faced with several strategic decisions that have environmental and economic implications. Will they change the types and/or sources of wood the firm uses in its products, or will they continue using wood harvested in ways that endanger forests? Will they invest in equipment to reduce the exposure of the workers to toxic fumes, will they invest in an employee smoking cessation program, or will they take no action because the firm is probably in minimal legal compliance and is rarely inspected? Will they report the illegal dump, begin legal proceedings against the previous owners, and take other measures to get it cleaned up, or will they ignore it because the authorities don't know about it and may never find out? How will they balance these environmental issues with the firm's financial goals and obligations and the demands caused by changing market conditions?

Ultimately, the decisions of the MEF executives will be based on factors such as what information they consider important, what values they hold concerning worker safety and environmental protection, and how much emphasis they give to the short-term and long-term consequences of their decisions. Thus, the thought processes of the MEF executives hold the key to what they might decide to do. Therefore, in this chapter we discuss human thought processes in some detail in order to explore the basic relationships between how strategic managers think about the natural environment and the decisions that they make about how to manage environmental issues. We present some important dimensions of human perception, including the role of values in complex strategic choices, and we discuss some of the vital considerations necessary for bringing long-term concerns for the health of the natural environment into the thought processes of strategic managers in business organizations.

Perceptions, Values, and Strategic Decision Making

There has been a dramatic paradigm shift in science during the 20th century. Theories of relativity and quantum physics have led scientists to understand that there is no such thing as objective reality; there are only perceptions of reality. Quantum physicist Sir Arthur Eddington once commented, " 'The frank realization that physical science is concerned with a world of shadows is one of the most significant of recent advances' " (quoted in Wilber, 1985, p. 9). Werner Heisenberg (1985a), also a quantum physicist, agrees, saying, "Understanding can never mean more than the perception of connections" (p. 56).

This new scientific paradigm has crept into management thought over the past two decades. Cognitive explanations of why and how individuals and organizations behave as they do, explanations that focus on the relationships between what people perceive and what they do, have begun to revolutionize the way many management scholars think about how decisions in organizations are made.

Perceptions and Organizational Behavior

During much of this century, theories of why people behave the way they do have focused primarily on the external environment (Luthans & Kreitner, 1985). These approaches advocate the idea that behavior is entirely shaped by the influence of environmental stimuli and reinforcement. Research on these models has been quite fruitful. However, even in the face of this considerable evidence, scholars and practitioners alike have resisted the idea that human beings are primarily motivated by rewards and punishments. Such theories leave little or no room for the influence of human thought processes, the very characteristic that separates humans from other species. Now a large body of cross-cultural research has emerged that refutes the idea that humans behave primarily for hedonistic reasons. This research suggests that perceptions play a primary role in human behavior (Ravlin & Meglino, 1987).

In understanding the role that perceptions play in human behavior, it is important to realize that people don't operate directly on objective reality. Instead, they operate on their *perceptions* of objective reality. That is, people scan their environment and create a mental picture of that environment; this mental picture involves applying values, assumptions, opinions, attitudes, beliefs, and knowledge to what is observed and developing perceptions of the situation from this process. Once perceptions are formed, people make their behavioral decisions based on these perceptions. Thus, human beings employ cognitive processes (mental processes involved in having and arranging thoughts) in order to understand and respond to given situations.

Perceptions are formed through a process called *categorization* (Ilgen & Feldman, 1983; Rosch & Lloyd, 1978). Categorization is essentially a process of reducing the information from the environment and storing it in mental categories. Categories are like mental compartments used to store a variety of information that relates in some way. People categorize information from their environment in two ways. Sometimes categorization is automatic; it occurs instantaneously for very familiar, over-learned information. Obvious characteristics, such as color, sex, and dress, are examples of the types of signals that people are likely to automatically categorize. However, people use a more thoughtful, controlled categorization process when dealing with problematic, novel, or unexpected information. Controlled categorization is complex; it requires that individuals pay close attention to information, consciously search their memory for the appropriate categories they use to interpret the information, and make conscious decisions about the information (Ilgen & Feldman, 1983). In fact, actual perception involves both automatic and controlled categorization processes in varying degrees depending on the situation.

Further, developing perceptions involves both logical, rational, conscious processes and unconscious, often nonrational processes (Gioia, 1986). Cognitive processing likely begins at the unconscious level, and most of what is processed probably remains at that level. Trying to consciously process all the information received from the environment would be overwhelming and incoherent. Cognitive psychologist Bernard Baars employed an excellent analogy to explain how unconscious and conscious processes interact to form conscious perceptions. He used a large number of experts in an auditorium, each with his or her own unique knowledge, to represent mental categories. The auditorium includes a blackboard, which in the analogy represents conscious thought. Just as human conscious thought is limited, the blackboard has a limited capacity to hold information; it can accommodate only a minute fraction of the information of the many experts in the auditorium. When the experts are faced with a problem, each one searches his or her own memory for information relevant to the problem. The experts who believe that they have relevant information then must find allies and face conflicts among the other experts in the auditorium; this is the only way that they can register the information they have on the limited blackboard space and have it applied to the problem. Thus, the analogy demonstrates that conscious perceptions result from a multitude of unconscious processes that involve both competition and cooperation among the many categories of information available (cited in Harman, 1990-1991).

If people's experiences were always the same, individuals would likely develop neat categories that could be called upon individually when needed. However, human experiences normally differ from previous ones, requiring people to integrate their mental categories in a wide variety of often unique and complex ways in order to develop meaningful perceptions of their various situations. The term *cognitive map* refers to the integrative mental processes people use when they are faced with behavioral choices; cognitive maps are networks of interconnected mental categories that interact in order to provide meaning and direction for the individual. Cognitive maps are used to translate experiences into knowledge and action just as road maps are used to explore the alternative routes people may want to take on a trip (Weick & Bougon, 1986).

Of course, people are the basic elements that form the nucleus of all organizations. Thus, since human behavior is guided by perceptions, organizations can exist only when their members share certain perceptions; they must perceive that they have common goals, they must perceive that there are common methods for goal accomplishment, and they must have a common perception of the roles of the organizational members (Weick & Bougon, 1986). In other words, organizations can exist only when the members share a common cognitive framework (Finney & Mitroff, 1986). Thus, organizations are essentially "networks of intersubjectively shared meanings that are sustained through the development and use of a common language and everyday social interactions" (Walsh & Ungson, 1991, p. 60). The popular term used when referring to organizations as cognitive networks is *organizational culture*

(Finney & Mitroff, 1986). Shared motives, shared experiences, shared visions, shared language, shared myths, and shared values all portray the cultural characteristics of organizations. With their emphasis on the word *shared*, these terms demonstrate the true cognitive nature of organizations.

Imagine these cognitive individual and organizational processes at work as the conversation unfolds around the conference table at Mountain Empire Furniture. Imagine the minds of these executives searching for ways to attach meaning to the environmental issues that face MEF. Imagine their cognitive maps emerging from the unconscious level as the executives choose what information to bring to the surface for consideration. Imagine them presenting this information within the web of shared cultural dimensions of the organization that define their interactions with their colleagues around the table. Imagining these things can provide insights into why paying attention to the thought processes of strategic managers is critical for understanding and improving the relationships between business organizations and the natural environment.

Strategic Decisions: Complex, Value-Laden Choices

One of the most common behaviors engaged in by human beings is decision making; people are faced with making choices all the time. Some choices are based on data that people have directly available; these choices require little more than an instantaneous, automatic response. Other decisions are quite complex. All the data needed are not directly available, meaning that individuals have to search their memory for knowledge and metaphors, and they have to consciously process the information available in making their choice.

Managers in business organizations are paid to make decisions, and the majority of the decisions that managers make are not automatic. Managerial decisions typically involve significant amounts of uncertainty and require extensive use of conscious, controlled cognitive processes. For example, decisions about the performance of employees (a standard managerial task) normally are made based on limited opportunities to observe the employees at work, and they require managers to search their memories for information that may be up to a year old (Ilgen & Feldman, 1983). Moving up the organizational hierarchy means facing even more problematic, uncertain issues that require managers to make decisions with increasingly significant consequences.

Values play a major role in complex managerial decisions (Liedtka, 1989; Rokeach, 1968; Schwenk, 1988; Yankelovich, 1981). Values are enduring, emotionally charged abstractions (categories) about matters that are important to individuals (Williams, 1960). Understanding values is no simple matter. Some have conceptualized values as existing in hierarchies; that is, some values are always more important to individuals than others. Others say that the importance of any individual value varies. They say that the real key to understanding how important values are in influencing decisions is to discern how important an individual's total system of values is to him or her. This approach views values from a holistic perspective in which the values people favor are influenced by the situation (Ravlin & Meglino, 1987). When people actually apply their values to their decisions, both of these frameworks are likely to come into play to one degree or another. No doubt, some values are more important to people than other values; at the same time, the total strength of people's value systems and the situations in which they find themselves are also important.

Social values seem to have a particularly strong influence on the complex choices that individuals make. Social values represent a broad array of behavioral norms that are best defined by their "oughtness." Social values deal with the ways people believe they should behave. Although social values may originally descend from pain and pleasure experiences, they become the social canons of a group, company, community, or society. As such, they serve to control and protect the behavior of individual citizens. This systemic support for social values gives them an existence well beyond any individual rewards or punishments. Because social values are expected within the larger group, behaving in accordance with these values is usu-ally endorsed by all the members. This is a very powerful motivational force (Ravlin & Meglino, 1987).

Values play major roles in the cognitive processes people go through when they make complex decisions. People search the characteristics of their situation, determine the conse-quences of these characteristics, and determine the desirability or undesirability of these consequences (Gutman, 1982). Cogni-tive choice processes involve choosing (consciously and uncon-sciously) what information to pay attention to; encoding, storing, and retrieving this information; and integrating the retrieved information into a final choice or decision (Denisi, Cafferty, & Meglino, 1984). Values have an especially strong influence on this process at two points. First, values are critical in helping people determine which elements of their environment are important to heed in making decisions. Second, values are the primary criteria used when individuals choose among the avail-able alternatives (Howard, 1977; Rosenberg, 1956). The more complex, ambiguous, and judgmental a decision is, the more prominent the role of values will become in the final choice (Jolly, Reynolds, & Slocum, 1988; Reynolds & Jamieson, 1984).

Strategic decisions are at the pinnacle of complex choices faced by business managers. They are made at the upper eche-lons of the organizational ladder, and their consequences are potentially vital to organizational success (Ansoff, 1980; Dut-ton, 1986). Further, successfully implementing strategic deci-sions rests on effectively integrating them into the culture of the organization. The complexity of strategic decisions is revealed in the fact that management scholars are not all that clear about what strategy really means. Dozens of definitions exist ranging from the concrete (i.e., Alfred Chandler's determining goals, developing processes, and committing resources) to the tran-scendental (i.e., Henry Mintzberg's patterns in streams of deci-sions) (Schwenk, 1988).

Typically, strategic decisions must be made about issues that are ill-defined, nonroutine, complex, and uncertain and that have the potential for multiple interpretations. Thus, stra-tegic decisions tend to be unique from situation to situation and from organization to organization. They require that managers have diverse capabilities and relationships; they require managers to integrate a variety of elements that include multiple goals, multiple stakeholders, multiple decision makers, multiple attitudes, and vague time horizons (Ansoff, 1980; Dutton & Dukerich, 1991; Dutton & Jackson, 1987; Grammas, 1985; Logsdon, 1985; Mintzberg, Raisinghani, & Theoret, 1976; Schwenk, 1988; Steiner, Miner, & Gray, 1986).

Thus, making strategic decisions in business organizations requires what Gioia (1986) calls the "art of management . . . the intuitive, insightful, perceptive, nonrational and holistic [processes] increasingly recognized as characteristic of the complete executive" (p. 339). These controlled cognitive processes related to strategic decision making have been the subject of several authors, one of whom is Charles Schwenk (1984, 1988). He says that strategic decisions are made by invoking a variety of cognitive simplification processes, such as ignoring or misinterpreting data that do not fit the decision maker's beliefs, anchoring final decisions on initial value judgments, and using analogies and images to identify problems and solutions. He also says that understanding the strategic decision-making process requires understanding its underlying assumptions. This means understanding the cognitive maps of the executives who make the decisions since these maps represent the mental structures through which strategic choices are filtered. These cognitive maps can provide a clearer picture of current and future strategic choices within the culture of the organization.

Finney and Mitroff (1986) discuss how strategic decisions are integrated into the culture of the organization. They say that if a firm wants to successfully implement its strategies, an organizational consensus is necessary concerning cognitive schema (mental frameworks that employees use to interpret information) and cognitive scripts (expected behaviors or sequences of events for certain situations). Without such a consensus, the organizational culture will not form around accomplishing organizational goals. Further, if strategic managers can understand the organizational schema and scripts, they may b comprehend how to integrate new or previously disregarded information into the existing culture of the organization.

Of course, the complex, novel, judgmental nature of cognitive processes used in making strategic decisions means that the strategic choices made by executives are highly judgmental and, as such, are both guided and limited by values (Christensen, Andrews, Bower, Hamermesh, & Porter, 1987; Hambrick & Mason, 1984; Schwenk, 1988; Sturdivant, Ginter, & Sawyer, 1985). Hambrick and Mason (1984) write, "Organizational outcomes—both strategies and effectiveness—are viewed as reflections of the values and cognitive bases of powerful actors in the organization" (p. 193). Values influence strategic decision makers either directly, by serving as guides to specific action (behavior channeling), or indirectly, by serving as screening mechanisms through which information and alternatives are filtered (perceptual screening). Perceptual screening is considered the more important of these two for strategic decisions because it is the primary way that people apply their values to ambiguous, open-ended, multifaceted situations (Hambrick & Brandon, 1987).

In a 1990 interview, Robert Haas, CEO of Levi Strauss, provided a practical explanation of why values and the cognitive nature of strategic decision making are so important for managers. He said,

> "What we've learned [at Levi Strauss] is that the soft stuff and the hard stuff are becoming increasingly intertwined. A company's values—what it stands for, what its people believe in—are crucial to its competitive success. Indeed, values drive the business. . . . In a more dynamic business environment, the controls have to be conceptual. . . . Values provide a common language for aligning a company's leadership and its people. . . . We have redefined our business strategy to focus on core products, and we have articulated the values that the company stands for—what we call our Aspirations. We've shaped our business around this strategy and these values, and people have started marching behind this new banner." (quoted in Howard, 1990, p. 134)

This brings us back to the case of Mountain Empire Furniture Company. The strategic choices faced by the MEF executives are complex, multifaceted, and uncertain. They are faced with a multiplicity of strategic choices, each with a potential for significant economic and environmental impacts. What they decide will depend on the outcomes of the complex thought processes that the executives apply when they scan their environment and make their choices. This means that, to a large degree, the decisions made by the MEF executives will depend on the strength of the values they hold concerning environmental protection and worker safety.

Valuing the Commons in Strategic Decisions

Without knowing the executives at MEF, it would be hard to predict the decisions they might make. However, at the current time, the strategic decision-making deck seems stacked against the environment. We discussed previously that the value of the commons (the air, water, and resources everyone needs for survival) is not adequately accounted for in current economic models; this means that the MEF executives will have to go beyond traditional business wisdom if they want to factor the environment more completely into their decisions.

As has been discussed in this chapter, the models that managers use to make complex strategic decisions are the result of cognitive processes whereby the managers apply their knowledge and values in order to develop their perceptions of reality and to determine the directions they will take in dealing with their environment. Why don't today's economic models adequately value the ecosystem? At the heart of the matter may be the insufficiency of current cognitive processes to account for the long-term, seemingly gradual changes that characterize most environmental problems (Ornstein & Ehrlich, 1989).

Most of the man-made changes in the environment have occurred during the Industrial Age, but the biological evolution of the human being was essentially complete thousands of years ago. The mental pictures that our ancestors used to comprehend their environment were developed in a very different type of world from the one that exists today. People lived in small groups in limited, stable, harsh environments. Most of their responses were geared to dramatic, short-term environmental changes. Thus, human beings developed cognitive processes that focused on the short-term. Long-term thinking for our ancestors was season to season; survival was based on their responses to events that occurred daily or moment to moment. They probably perceived gradual global patterns, but they had to suppress these perceptions in order to focus on their immediate situations. For most of human history, these short-term mental processes were adequate for survival. The planet was not overpopulated, and there was safety in numbers. People had neither the potential to create long-term global changes nor the ability to deal with these changes when they occurred (Ornstein & Ehrlich, 1989).

Whereas most species evolve only biologically, human beings also evolve culturally and technologically. Even though human biological evolution has occurred very slowly, cultural and technological rates of development have been nothing short of phenomenal, especially during the Industrial Age. Humans now have an exponentially growing population, a global culture based on a shared belief in the virtues of economic growth, and the technology to create long-term global changes. These are, of course, the three key ingredients for continued environmental degradation (as discussed in Chapter 2). Unfortunately, human perceptual processes are still tied to the old world of short-term, dramatic change; people still suppress long-term perceptual processes to a great extent. Thus, it is hard to perceive the impacts of the global changes that are occurring. Humankind continues to reproduce rapidly even though it knows that overpopulation is one of the most serious long-term problems; humans continue to use resources and pollute at incredible rates even though they know that there will be dire long-term consequences. As Ornstein and Ehrlich (1989) say,

> There is now a mismatch between the human mind and the world people inhabit. . . . We are out of joint with the times, our times.

. . . The same mental routines that originally signaled abrupt physical changes in the old world are now pressed into service to perceive and decide about unprecedented dangers in the new. . . . The human predicament requires [that we] detect threats that materialize not in instants but in years or decades. We need to develop "slow reflexes" to supplement the quick ones. We need to replace our old minds with new ones. (pp. 10-12)

Ornstein and Ehrlich (1989) contend that people need to take advantage of the flexibility and trainability of the human mind to achieve the changes necessary in their mental pictures of reality. Human beings are the most adaptable of the species, and they have the potential to synthesize large amounts of information. Education about the problems faced by human-kind is important, but education about the way people think may be even more important. If people can learn how they learn, if they can understand how their values and perceptions influence their view of the world and their reactions to it, then they may be better equipped to modify their cognitive struc-tures to fit the demands of their current environment.

Thinking in Circles

Argyris and Schön (1978) refer to the cognitive process described previously—in which environmental data are per-ceived through the senses, interpreted through the cognitive filters, and acted upon based on these interpretations—as sin-gle-loop learning. Single-loop learning is essentially an adap-tive process in which individuals base interpretations and the resultant behavioral decisions on currently held mental frame-works (Senge, 1990). This adaptive process is generally very effective in helping people to avoid pain and immediate threat but has little value in revealing and changing the nature of the learning process itself (Argyris & Schön, 1978). If, as Ornstein and Ehrlich (1989, p. 12) contend, it is necessary for people to develop "new minds to replace the old ones," then *double-loop learning* processes are necessary. These processes allow people to reflect on, inquire about, and change the fundamental mental frameworks that determine how they interpret and act upon environmental data (Argyris & Schön, 1978).

Reflection and inquiry about the assumptions, values, experiences, and social norms that frame people's thought processes allow people to transcend from adaptive, single-loop learning processes, which focus on the analysis of events and behavioral patterns, to generative, double-loop learning processes, which focus on the systems structures that "address the underlying causes of behavior" (Senge, 1990, p. 53). At this generative, "learning to learn" level, the patterns of people's learning methods are revealed, permitting their understanding and modification (Senge, 1990).

Systems Thinking: The Processes of Learning to Learn

According to Senge (1990), at the heart of generative learning is systems thinking, a conceptual framework that focuses on the "invisible fabrics of interrelated actions" (p. 7) that reveal the long-term, holistic nature of things. The language of systems thinking helps people to "see the deeper patterns lying between the events and the details" (Senge, 1990, p. 71). Systems thinking rests on the notion of mutual causality; that is, within a system each part is both cause and effect. Thus, systems are circular patterns of dynamic interrelationships rather than linear patterns of discreet causes and consequences. Systems thinking helps people to realize that they are parts of rather than separate from their environments; that is, they are active participants in the underlying circular dynamics of their world (Senge, 1990).

The circular dynamics of a system are sometimes *reinforcing* and sometimes *balancing*. The dynamics of reinforcing systems begin as small changes, but they amplify over time, potentially spiraling out of control if not checked. These cycles can be either *vicious* reinforcing loops, in which things go from bad to worse over time, or *virtuous* reinforcing loops, in which things go from good to better over time. Vicious cycles characterize the nature of many environmental issues, such as population growth, ozone depletion, and the growing presence of greenhouse gases in the atmosphere. This is of primary concern because vicious reinforcing dynamics have the potential to mask problems until they become serious, even unsolvable (Senge, 1990).

Balancing dynamics are those processes that act to maintain stability and status quo in systems. A balancing process generally includes some goal, target, or limit that allows the system to self-correct and/or holds it in check. Although they are simple enough to understand, balancing processes are often implicit, subtle, and very hard to detect (Senge, 1990). For example, as the researchers at Hawthorn demonstrated over 60 years ago, hidden, implicit social norms can stop organizational change efforts dead in their tracks.

A primary reason why balancing processes are often hard to detect is that there may be *delays* in the loop. In fact, complex systems seldom operate in ways that allow cause-effect relationships to be easily observed. More often, causes and effects are separated by significant amounts of time and/or space, which make them very difficult to tie together (Senge, 1990). In the same vein as Ornstein and Ehrlich (1989), Senge (1990) points out that unnoticed systems delays represent the fundamental mismatch between predominant human thought processes and the true nature of reality. He says, "The first step in correcting this mismatch is to let go of the notion that cause and effect are close in time and space" (p. 63).

Given that delays often underlie the insidious nature of systems dynamics, identifying these delays can be the key to finding the *leverage* necessary to change the dynamics of the system. Leverage is that point in the structure of the system where changes will result in long-term improvements. Because delays are largely responsible for the long-term, often hidden nature of the systems structures that underlie human activity, it is within these delays that the leverage necessary for finding long-term solutions generally reveals itself (Senge, 1990).

Systems thinking is important precisely because "structures of which we are unaware hold us prisoner" (Senge, 1990, p. 94). In other words, the key to effectively moving from an adaptive, single-loop learning mode to a generative, double-loop learning mode involves recognizing, analyzing, and potentially modifying the systems structures that underlie how humans think and act. At first glance, this task seems rather daunting given the virtually infinite ways in which reinforcing loops, balancing loops, and delays can manifest themselves over time. However, Senge points out that although there are certainly many ways to cast and recast the dynamics of a system, at the heart of almost all these structures are a few system *archetypes* that recur regularly in most management situations.

The two archetypes that Senge (1990) focuses on most closely are "shifting the burden" and "limits to growth." The first of these involves two balancing loops, one providing a symptomatic solution and one a fundamental solution to the problem at hand. Choosing to operate within the symptomatic loop may produce relief from the problem over the short run, but it also leads to unintended, often disastrous, side effects. Long-term solutions are found only by operating in the fundamental solution loop. For example, an individual may attempt to manage job stress by coming home each day and consuming alcoholic beverages. This symptomatic solution will likely work for a while, but the cycle will eventually "shift the burden" on the individual from job stress to alcoholism, family problems, and so on. Only by focusing on the fundamental solution, finding and rectifying the causes of the job stress, can such a shift be avoided and a long-term solution found.

In the limits-to-growth archetype, a reinforcing loop is in full swing, culminating in rapid growth in the system. For example, if an organization gains a reputation for high quality, this can lead to increased sales, which in turn result in an even wider reputation for high quality, which reinforces sales further, and so on. Unfortunately, such rapidly growing reinforcing loops are likely to have side effects that eventually produce a balancing loop, bringing the rapid growth to a grinding halt. In the above example, the increased sales may eventually strain the organization's production capacity, which in turn limits sales growth. A key to recognizing and managing limits-to-growth archetypes is to understand that the balancing loop almost always contains a delay. In the above example, a delay in the balancing loop is a virtual certainty because increasing production capacity almost always takes time. Leverage in limits-to-growth archetypes is most easily found, not by focusing on the dynamics of the reinforcing loop, but by focusing on the delay in the balancing loop. Again returning to the example, if the organization tries to push the reinforcing process by stretching the limits of its current production capacity further, then it will likely suffer a reduction in quality, changing its virtuous, high-quality-to-increased-sales loop to a vicious, low-quality-to-decreased-sales loop. If high quality, the driving force behind the organization's sales growth, is to be maintained, then increasing production capacity emerges as the most appropriate solution because, although it may be costly and time-consuming in the short run, it is the only way to maintain quality in the face of increasing sales in the long run (Senge, 1990).

Ecological Limits to Growth

How would the decisions of the Mountain Empire Furniture executives be influenced if they were to apply long-term, double-loop, generative learning processes that would not only help them to examine the issues at hand but that would also help them to reflect on the underlying dynamics of the system in which these issues exist? Would they see more clearly the relationship between the long-term preservation of tropical forests and the long-term economic success of the firm? Would they be more aware of the long-term benefits of employee health and safety on the firms' product quality and profits? Would the long-term advantages of voluntarily reporting the previously buried toxic wastes and taking expedient actions to ensure their cleanup be more obvious to these executives? Would seeing long-term interrelationships such as these help the executives to understand why an underlying mental framework based on sustainability is so important to their firm's long-run economic survival?

There are no sure answers to these questions, but the chances that the MEF executives would see the important long-term implications of their decisions would certainly be im-

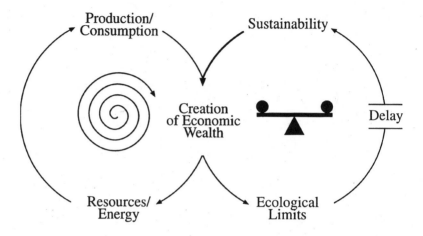

Figure 5.1. Ecological Limits to Growth

proved if they applied a generative thought process such as the one depicted in Figure 5.1. In it, a limits-to-growth archetype is chosen to portray the growing stress between business and the natural environment. It depicts humankind in a reinforcing cycle that has been operating at full throttle throughout the Industrial Revolution. Natural resources and energy, perceived to be vast and unlimited, have been converted at increasingly rapid rates into goods and services, and economic wealth has continuously increased as a result. Humankind is now becoming aware that the ecological side effects of these economic activities will, after a delay, limit this reinforcing cycle by eating away at the natural capital that lies at its foundation. Although these ecological limits may be manageable now, their power to limit economic growth will continue to increase over time. Thus, if something is not done to remove or reduce these limits, the reinforcing cycle of economic growth, at some point, will likely reverse itself into one of economic decline. Of course, as discussed in depth in Chapter 4, reducing or removing these limits is possible if humankind will embrace sustainability as the central concept in the design and operation of the economic system.

Conclusions

Relativity and quantum theory have vanquished the idea that everything, from the structure of the universe to the behavior of human beings, can be reduced to mechanical processes governed by deterministic laws. People can view their world only through their perceptions. Perceptions result from complex mental processes that involve filtering environmental data through intricate cognitive frameworks in order to ascertain meaning and choose courses of action. These cognitive frameworks are value-laden, especially in the complex, uncertain, unfamiliar, ill-structured situations faced by strategic managers in business organizations.

Adequately including the ecosystem in the mental pictures that guide managers in their strategic decisions can be achieved only by refocusing their mental frameworks on gradual, long-term processes. Doing so will require changing the way managers think. Adopting generative, double-loop processes will allow strategic managers to perceive the long-term, mutually causal interconnections between their organizations and the natural environment.

As depicted in Figures 1.1 and 5.1, perceiving these long-term interconnections means broadening the perceptions of strategic managers beyond the sphere of the economic subsystem to encompass the greater social system and the natural environment. This means that new models are needed within the managerial disciplines to more accurately reflect these long-term interconnections. Given that the managerial disciplines are contained largely within the frameworks of economics, their professed mother discipline, the development of new economic models that reflect these long-term, interconnected relationships is a critical step toward more ecologically sensitive strategic decision-making processes in organizations.

Note

1. There are hundreds of furniture manufacturers in the small mountain communities of northeast Tennessee that specialize in producing fine wood products. Many are old and have poor ventilation. Because of their rural isolation, number, and relatively small size, these firms are seldom inspected by government agencies responsible for employee and environmental protection. In 1990, it was discovered that one such firm, the East Tennessee Chair Company, located in Carter County, Tennessee, had been illegally dumping toxic chemicals on its property for years. The dump has since been classified as a state Superfund site. The fictitious Mountain Empire Furniture case in this chapter was generally conceived based on this incident, but the specific details of this fictitious case in no way portray the actual events at East Tennessee Chair Company.

Chapter 6

Economics As If the Planet Mattered

E. F. Schumacher (1979) often told a story about an economist who, while strolling through the park one Sunday afternoon, came face-to-face with the Lord. The economist was understandably frightened by this encounter and became completely speechless. However, after the Lord assured the economist that He was not going to take him to heaven, the economist regained his composure and decided to ask the Lord a question. "When I was a child," said the economist, "the priests always told us that a thousand years on Earth was only a minute to you. Is that so?"

"Yes, that is so," responded the Lord.

Gaining some more confidence, the economist decided to ask another question. "If a thousand years for us is but a minute to you, then it must also be true that a million dollars to us is but a penny to you. Am I correct about this?"

"You are correct," responded the Lord, patiently.

Now the economist got very bold. He saw this as his big chance for instant economic wealth, so he said, "Well then, Lord, since you plan to leave me on this Earth for a while, would you be so kind as to give me one of your pennies?"

"No problem," said the Lord. "I'd be happy to oblige you. Unfortunately, I have no pennies with me right now, but if you will wait just a minute I'll get one for you."

Just as there were major discrepancies between the perceptions of the Lord and the perceptions of the economist, there are major discrepancies among the assumptions of current economic theory, the preservation of the ecosystem, the happiness of the planet's human inhabitants, and the dynamics of the global marketplace. As Peter Drucker (1980) points out, there is a crisis in economic theory today because of the "failure of the basic assumptions of the paradigm" (p. 9). He says, "Reality and the available economic theories have been moving further and further apart" (Drucker, 1989, p. 160). Economist Herman Daly (1977, 1991b) says that applying the assumptions of modern economics is like "seeking the optimal arrangement of deck chairs on the Titanic" (p. 89).

Current Economic Assumptions: Shoes That Don't Fit

In addition to Drucker and Daly, several other scholars have criticized the assumptions of modern economic theory, addressing a broad spectrum of concerns that ranges from the role of the individual and the firm to the true nature of international trade to the relationship between the economy and the ecosystem. In short, just as children outgrow their shoes, the realities of the marketplace have outgrown economic theory.

Economic Growth: Pie-in-the-Sky Gluttony

As we discussed in detail in Chapters 2 and 3, the assumption that the economy can grow forever is having major negative ramifications on the health of the ecosystem. The environmental costs of this assumption include the rapid depletion of nonrenewable energy, the depletion of natural resources, and pollution of the natural environment.

Microeconomic theory teaches that organizations should strive to maintain an optimal size determined by several external factors (capital intensity, proximity to customers, etc.). Managers know that striving to have the biggest organization possible regardless of the realities of the business environment is not rational; they know that beyond some size, the marginal costs will be greater than the marginal revenues. Yet the idea of optimal size is somehow lost in the shift to macroeconomic theories of the total economy, where it is assumed that the benefits of growth will outweigh the costs of growth regardless of how big the economy gets.

One way that many economists try to circumvent the reality of limits to growth is to assume that new technologies will continually appear to counteract the ecological problems. For example, they may assume that less intrusive oil-drilling methods can be developed that will allow oil exploration in wilderness areas with less environmental impact, or they may assume that cleaner ways to mine and burn coal can be developed that will allow its continued use as a primary energy source. As Daly (1991b) says, "Technology is the rock upon which the growthmen built their church" (p. 105). Technological innovations (such as the efficient collection and storage of solar energy, cleaner and more efficient production processes, and nuclear fusion) certainly need to be pursued. However, as we discussed in Chapter 2, humankind cannot expect sufficient technological advances to neutralize all of the negative impacts of increasing economic wealth for the growing number of people on the planet. Indeed, technology can often cause as many problems as it alleviates. For example, nuclear energy was considered the salvation from fossil fuel dependence in the 1950s, but in the 45 years since then, no technology has emerged to safely and effectively dispose of the high-level wastes from the process and none seems forthcoming. As Daly and Cobb (1989, 1994) say, "The assumption that new technologies will solve the problem . . . does not hold up" (p. 311).

Given the seriousness of our current environmental problems, it seems time for the field of economics to embrace concepts such as living-systems theory and thermodynamics, which clearly point to the fact that unlimited growth in a finite space is not possible over the long term. Incorporating these concepts into economic theory means discarding the unlimited growth assumption in favor of a more realistic model of the macroeconomy that recognizes that the total size of the economy does have limits defined by the ecosystem. Again, we quote Peter Drucker (1989):

> The final new reality in the world economy is the emergence of the transnational ecology. Concern for the ecology, the endangered habitat of the human race, will increasingly have to be built into economic policy.... We still talk of "environmental protection" as if it were protection of something that is outside of, and separate from, man. But what is endangered are the survival needs of the human race. (p. 133)

Ignoring Natural Capital: An Ecological and Social Nightmare

We have argued in previous chapters that the assumption of unlimited growth can exist only if the value of the Earth's natural capital is ignored. As you may recall from our discussion in Chapter 3, natural capital in current economic theory is assumed to be virtually unlimited because it is considered to be a near perfect substitute for human-made capital. One dimension of this problem not yet discussed is the fact that some of the most devastating social and ecological effects of assuming away resources in Nature are occurring in developing nations. The industrial nations seldom have all the natural resources they need to fuel their economic machines. Japan, for example, has almost no resources of its own, and the European Community is not much better off. Even resource-rich America imports large quantities of oil, platinum, and other resources from abroad. A high percentage of these resources are imported from developing nations that often have an abundance of natural capital but few financial resources. Under the current economic system, the rational thing is for the cash-rich industrial nations to purchase their natural resources from the cash-poor developing countries.

However, this solution is flawed for two reasons. First, the resources being traded by these developing nations, for the most part, are limited and are being depleted at nonrenewable rates. Because current economic systems have no provisions for the loss of natural resources, developing nations unwittingly transfer huge amounts of their nonrenewable wealth to industrialized nations in return for financial capital. According to economist Robert Repetto of the World Resources Institute, " 'A country could exhaust its mineral resources, cut down its forests, erode its soils, pollute its aquifers, and hunt its wildlife and fisheries to extinction, but measured income would not be affected as these assets disappeared' " (quoted in Hinrichsen, 1991, p. 3). Of course, these countries can collect cash only so long as the resources last; once they are gone, they have no other sources of income, and the land is usually left scarred and devastated. This is precisely what is happening to rain forests all over the world. Brazil, Malaysia, and other nations with significant amounts of rain forests are cutting them down and shipping them to Japan, Europe, and the United States for money that will dry up when the forests are gone.

Second, the cash that is paid for these resources seldom adds much to the social welfare of the citizens of the developing nations. The resources are normally owned by a few land owners who may become wealthy themselves but who often invest little of their money back into the local or national economies. The jobs that result from trading nonrenewable resources for cash are typically low paying, and the returns on their investment are normally below average (Porter, 1990). New firms in the developing country are normally tied to the excavation or harvesting of resources and thus will disappear when the resources are depleted. Economist James Robertson (1990) sums up this problem: "In recent years the world economy has devastated the lives of millions of innocent people, it has been transferring resources systematically from poor countries to rich countries, and it is destroying the Earth" (p. 68).

Selfish Human Beings: Please, Play It Again, Adam Smith

One of the economic assumptions criticized most often concerns the relationship between self-interest and the common good. In current economic theory, self-interest, the "invisible hand" that efficiently guides the market system toward a fair allocation of resources, is interpreted as the selfish pursuit of individual goals. This assumption of selfish individualism is supported because, in theory, maximizing individual wealth is the most direct route to maximizing the welfare of society. Individuals are depicted as self-contained entities that have no need to consider anything beyond themselves when they make their choices. Further, it is assumed that individuals are essentially value neutral; they are perceived to have no values except those that can be expressed monetarily. Human beings in economic models are similar to the lemmings described in Chapter 1; they're satisfied only when they are consuming.

In his classes at Louisiana State University, Herman Daly used to say that the selfish individualism embedded in current economic assumptions acts as an "invisible foot that kicks the heck out of the common good" because morality, quality time, meaningful relationships with others, and spiritual enlightenment play no part in the model. As Daly and Cobb (1989, 1994) say, the radical individualism of current economic theory "excludes concerns for other people's satisfaction and sufferings that do not express themselves as one's market activity. . . . [It] knows neither benevolence nor malevolence, only indifference" (p. 86). Etzioni (1988) agrees, saying, "There is more to life than a quest to maximize one's own satisfaction" (p. 13). He says that morality that evolves from the greater community is as important as individual pleasure in guiding human behavior.

One of the most interesting aspects of the neoclassical economic assumption that social welfare will improve if human beings will behave as selfish profit maximizers is that it is a fundamental misinterpretation of what Adam Smith says in both *Wealth of Nations* and *Theory of Moral Sentiments* (Collins & Barkdull, 1995). Collins and Barkdull (1995) point out that Adam Smith's concept of self-interest did not mean selfishness. According to Smith, *self-interest* was a rational pursuit of human desires constrained by considerations of justice, morality, and the impact of one's actions on others. By contrast, Smith defined *selfishness* as the immoral pursuit of one's goals without regard for the interests of others. Smith wrote in *Wealth of Nations,* " 'Every man, as long as he does not violate the laws of justice, is perfectly free to pursue his own self interest' " (quoted in Collins & Barkdull, 1995, p. 232); and he writes in *Theory of Moral Sentiments,* " 'One individual should never prefer himself so much even to any other individual, as to hurt or injure that other in order to benefit himself' " (quoted in Collins & Barkdull, 1995, p. 234).

International Trade: Vanilla Theories in a Banana Split World

We discussed previously that ignoring the value of natural capital creates a devastating distortion in the trade relationships between developed and developing nations. Other economic assumptions of international trade have been criticized as well. Michael Porter (1990) points out that the current theory of comparative economic advantage among nations assumes that capital and labor cannot cross international boundaries, technologies everywhere are identical, products are undifferentiated, no economies of scale exist, and the pool of factors of production in a nation is fixed. The absurdity of these assumptions renders the theory of comparative advantage virtually useless as a tool for understanding international trade. Porter says, "It is not surprising that most managers exposed to the theory find that it assumes away what they find to be most important and provides little guidance for appropriate company strategy" (p. 13).

Peter Drucker (1989) says that the transnational world economy is, for all practical purposes, ignored in current economic theory even though it obviously influences and sometimes even controls national economic activity. Economic theories have been developed within closed national markets and then fallaciously applied to the international marketplace. To exemplify his point, Drucker (1989) uses President Reagan's decision to raise the value of the dollar in the early 1980s. Rather than taking this as an opportunity to sell their products for less in order to protect their international market shares, most American exporters raised their prices to compensate for the money they would lose due to the revalued greenback. In the short-term, they were able to protect their dollar profits, but the higher prices eventually led to decreasing sales as the world market adjusted to the higher valued dollar; within 2 years they were experiencing profit losses. Four years later, the yen went up in value just as the dollar had done. In contrast to the American response, the Japanese sacrificed short-term profits in order to maintain market share; their sales did not go down (they actually rose), and their long-term profits increased.

One of the most confounding dimensions of international trade as it relates to the natural environment involves the emergence of free trade, supported by agreements such as the Uruguay Round of the General Agreement on Tariffs and Trade (GATT) and the North American Free Trade Agreement (NAFTA). Many argue vehemently that the free-trade principles embodied in such agreements are incompatible with protecting the natural environment. A few years ago, an anonymously penned poster mysteriously appeared in capitols all over the world portraying "GATTzilla," a horrendous monster devouring the planet by spreading wastes, destroying species, polluting water, and crushing democracy. Many believe that GATT officials are doing their best to live up to the GATTzilla image, citing actions such as the 1992 ruling that the United States's 1988 amendment to the Marine Mammal Protection Act was in violation of GATT because it banned imports of tuna into the United States from nations not using dolphin-friendly fishing methods (Reinhardt & Vietor, 1996).

On the other side of the argument are those who believe that free trade is, in fact, a primary requirement for a sustainable world economy. They argue that free trade provides developing countries with the opportunity to develop strong economies that will not have to rely on the exploitation of natural resources and cheap labor as the basic foundations of economic success. However, Daly (1993) believes that this conclusion is flawed because it rests on the same fallacious assumptions of the theory of comparative advantage that Porter (1990) criticizes as unrealistic, especially the assumption that capital and labor are immobile. Daly (1993) says, "Free traders are using an argument that hinges on the impermeability of national boundaries to capital to support a policy aimed at making those same boundaries increasingly permeable to both capital and goods" (p. 51).

According to Daly (1993), free trade conceived under this incorrect comparative-advantage assumption creates three problems. The first is the inefficient allocation of resources. For example, international trade typically involves excessive transportation costs. Commenting on this, Daly (1993) says, "Americans import Danish sugar cookies, and Danes import American sugar cookies. Exchanging recipes would surely be more efficient" (p. 51). Second, Daly (1993) points out that free trade can lead to the unfair distribution of resources. The comparative advantages that nations would enjoy if capital and labor markets were truly impermeable would give way to absolute advantages of some nations over others as capital and labor followed lower production costs. Daly's third criticism of free trade is that it flies in the face of sustainability because there are no workable mechanisms built into the current free-trade formula to account for the often broad differences in how environmental and social costs are internalized and externalized in different nations. Those nations that allow these costs to be born by society and the ecosystem rather than including them in the price of goods and services will have significant cost advantages in a free-trade marketplace. He says, "Free competition between different cost-internalization regimes is utterly unfair. . . . Attaining cheapness by ignoring real costs is a sin against efficiency" (Daly, 1993, p. 52). According to Daly (1993), these free-trade fallacies mean that wage rates for labor (nonsupervisory personnel) in high-wage countries will stagnate, that the cultural and economic bases of individual communities and nations will likely erode, and that ecological problems will be intensified.

Why Don't the Shoes Fit? Misplaced Concreteness

Alfred Korzybski (1933) stated years ago that "the map is not the territory." He counsels that it is not wise to confuse signs, symbols, models, and language with the reality they represent. Our languages and our models are mere abstractions of reality, and they can never be completely accurate in expressing all the intricate dimensions of what they are meant to describe. All complex subjects require that abstract models be developed that simplify them; understanding requires breaking a subject down into elementary parts that can be examined. No science, physical or social, can evolve in any way other than through the careful development of abstract models that explain the basic elements of the processes involved.

Economics is a highly abstract social science that attempts to explain an incredibly complex subject—how all of the 5.64 billion people in the world tend to behave as they go about satisfying their economic needs and wants. Drucker (1989) believes that economics is already so complex that managers usually cannot develop a meaningful working knowledge of it. Much criticism is leveled at economics because it omits so many important factors, yet everyone can agree that it cannot possibly include everything.

However, the crisis in economics is not so much related to its complexity and abstraction as it is to the failure of economists to recognize this characteristic. Very abstract and incomplete economic concepts are often presented as if they were complete representations of reality. This problem has been exacerbated by a number of factors, including the current isolation of economics into an academic discipline and the strict adherence to the scientific method in economics (economists such as Adam Smith operated in an interdisciplinary world in which few distinctions among disciplines were made, while the scientific method is reductionist by nature and therefore difficult to apply to broad, holistic situations) (Daly & Cobb, 1989, 1994). This problem is known as *misplaced concreteness* (Whitehead, 1925), which means confusing abstract conceptual measures with the reality they are designed to describe—confusing the map with the territory. As Kenneth Boulding (1970) writes, "The danger of measures is that they become ideals" (p. 157).

We have already alluded to several of the problems with misplaced concreteness in economics. The dogmatic assump-

tions that individuals are nothing but money-motivated consumers with no moral fiber, that international trade is played
on a vanilla playing field, and that natural resources have value
only when they are mined or chopped down have all led to
major economic, social, and ecological problems. However, we
would like to focus particular attention on two outcomes of misplaced concreteness: the misuse of GNP and extreme egoism.

GNP: Misplaced and Misunderstood

Assuming that the economy has the unlimited resources
and environmental capacity to grow indefinitely was a rational
and harmless simplification of reality when the field of economics was emerging in the 1700s and 1800s. At that time, only a
few nations were involved in significant economic activity,
newly discovered natural resources seemed endless, and the
population was much smaller. Over time, however, unlimited
growth was transformed by economists from a harmless assumption into a fact. Finally, in 1929 a statistical standard called
the *gross national product* (GNP) emerged as an official measure
of economic growth (Boulding, 1970). Since then, the GNP has
become the primary indicator by which societies measure the
human welfare of nations; efforts to show significant increases
in the GNP drive virtually every monetary and fiscal action
taken by the political and economic machinery. Prevailing economic thought says that increasing GNP is the primary mechanism necessary for achieving prosperity for all the world's
people.

However, according to Hazel Henderson (1991, 1992), GNP
is an undifferentiated measure of growth. She says that using
GNP as the only measure of human welfare is "like flying a
Boeing 747 with nothing but an oil gauge" (Henderson, 1992).
GNP simultaneously includes in its measurement of total economic activity a great deal that, in reality, detracts from national prosperity; at the same time, it leaves out many factors
that actually contribute to national well-being. Though some of
the money that changes hands within the economy results in
healthier and happier human beings, not every dollar is spent

to improve human welfare. In a typical industrial cycle, scarce resources are converted into products, and the products are then sold, consumed, and discarded as wastes. Money is spent throughout this process for a variety of things. The customers, employees, and firms will be temporarily, even permanently, better off because of the money they receive; however, money is also spent to deplete scarce resources, pollute the environment, and dispose of wastes. All of these are added into GNP. Depletion and pollution costs are masked as income and added into the GNP, and everyone is presumed to be better off because of it. Thus, every time organizations have to drill deeper or invade more wilderness to acquire resources, every time they dump wastes in a landfill, the air, or waterways, GNP goes up. The $2 billion that it cost to clean up the *Exxon Valdez* oil spill was actually added to the GNP of the United States (Postel, 1990). Daly (1991b) says, "We take real costs . . . of protecting ourselves from the unwanted side effects of production and add these expenditures to GNP rather than subtract them. We count real costs as benefits" (p. 99).

Why is GNP so unrelentingly worshiped in economics? The belief that increasing GNP and improving human welfare go hand-in-hand has persisted despite overwhelming evidence that the economy cannot grow big enough or fast enough to benefit the majority of the world's exponentially growing population, and if it did, the ecosystem could not absorb the stress. World GNP grew (in real dollars) from $3.8 billion in 1950 to $20.1 trillion in 1994, and the trend is expected to continue for the remainder of the 1990s (Brown, 1995c). If the trend does continue as expected, then the economy will grow to over $100 trillion over the next generation (Goodland, 1992). Yet as pointed out in Chapter 2, the number of people on the planet living in abject poverty continues to expand. According to Daly's (1993) calculations, world resource use will have to increase almost 36 times in order for 10 billion people to live on the planet at the same levels of per capita income currently enjoyed in the high-income nations. This is why Boulding (1970) says, "The GNP is like the Red Queen in *Alice Through the Looking Glass:* it runs as fast as it can to stay where it is" (p. 158).

Unfortunately, as long as unlimited growth is assumed to be a reality rather than a simplifying assumption, GNP will continue to be falsely considered synonymous with human welfare. There will continue to be no distinctions made in economic theory between the quantitative and qualitative dimensions of growth. Schumacher (1979) is quite graphic on this point:

> How can anybody assert that growth is [always] a good thing? If my children grow, this is a very good thing; if I should suddenly start growing, it would be a disaster. . . . Therefore, the qualitative discrimination is the main thing; it's far more important than some mysterious adding-up of everything. (p. 125)

Egoism Gone Wild: Roll Over in Your Grave, Adam Smith

Etzioni (1988) points out that exchanges seldom occur among equals; usually one party has a power advantage over the other. This often means that powerful individuals, firms, and so on can dominate the free market. If this domination is not tempered with Adam Smith's imperative not to do harm to others, then powerful executives and organizations can easily conclude that their primary purpose is to serve their own personal interests, implementing what Freeman and Gilbert (1988) call managerial prerogative strategies. The misplaced concreteness of this distorted neoclassical economic view of self-interest has had predictably dire consequences.

Examples abound of how strategic decisions made "for the good of the company" have left closed plants, unemployed workers, ripped-off customers, devastated communities, and natural disasters in their wakes. We mentioned in Chapter 3 how Unisys made an economic decision to close its profitable Bristol, Tennessee, plant, leaving behind unemployed workers and an illegal toxic waste dump. Even after the *Valdez* oil spill, Exxon, citing the high costs of the transition, said that it would take the firm about 20 years to replace its fleet of single-hulled tankers with double-hulled tankers. This decision was made even though other oil firms, like BP, had already invested in double-hulled tanker fleets, and in spite of clear evidence that double-hulled tankers can reduce the risk of oil spills by about 80% (Stead & Stead, 1994b). In 1986, Frank Lorenzo bought Eastern Airlines for $620 million ($280 million of which was his own cash). He bled Eastern Airlines dry while infusing capital into Texas Air, which he also owned. Eastern was saddled with $500 million in new debt, was stripped of its assets, and eventually bankrupted. Many people lost their jobs, but Lorenzo cleared $200 million (Gibney, 1989). However, the most blatant example of egoism in business may be Charles Keating, former CEO of Lincoln Savings and Loan of California. While Keating was lavishing huge salaries, yachts, and other perks upon himself, Lincoln Savings and Loan was losing $2.6 billion of its depositors' money in the junk bond market. At one of the court hearings concerning the fraudulent practices by Keating, an internal memo from Keating to his junk bond salespersons was presented as evidence. It read, " 'Always remember, the weak, meek and ignorant are always good targets' " (quoted in Martz, 1990, p. 22).

New Economic Models

In sum, current economic theory is having a destructive impact on the natural environment, favors egoism over the moral standards of the greater community, has led to abuses of power, and provides an inaccurate picture of the international trade arena. Drucker (1989) is very pessimistic about the role that economic theory will play in the future. He says, "To give us a functioning economic theory, we need a new synthesis. . . . And if no such synthesis emerges, we may be at the end of economic theory" (p. 157). Economists and noneconomists alike have labored diligently over the last few years to foster new economic theories based on more realistic assumptions about the greater environment in which the economic system is embedded.

Replacing Unlimited Growth With Sustainability

More than anyone else, E. F. Schumacher brought the world's attention to the problems of unlimited economic growth. His publication of *Small Is Beautiful* in 1973 was a wake-up call for the world. He says that the first assumption of economics should be that there is such a thing as "enough." Once such an assumption is in place, then economists and other scientists can go about the business of defining what "enough" is (Schumacher, 1973). Herman Daly (1977, 1991b) proposes that *enoughness* needs to be a primary value upon which economic theory is based if humankind is to achieve a sustainable balance between the economic system and the ecosystem.

Enoughness implies that there is a sufficient level of economic consumption beyond which human welfare and ecological balance are significantly eroded. As was made clear in the discussion of sustainability in Chapter 4, defining sufficiency is no easy task. However, the results of ignoring sufficiency are a great deal more ominous than assuming that it exists, albeit imprecisely. Daly (1986) says, "Perhaps the only thing more difficult than defining sufficiency is our present attempt to get along without the concept by pretending that there is no limit to either the possibility or desirability of growth" (p. 43).

Daly (1977, 1991b) says that if the scarcity and aesthetic value of resources and the relationship between economic satisfaction and human fulfillment can be added into the economic formula, then the concept of sufficiency would take on real meaning. That is, enoughness will be definable when economic models include the following assumptions: (a) Human beings want happiness, fulfillment, enlightenment, and a sense of purpose, not just more things; and (b) the Earth has a limited amount of resources and a limited waste-processing capacity.

Accounting for Nature

Achieving sustainability requires the development of meaningful economic models and tools for including the value of

Nature. One approach, commonly referred to as *environmental economics*, tries to internalize the environmental costs of doing business, which, in the past, have been considered external to the economic system. Environmental economics proposes that regulations, taxes, and market incentives can be used as mechanisms for assigning value to resources, pollution, and wastes. Once this occurs, the natural environment is brought into the circular-flow model, allowing for the application of neoclassical economic theory in determining the optimum levels of resource depletion, pollution, and waste generation that the planet can bear (Costanza, 1989).

One example of an environmental economics approach is James Robertson's (1990) suggestion of a three-pronged tax system designed to internalize environmental costs. His first proposal is a land occupation tax based on the site value of the land (the value of the land prior to any improvements such as buildings). Using the site value allows the tax to be levied on the value of the property before it enters the traditional economic cycle. Second, he suggests taxing energy and resources before they are mined or harvested, again accounting for their value in Nature prior to their entry into the economy. These taxes should be based on the calorific value of the resources (calories are a measure of the amount of potential energy something contains) rather than the dollar value. Third, Robertson would tax pollution and wastes. He acknowledges that implementing pollution and waste taxes will be more difficult than implementing the first two. Such taxation will require a plethora of taxes, each focusing on specific waste and pollution problems—that is, garbage taxes, soil erosion taxes, air pollution taxes, water pollution taxes, and so on. He says, "Certainly, it could provide meat and drink for a small army of environmental economists and bureaucrats" (p. 108). However, he points out that the complexity of the waste and pollution tax system can be at least partially offset by the energy and resource taxes; these are designed to encourage organizations to be energy and resource efficient, and greater efficiency means fewer wastes and less pollution to tax.

Another approach, which is currently getting more attention than tax approaches such as Robertson's, is the use of market incentives to control environmental problems. Such approaches are designed to reward firms for controlling wastes and pollution before they occur. One approach is to issue pollution credits that allow a firm to emit a certain amount of pollutants into the environment. These credits are tradable assets; that is, companies whose emissions are below that allowed by their credits can sell the excess credits to other firms. For example, the 1990 Clean Air Act provides for tradable sulfur dioxide credits.

Daly (1977, 1991a, 1991b) and Costanza (1989) believe that these market mechanisms (both taxes and market incentives) are good ideas but that they don't go far enough in internalizing environmental costs into the economic system. They say that environmental economics alone cannot be counted on to solve all of our ecological ills because it doesn't directly address the issue of absolute scarcity of resources. They suggest adding the basic principles of ecology to the tenets of environmental economics, resulting in what they refer to as *ecological economics*. Essentially, ecological economics is based on the following: (a) a dynamic, holistic evolutionary view of the world; (b) multiscale time frames that recognize both the short-term dimensions of day-to-day economic decisions and the evolutionary dimensions of Nature's processes; (c) the recognition that humans are a part of Nature; (d) a macroeconomic goal of sustainability and appropriate microeconomic goals to support this; (e) a belief that technology is important but not a panacea for achieving sustainability; and (f) a belief that solutions to ecological problems must transcend traditional disciplinary boundaries (Costanza, Daly, & Bartholomew, 1991).

Daly (1977, 1991b) proposes a model of ecological economics that he calls a *steady-state economy* (SSE). An SSE is based on two physical magnitudes—the physical stock of capital (comprising both people and products) and the flow of throughput. By adding throughput into the formula, an SSE is able to operate on the assumption that the entropy law imposes absolute limits on the capacity of the economy. Daly (1991b, p. 199) says, "To deny the relevance of the entropy law to economics is to deny the relevance of the difference between a lump of coal and a pile of ashes." Daly (1991b) defines an SSE as

> an economy with constant stocks of people and artifacts, maintained at some desired, sufficient levels by low rates of maintenance throughput, that is, by the lowest feasible flows of matter and energy from the first stages of production (depletion of low-entropy materials from the environment) to the last stage of consumption (pollution of the environment with high-entropy wastes and exotic materials). (p. 17)

Daly (1991b) notes that an SSE is a concept that can help to differentiate between physical, quantitative growth and non-physical, qualitative development. An SSE develops but does not grow, just as the planet develops but does not grow. However, things such as culture, knowledge, genetic inheritance, technology, and so on are not held constant but can grow. Neither are the product mix nor the distribution of the capital stock held constant. The constant, physical stock of people and products does require that deaths equal births and that new production offsets physical depreciation. However, in an SSE, "limits to growth do not mean limits to development" (Daly, 1991b, 243). Daly (1993) says, "Development without growth is sustainable development" (p. 57).

Regarding the value of capital, Daly (1977, 1991b) takes issue with the neoclassical assumption that reproducible capital is a near-perfect substitute for land and other low-entropy resources. He notes that capital requires resources (matter and energy) for its production; that is, it requires throughput. Since current macroeconomic theory ignores the role of throughput, human-made capital and low-entropy resources are seen as almost perfect substitutes. In reality, however, the entropy law places limits on factor substitution. Daly and Cobb (1989, 1994) suggest that by replacing the term *land* with *Nature* in economic theory, the differences between reproducible economic capital and nonreproducible natural capital can be taken into account more easily. After all, whereas land is something humans can buy, sell and live on, humans can never own Nature; they must live with her.

Depletion quotas are one of the specific aspects of Daly's (1977, 1991b) SSE. Depletion quotas impose limits on the absolute amount of resources that can be extracted in a given period of time. Like Robertson's land and energy resource taxes, depletion quotas recognize the value of resources in their natural state. Like pollution credits, depletion quotas would be tradable on the open market, providing positive incentives for organizations to save resources. Thus, these depletion quotas would provide control over scarce resources while maintaining a free-market system to allocate them.

One of the real barriers to the global implementation of ecological economics is redefining GNP in order to truly account for Nature and human welfare. This is certainly no simple matter. Such an index needs to include things for which there are currently no generally accepted measures. According to Hazel Henderson (1991), human welfare and the natural environment can truly be measured only if GNP can be replaced with measures that account for (a) the psychological as well as the physical needs of human beings, (b) the aesthetic value and carrying capacity of Nature, and (c) intragenerational and intergenerational equity regarding opportunities for self-development and fulfillment. She cites three specific efforts currently under way designed to accomplish this, including Japan's development of the Net National Welfare (NNW) index, the Overseas Development Council's Physical Quality of Life Index (PQLI), and the U.N. Environmental Programme's Basic Human Needs indicator (BHN) (Henderson, 1991).

Daly and Cobb (1989, 1994) propose an alternative approach to GNP called Hicksian Income (HI). The concept was named for Sir John Hicks, who wrote over 40 years ago that sustainable income is the only kind of income that has any real meaning. Simply stated, when people cannot sustain their income, they become poor. HI begins by calculating the net national product (NNP), which is GNP minus standard depreciation costs. NNP alone is a better measure of sustainability than GNP because it recognizes that growth has some costs associated with it—wear and tear, repairs, replacement, and so on. However, it does not include either depreciation of natural capital (DNC) or defensive expenditures (DE), income spent to protect ourselves from the ecological side effects of production, such as money to clean up an oil spill or toxic waste dump. HI is thus calculated by subtracting DNC and DE from NNP.

Replacing Egoistic Lemmings With Moral Human Beings

Amitai Etzioni (1988) proposes that the assumption of radical individualism that is prevalent in current economics should be replaced with what he refers to as the *I/We paradigm*. The I/We paradigm recognizes that human beings make rational economic choices designed to satisfy their individual needs and desires, but it also recognizes that individual economic satisfaction can occur only within the moral dimensions of a meaningful community structure.

The I/We paradigm makes three assumptions that foster a more realistic perspective of human beings. First, it assumes that people have many needs and wants. In addition to economic desires that can be measured in dollars and cents, people also want to live up to moral values that are unrelated to the economic system. Second, the I/We paradigm assumes that people typically make their choices primarily on the basis of value judgments and emotions and only secondarily through empirical logic. Third, it assumes that people exist as parts of social collectives that impose moral standards of conduct. Individual relations are largely molded by the community in which they take place. Thus, human beings are perceived in the I/We paradigm to be multidirected, emotional, value-laden, and unable to function effectively except within the acceptable moral limits of the community (Etzioni, 1988).

Daly's and Cobb's (1989, 1994) *person-in-community paradigm* is similar to the I/We paradigm. They point out that people are both consumers and workers in an economic community where relationships with one another are important.

Further, the economic community is a smaller part of larger social, political, and ecological communities, and thus it should serve the moral priorities of these larger communities. The foundation unit of the economic system within their paradigm is the self-sufficient community, not the selfish individual.

Daly and Cobb (1989, 1994) recommend several steps for implementing the paradigm, including implementing land taxes, resource taxes, waste taxes, and depletion quotas (discussed earlier) and changing the nature of free trade (which will be discussed in the next section). Further, they suggest that more political and economic powers be pushed down to the state and local levels; they say that this would encourage people to be more active in democratic processes because it would allow individuals a greater sense of identity with their communities.

Two of their recommendations address the problems associated with extreme egoism. First, they suggest a return to previous governmental policies designed to prevent consolidation of economic power into the hands of a few individuals and organizations; tax and ownership laws should be structured to encourage spin-offs and discourage mergers. Second, they propose that income tax laws should be modified so that the income gaps between the rich and the not-rich are less extreme. They clearly state that income differentials are important free-market incentives that should not be abandoned; however, extreme income differentials ignore the important interdependencies among the members of the community (Daly & Cobb, 1989, 1994).

One feature of the person-in-community paradigm that is of particular interest to business managers concerns labor-management relations. Daly and Cobb (1989, 1994) say that management and labor constitute a single community of mutual interests. They advocate small, employee-owned organizations that are energy-efficient and that provide real opportunities for personal employee satisfaction with their work. Such organizations tend to do less environmental damage, foster the group over the individual, and help to restore thought, skill, and initiative to the workplace.

Addressing the Realities of the Global Market

Michael Porter's *The Competitive Advantage of Nations* (1990) is probably the most complete attempt to dislodge the current economic theories of international trade. He proposes that current theories do not even address the right question. Current theories focus on understanding why some nations are more competitive than others, but Porter points out that nations do not compete. Industries and industry segments are the competitors in the global market. For example, Japan is not a competitive nation; it has many competitive industries and many noncompetitive industries. The same is true of Germany, Italy, and the United States. The role of the nation is to serve as the *home base* of the competitors. Thus, the proper question is, why do particular nations provide favorable environmental conditions (a good home base) for the emergence of globally competitive firms and industries?

He dispels many fallacies about international trade. For example, he points out that many nations are quite well off despite high trade deficits or high exchange rates for their currencies. He also shows that an abundance of cheap labor or natural resources is usually a poor mechanism for achieving advantages in the global marketplace. The advantages once provided by low wages and cheap natural resources are being replaced by the ability to adopt new technologies that bypass or reduce dependence on these factors. He says that nations such as India and Mexico have built their economies on cheap labor, but they are not exactly ideal industrial role models. He says, "The ability to compete *despite* paying high wages would seem to represent a far more desirable national target" (Porter, 1990, p. 3).

Porter (1990) identifies four determinants of a nation's ability to provide an effective home base for particular firms and industries. First are factor conditions; a nation should be able to adequately create, upgrade, and specialize its human, physical, knowledge, and infrastructure (communications, transportation, etc.) factors to meet the needs of its industries. Of these, the most important are *advanced factors,* such as sophisticated electronic communication capabilities, highly educated personnel, and a strong commitment to scientific research. The second determinant is the demand conditions that exist within the home-base nation. Firms and industries that are required to constantly innovate and improve in order to be competitive at home typically will be better equipped to compete abroad. The third determinant is the presence of strong related and supporting industries (suppliers, software firms to support computer manufacturers, etc.), and the fourth determinant is how well the strategies and structures of the firms in the industry fit the dynamics of the global market as well as how much rivalry exists among the firms in the industry.

Porter makes two points about the ecological dimensions of international trade. As mentioned, he warns against basing competitive advantages on cheap natural resources (Porter, 1990); he also argues that strong environmental regulations in home-base nations can provide global competitive advantages for firms in industries affected by the regulations (Porter, 1991). He points out that Germany, with the world's strongest environmental laws, supplies 70% of the air pollution control equipment sold in the United States.

Daly and Cobb (1989, 1994) agree with Porter that low wages are not an appropriate competitive advantage and that international trade takes place among individual firms and industries rather than among nations. They also agree with Porter that basing trade on cheap natural resources can create problems. They note that massive debts accumulated by developing nations (i.e., Brazil) have forced them to overharvest rain forests and other natural resources to meet their financial obligations. However, they break with Porter by suggesting that ecological and social dimensions would be more prominent in international trade if it were conducted among national communities rather than individual firms. Nations could more effectively seek multilateral balances based on the physical amounts of resources traded (as opposed to financial balances). This would allow a nation to have resource deficits or surpluses with specific nations while maintaining an overall balance. Such balances could be achieved by auctioning import quotas to firms in amounts relatively equal to what a nation expects to export in a given period of time; these quotas could be resold or traded to others, but no more quotas would be issued during the trading period. Thus, positive incentives are provided to firms, and global natural capital transfers are kept to a sustainable level (Daly & Cobb, 1989, 1994).

With regard to dealing with the social and ecological inefficiencies related to free trade, Daly (1993) argues that those nations that have regulations and other mechanisms designed to internalize social and environmental costs into the price of their products and services should be allowed to charge tariffs on imports from nations that do not. He points out that such tariffs would simply extend the already accepted free-trade practice of levying tariffs for *dumping*, selling products in other countries below actual production costs. These tariffs would essentially expand the definition of dumping to include full environmental and social costs as well as more traditional production costs. Using this concept, the United States should have every right to charge tariffs on imported tuna that were caught without regard for the number of dolphins killed in the process. Whereas many free traders would argue that such tariffs constitute protectionism, Daly (1993) makes it clear that there is a major difference. Protectionist tariffs are levied to protect inefficient industries from more efficient foreign manufacturers, but the tariffs suggested by Daly are designed to assure that all costs, including social and environmental costs, are included in the definition of efficiency.

Conclusions

We began with a story, and we will end with one. A cruise ship sank in a storm several years ago, and one of its rafts was left adrift with three people aboard—a physicist, an engineer, and an economist. The raft was stocked with a survival kit that included canned goods, but the can opener was missing from the kit. The physicist said that this presented a very perplexing problem because they had no way to separate the strong metal molecules of the cans in order to get to the food inside. The engineer agreed, lamenting that there were no sharp instruments on board that they could use to open the cans. The economist, however, dismissed the pessimistic realities of his fellow passengers, saying, "All we have to do is assume that the cans are already open. Then we can eat to our hearts' content."

The fallacious assumptions that frame a great deal of our current economic thought make it extremely difficult to apply traditional economic models with any degree of success. In this chapter, it has been documented that new economic models are springing forth from both inside and outside the discipline of economics. Because strategic managers make the vast majority of the decisions within the global economic system, they are the ones most in need of new models. Concerns for the Earth are now being shouted at business organizations by a plethora of environmental stakeholders. Managers are left with no choice but to apply new models, values, and methods to deal effectively with these concerns. The survival of their firms and their species depends on it.

Chapter 7

Values for a Small Planet

As we have demonstrated throughout the book, the long-term survival of the economic system and the ability to sustain the ecosystem are intricately intertwined. The ability of the planetary ecosystem to support human life is being directly threatened by current levels of economic activity. Economic system *and* ecosystem survival are directly tied to humankind's willingness to evolve to an economy that better accounts for the moral as well as the economic needs of the human community and that is in sync with the evolutionary biophysical processes of the Earth. A key ingredient in all of this is the emergence of ecologically sensitive business organizations, organizations willing to tie their economic success and their environmental responsibility together into one package. This means, of course, that economic success for business organizations in the future will require the formulation and implementation of strategic management processes that account for the limits of the Earth.

We discussed in Chapter 5 that successfully integrating concern for the planet into an organization's strategic processes requires that strategic managers refocus their values, ethical systems, and thought processes to account for the mutually causal interconnections between the organization and the evo-

128

lutionary biophysical processes of Nature. Given this, the first step toward implementing ecologically sustainable strategic management processes is to identify and adopt a set of organizational values that, collectively, comprise an ethical system that allows for positive synergy between the organization's ecological concerns and its economic goals.

Ethical systems are generally composed of complex networks of related values. At the heart of these networks are *core values* that define the essence of the ethical system. The role of a core value is to create the overarching moral framework for differentiating between right and wrong. This core value represents a kind of moral vision within which ethical decisions can be framed. Once the core value of the system has been identified, then relevant *instrumental values* can be identified that more clearly define the behavioral principles associated with behaving within the ethical boundaries implied by the core value (Freeman, 1984; Milbrath, 1989). In this chapter, we suggest a system of core and instrumental values that we believe can facilitate the efforts of strategic managers to successfully manage within the limits of the planet.

The Manager's Divergent Dilemma

From Schumacher's (1977) perspective, any environmentally sensitive ethical system will have to span the divergent ecology-economy dichotomy that currently keeps business at odds with the natural environment. Hawken (1993b) describes the linear thinking that characterizes this divergence in this way: "Business believes that if it does not continue to grow and instead cuts back and retreats it will destroy itself. Ecologists believe that if business continues its unabated expansion it will destroy the world around it" (p. 9). The outcomes of couching the ecology-economy debate in such linear terms are predictably unsolvable arguments: growth versus no growth, wealth versus beauty, Nature versus humankind, and Nature as means versus Nature as ends. Such arguments leave managers faced with seemingly insolvable conflicts between environmental protection and economic success. They do not necessarily want to ignore the environment, but they have a difficult time putting the environment in its proper perspective.

Sustainability: The Transcendent Core Value

For Schumacher (1973, 1977, 1979), Hawken (1993b), and Milbrath (1989, 1990) these left-versus-right, ecology-versus-economy debates have gotten humankind nowhere in its search for an ecologically rational economic system. Effectively integrating Nature into the consciousness and decision-making processes of strategic managers begins with identifying a core value that provides a valid moral vision for transcending the linear traps of the economy-ecology debate. Milbrath (1990) says that the answers lie "neither to the left nor to the right, but out front." Hawken (1993b) says that humankind has to seek "a third way, a path that restores the natural communities [by using] many of the historically effective organizational and market techniques of free enterprise" (p. 9). Schumacher counsels that the answer lies in finding "the middle way," the enlightened path through the maze of conflicting issues that plague this divergent problem (Schumacher, 1973; Wood, 1984).

As would be expected from our discussions in previous chapters, we believe that sustainability represents the appropriate core value for an ethical system that allows for positive synergy between economic success and environmental responsibility in business organizations. This is not our original thought, of course: Milbrath (1989), Daly and Cobb (1989, 1994), Buzzelli (1994), Gore (1992), and a multitude of others have made the same argument. They all argue that sustainability can transcend the growth-versus-no-growth, money-versus-beauty, humans-versus-Nature, means-versus-ends dichotomies that have so long characterized the economy-ecology debate.

Thus, as a core value, sustainability can provide the understanding that economic success and ecosystem survival are both worthy and necessary goals for individuals, organizations, societies, and Nature. Such an overarching understanding al-

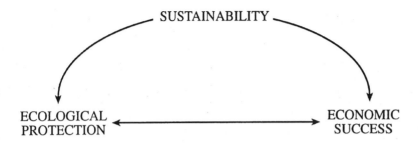

Figure 7.1. Transcending the Divergent Problem

lows previously opposing forces (e.g., environmentalists and strategic decision makers in business organizations) to recognize that they have common goals and expectations. Cooperation founded on common goals and expectations is a basis for synergy among human beings; therefore, cooperation between these traditionally opposing forces is more likely to lead to meaningful actions than either group acting alone. Indeed, in the genre of the French Revolution, "ecology, economy, sustainability" can be heralded as the appropriate overarching vision upon which to base business activity in the future (see Figure 7.1).

Instrumental Values for a Small Planet

Thus, sustainability defines the essence of an ethical system for solving the divergent dilemma faced by society as it tries to balance economic and ecosystem survivability. It is the basic principle upon which an ecologically balanced economy can be defined. However, implementing sustainability as a core value requires a set of instrumental values that allow humans to behave in sustainable ways. Instrumental values are essentially more numerous and more personal than core values. Thus, as many have reminded us over the past few years, there are many instrumental values and combinations of instrumental values that can help to define how to behave in the context of sustainability. With this admonition in mind, we offer six instrumental values that we believe allow for human decisions based on sustainability: wholeness, posterity, smallness, community, quality, and spiritual fulfillment.

Wholeness

Wholeness is a critical aspect of environmental ethics. Conceptually, wholeness is about interconnectedness, relatedness, balance, mutual causality, and the connections between past, present, and future. Wholeness reminds humans that they are products of their collective past and architects of their collective future. It reminds them to connect with all elements of their environment and to consider their impact on these elements in the decisions they make.

Thus, a value of wholeness helps people recognize that all of the Earth's living subsystems are parts of a supranational ecological system. Wholeness also helps people remember that survival depends on successfully interacting with the other living subsystems on the planet, since the whole cannot survive if its parts are destroyed. Further, since the whole is defined by how its parts interact with one another, valuing wholeness will help people to better perceive and attend to the relationships with other elements of the environment.

Rene Dubos, who developed the first antibiotics, provides an excellent example of how holistic thinking can be beneficial. Whereas most physicians of his time believed that the ability to cure and/or eliminate diseases rested in isolating organisms and breaking them down into their smallest components, Dubos believed that no living organism could be understood except within the context of its relationships with the ecosystem. He revolutionized the medical profession with his theories that human disease is not usually caused simply by the presence of some particular disease-causing organism; rather, he showed that the causes of disease are related to how humans interact with their total environment. Dubos believed that human health would not significantly improve until humankind learned to understand and sustain its environment. Because people have to continuously adapt to things such as increasing crowding and environmental pollution, he thought that serious disease of some type would always be present in society. His development of antibiotics resulted from his holistic perspective on the problem of controlling infectious diseases. He decided that the solution to effectively fighting these diseases was to find substances that would destroy whole bacteria rather than specific cells. This insight led to one of the most important medical advances of the 20th century (Moberg & Cohn, 1991).

In one of his 16th-century essays, philosopher Michel de Montaigne elegantly appealed to the need for decision makers to adopt wholeness as a value. He believed that people can comprehend the true impact of their decisions only if they account for the wholeness of the Earth and their role in it. On this point, he says,

> Whoever calls to his mind, as in a picture, the great image of our mother Nature in all her majesty; whoever reads in her face her universal and constant variety; whoever sees himself in it . . . like a dot made by a very fine pencil; he alone estimates things according to their true proportions. (Montaigne, 1580/1958a, p. 63)

Montaigne also believed that decision makers need to realize when they make decisions that their actions will always have an influence (usually negative) on someone and/or something else:

> No profit can be made except at another's expense. . . . As I was reflecting on this, the fancy came upon me that here Nature is merely following her habitual policy. For natural scientists hold that the birth, nourishment, and growth of each thing means the change and decay of something else. (Montaigne 1580/1958b, pp. 48-49)

Thus, Montaigne and Dubos captured two reasons why valuing wholeness is advantageous for a sustainable balance between economic success and environmental protection. First, a value for wholeness can provide business organizations with the broad perspective they need to remain competitive in today's global network of business activity. Thinking of the world as an interconnected whole can provide a much clearer understanding of the cooperative, participative relationships that organizations need to develop with their employees, customers, suppliers, and other stakeholders. It can also give organizations a better viewpoint from which to observe and analyze today's complex, dynamic, international business environment. Further, as Dubos adroitly demonstrated when he discovered antibiotics by looking at the whole bacterium, holistic thinking can be of tremendous benefit to novel, creative efforts. New products, new services, and new methods can all spring from the value of wholeness. Thus, valuing wholeness can contribute significantly to a firm's economic success in a very competitive world.

Second, Montaigne and Dubos make it clear that if people think holistically, they can't help but recognize and consider the impact of their decisions on other parts of the ecosystem. Understanding (a) how the organization fits into the ecosystem and (b) that most organizational actions will have some negative effect on other subsystems of the planet can give strategic managers an ecological perspective upon which to base their decisions. They will be more likely to examine the impact of their decisions on other people, communities, societies, and the Earth.

Posterity

"We didn't inherit the Earth from our parents; we borrowed it from our children." This well-known Kenyan proverb clearly describes why posterity is an important value for achieving sustainability. Valuing posterity, believing that future generations of human beings and other species are prominent factors in strategic decisions, can be instrumental in attaining a sustainable economic and ecological balance. It's no wonder that the basic definition of sustainability, "development which meets the needs of present generations without compromising the ability of future generations to meet their own needs" (World

Commission on Environment and Development, 1987, p. 8), is essentially a restatement of this proverb.

People who grew up in middle-class America during the 1950s and 1960s remember the magnificent portrait of the American dream painted by their parents. "We want things to be better for you than they were for us," their parents said. This positive portrait, based on creating a solid economic base for their children, provided the impetus for members of that generation to work very hard in order to achieve their economic goals. Unfortunately, the future does not look as bright for the current generation of children as it did for the previous one, and the environment is a major reason why. Many polls have concluded that the public believes that the world will be a worse place to live in the future because of the deteriorating environment (see, e.g., "Research Alert," 1991). An image of society based on unlimited economic growth has caused humankind to fall into ecological traps, raising serious concerns about the quality of life for our future generations. Assuming that social scientists are correct in concluding that a positive image for future generations is critical to the survival and health of a society, there is every reason to be concerned.

Ornstein and Ehrlich (1989) make it clear that people's picture of the future will have to change drastically if they wish to develop a positive view for their children and their children's children. It may help if people realize how old (or young) humankind really is. The Earth is 4.5 billion years old, but human civilizations did not appear until 10,000 years ago, written histories have been around for only 5,000 years, and the Industrial Age began only 350 years ago. Milbrath (1989) effectively demonstrates this point by using the popular image of a 1-year movie encompassing the Earth's entire history. If the movie began on January 1, dinosaurs would not appear until December 13, mammals would enter the scene on December 15, and *Homo sapiens* would make their movie debut at 11 minutes before midnight of December 31. Civilized human activity would not emerge until the last 2 minutes of the movie, recorded history would begin 1 minute before the curtain comes down, the Industrial Age would dominate only the last 1.5

seconds, and our own lifetimes would flicker by during the final half second of the film. Maybe this movie can help to put what is called long-range planning into its proper perspective.

A value for posterity can be an important ingredient in effectively managing the change and turbulence that all organizations now face and will continue to face in the 21st century. Adopting posterity as a value encourages business organizations to develop a vision of what they are and what they want to become. Having a clear vision of the future has proven to be a critical factor for successful organizations. Visions serve as common denominators around which strategic decisions are shaped and implemented. A shared vision in an organization encourages employees to think strategically; when strategic thinking is a part of an organizational culture, the company is better prepared to manage its opportunities and threats in ways that are advantageous to its survival and prosperity (Ernst & Baginski, 1989/1990).

In addition to supporting economic success, posterity is also important for achieving ecological sensitivity in organizations. Taking future generations into account in strategic decisions will significantly influence a wide range of choices. If strategic managers believe that clean water, clean air, abundant resources, biodiversity, and natural beauty are the birthrights of all generations, not just their own, then the decisions they make are bound to better reflect a concern for the Earth. The Iroquois Confederacy had a seven-generation planning horizon; they tried to predict the effects of their decisions for the next seven generations to follow. This type of long-range planning by business organizations would tremendously enhance the sustainability of the small planet, Earth.

Smallness

As we discussed, sustainability is a matter of scale. Humans live on a small planet, one that is becoming overburdened with population and economic activity; thus, thinking in terms of a smaller scale seems necessary. Schumacher (1973) brought the world's attention to the ideals of smallness. He says, "Small-scale operations, no matter how numerous, are always less harmful to the natural environment than large-scale ones, simply because their individual force is small in relation to the recuperative forces of Nature" (p. 36). Thinking small is no easy task for humankind in today's world. Daly and Cobb (1989, 1994) say that the conviction that bigger is better is a deep social ideal that permeates the hearts and souls of most people today; changing values from bigness to smallness will mean examining the basic differences between wants and needs in society.

Given that economic scale is ultimately defined by the amount of energy and resources transformed from their natural state into outputs, including wastes (Daly & Cobb, 1989, 1994), a value for smallness has implications for every aspect of the economic cycle. At the production end of the cycle, smallness will help managers more accurately account for the value of the scarce natural resources that form the foundation of all economic capital. A value for smallness will encourage strategic decision makers to implement policies aimed at using as little as possible of the Earth's nonrenewable resources. Organizations applying smallness are more likely to focus a great deal of attention on searching for ways to save energy and to use more renewable energy sources in the production and delivery of their products and services. Smallness will also encourage organizations to look for ways to reduce the materials that go into their products, including packaging.

Valuing smallness in the production of goods and services has tremendous implications for the technologies used by organizations. Production technologies based on industrial-ecosystem models (discussed in depth in Chapter 9) would emanate from such a value. Renewable energy technologies, resource conservation and recycling technologies, interorganizational waste-resource loops, and so on, would become the focus of attention. This means that technological development would move toward "human technologies functioning in an integral relationship with Earth technologies" (Berry, 1988, p. 65). This, by itself, is an economic boon; there was unanimous agreement among the participants of a *Business Week* conference on the natural environment in 1990 that new environmental technologies will provide many business opportunities for decades to come (Brown, 1990; Sarney, 1990).

No doubt, as Daly and Cobb (1989, 1994) warn, moving from a culture based on bigness to a culture based on smallness will not be easy. However, smallness is already emerging as a basic consideration in the way business is being done. Peters and Waterman (1982) repeatedly found that the efficiency provided by smallness was consistently profitable for the excellent companies they investigated. Organizations are discovering the economic benefits of small work teams, energy efficiency, and growth based on quality rather than quantity. As smallness becomes a more significant influence on both the production and consumption sides of the economic formula, there is a distinct possibility that the resulting synergy may lead to smallness dominating our social consciousness in the same way that bigness does now. If this can happen, then both economic and ecological sustainability are possible.

Community

Communities are not simply groups of people occupying patches of land. They are complex social systems composed of diverse individuals and organizations. Members of a community share at least three characteristics: (a) They are conscious of their relationships with others in the community; (b) they are conscious of the limits of the community; and (c) they are conscious of the differences between themselves and those who live outside the community (Daly & Cobb, 1989, 1994). Thus, although communities usually share a common geography, the essence of a community lies primarily in the complex cognitive networks that form around the values and expectations of the individuals and organizations that constitute it. As Etzioni (1991) says, communities are identified by their "sense of we-ness" (p. 5).

Since communities are more cognitive than physical, they exist in many forms. The local community, business community, religious community, and European Community all fit the definition. In this sense, there is no need to differentiate between the terms *community* and *society*; communities simply represent the underlying social form on which societies are based (Daly & Cobb, 1989, 1994). Etzioni (1991) says, "Communities exist like Chinese nesting boxes, in which smaller ones—families—are embedded in more encompassing ones—say, villages—and these in still more encompassing ones—some national societies" (p. 5).

The shared values and expectations that make up the essence of communities lead to their strongest force, the establishment of ethical standards. As physicist Werner Heisenberg (1985b) once said, "Ethics is the basis for the communal life of men" (p. 44). Communities themselves have no power to coerce people to behave in socially acceptable ways (communities may have police forces with coercive powers, but the powers of the police result from shared community values for law and order, public safety, etc.); however, the moral codes of communities serve as public barometers by which the behaviors of the individual members are judged and controlled (Etzioni, 1991).

As we discussed in some detail when we explored the field of economics in Chapter 6, many ecological problems stem from the neoclassical assumption of radical individualism, the belief that selfishly serving one's own interests will necessarily result in the collective good. We are fostering the opposite notion: Individuals, organizations, and economies are parts of a greater community; thinking only of themselves can lead to individual actions that are detrimental to the encompassing systems of which they are a part (Hardin, 1968). Daly and Cobb (1989, 1994) say, "In the real world the self-contained individual does not exist" (p. 161). They reject the idea that organizations are like Robinson Crusoe, earning their way solely by their own guile, in favor of the belief that organizations are integral parts of interlocking communal systems composed of individuals, families, towns, cities, nations, international coalitions, and ecological systems bound by a common desire for survival and a high quality of life.

Thus, strategic managers who value the greater community are better equipped to make decisions compatible with achieving sustainability. Valuing the more comprehensive communities to which they belong helps them to be more aware of the interconnections between their decisions and the quality of life in the communities where they operate. From this, strategic managers are better able to recognize that their organizations can prosper over the long run only if the community can maintain a balance among a healthy natural environment, ample opportunities for human development and fulfillment, a meaningful code of ethics, and a healthy system of economic activity. Accordingly, strategic managers who value community will likely benefit from numerous economic advantages, such as customer loyalty, a positive public image, and employee commitment, while contributing to the protection of the natural environment. They are also more likely to become involved in the community-based decision-making structures (discussed in Chapter 4) that so many scholars believe are so critical for protecting the commons (Daly & Cobb, 1989, 1994; Etzioni, 1988; King, 1995; Starik & Rands, 1995).

Quality

Robert Pirsig (1974) engaged in a fascinating (and often frightening) search for the true meaning of quality in *Zen and the Art of Motorcycle Maintenance.* His schizophrenic inquiry led him to the conclusion that quality does not result from something people do or see. It is not an objective measure. Rather, it is a perception with deep cognitive roots. This conclusion disturbed him; quality is, no doubt, a subjective mental image, but its basic purpose is to improve objective awareness of the world—that is, to provide observable criteria for making choices. How can it possibly be both subjective and objective? His final breakthrough (as well as his mental breakdown) came when he realized that quality could not exist either solely as a subjective mental picture or solely in the objects of the real world; quality existed in the interactions between the mind and its surrounding environment. He said,

> Quality couldn't be independently related with either the subject or the object but could be found only in the relationship of the

two with each other. It is the point at which subject and object meet. Quality is not a thing. It is an event. (p. 239)

This perspective on quality has rapidly become the standard in industry. Quality today is becoming less and less the exclusive bailiwick of quality control engineers applying absolute standards; instead, quality is more often being determined through interactions among executives, operational employees, customers, suppliers, quality control personnel, and others. Quality, according to this definition, is not an absolute percentage of defective products, and the like; rather, it is an overall perception of what the firm's products and services should be. As such, quality serves as the guiding force behind the firm's operations and its relationships with its stakeholders.

Primarily because of the influence of Edwards Deming, the Japanese initiated this trend toward an interactive definition of quality with their philosophy that quality is defined by the customer. Implementing this philosophy requires forming strong customer-organization-supplier networks that are cemented by a shared vision of quality. Essentially, an organization makes a concerted effort to identify customers' perceptions of what constitutes quality in relation to the organization's products and services. These perceptions are passed on to operational employees who use them as guides for continuously improving the firm's products and services. These perceptions are also instilled in suppliers so that they can include them in producing the parts and services they provide the organization. Thus, the perception of quality in this process begins with the customer, but it transcends its roots and serves as an overriding image that determines the relationships between the organization and its stakeholders.

As an instrumental value that supports sustainability, quality integrates many of the elements of wholeness, posterity, smallness, and community. That is, valuing quality means valuing networks over dominance, tomorrow over today, and better over more. Once organizations adopt a philosophy that how well products are made and how well customers are served are more important than how many products are produced and how many customers they are sold to, then the proper scale of their operations can be defined by something other than physical growth. When quality is the nucleus around which organizations revolve, they are likely to adopt a scale of operations small enough to focus on developing individual relationships within their stakeholder network. Improved customer loyalty, more stable supplier relationships, more participative interactions among organizational members, and improved operational efficiency are all possible outcomes for organizations that adopt quality as a key value in their strategic decision-making processes.

A value of quality will best support sustainability if it includes three basic dimensions—quality of products and services, quality of work, and quality of life. As we discussed above, the economic well-being of the firm is enhanced by improved customer loyalty, increased efficiency, and so on that come with high-quality products and services. Quality products and services also support ecological sustainability because they last longer, are worth repairing, and can be exchanged more readily in secondhand markets, such as flea markets and garage sales. A preponderance of durable, long-lasting products in the economic system will help to reduce the perception that constant style changes are necessary; it will also help to reduce wastes because fewer of these products will enter the system and more of them will remain in the system for longer periods of time (Daly & Cobb, 1989, 1994). Thus, high-quality products and services are definitely important for achieving a sustainable balance of economic activity and ecological protection.

Attaining the sustainability promised by focusing on quality products and services is not possible unless organizations also value quality of work over quantity of work. Quality products and services are simply not possible without quality work. Structuring jobs around the concept of *good work* (Schumacher, 1979), work that satisfies human needs as well as organizational needs, can no doubt improve the quality of products and services. This is because it encourages employees to be creative and to contribute their best efforts to accomplishing the organization's economic goals and objectives. Further, the psychological satisfaction that people derive from good work often reduces their desire to derive satisfaction from consuming more and more goods. As Daly and Cobb (1989, 1994) say, "Satisfaction derived from work is of equal importance with satisfaction derived from consumption" (p. 305). Thus, good work also contributes to a sustainable economic-ecosystem balance.

Achieving sustainability through quality is also enhanced by valuing the quality of life in general; this value encourages strategic managers to recognize that all of their stakeholders have rights of physical well-being, long-lasting happiness, personal fulfillment, and a hopeful future (Milbrath, 1989). Such a value can focus the attention of strategic decision makers on how intricately interwoven economic sustainability and ecosystem sustainability really are. Valuing quality of life brings a wide variety of economic and environmental issues to the attention of organizations, including job design, organizational reward systems, employee health and safety, shareholder wealth, community economic development, pollution, waste control, and so on. This range of issues can provide managers with the overall perspective they need to balance their economic activities with the limits of the planet.

Spiritual Fulfillment

Implicit in the above paragraph is that the concept of quality of life goes well beyond material dimensions. As Schumacher (1977) and so many others have made us aware, we have been operating for most of the Industrial Revolution in a world falsely separated into *spiritual* and *secular* parts. Organizations in this divided world have fallen comfortably into the secular segment, and the results have been obvious and predictable. The economic goals of organizations have typically been seen as ends in themselves, and the relationship between organizations and their stakeholders has primarily been an economic one. Organizations seeking to meet the higher-level, spiritual needs of humankind have been relegated to positions outside the economic arena. The result is an economy made up largely of organizations designed to serve no purpose beyond providing economic prosperity and physical comfort.

Daly (1977, 1991b) points out that the problem here lies in the fact that wealth and comfort are *intermediate ends* and, as such, do not directly satisfy spiritual needs. Rather, the value of intermediate ends lies in how much they contribute to the fulfillment of humankind's *ultimate ends,* such as happiness, peacefulness, and joy. Unlike intermediate ends, ultimate ends have intrinsic value; they are good in and of themselves. It is through the satisfaction of these ultimate ends that spiritual needs are met. Wealth and comfort have been erroneously elevated to ultimate ends during the Industrial Revolution, and this has led to the false perception that they have value in and of themselves and that unlimited quantities of them will satisfy the human spirit.

Many are now saying that kindling the flames of the human spirit is critical for modern organizations. They say that organizations today need to focus beyond wealth and comfort. They need to focus more clearly on their roles in contributing to the quality of life in the larger community, and they need to create structures, processes, and outputs designed to fulfill the spiritual as well as economic needs of the humans whose lives they touch (employees, customers, etc.) (Capra, 1982; Freeman & Gilbert, 1988; Halal, 1986; Handy, 1989; Schumacher, 1973, 1979; Senge, 1990; Starik & Rands, 1995).

The role of organizations in fulfilling the human spirit can be examined through the lens of process theory. Process theory is a product of philosopher Alfred North Whitehead (Lowe, 1990; Urmson & Ree, 1989). Whitehead based his philosophy on a quantum physics view of the world, saying that reality is essentially a creative process in which everything from quantum particles to societies are products of interactions that tie together the past, present, and future. Within this process, each entity has both the freedom and responsibility to create its own niche in the greater scheme of things (Cobb, 1995; Lowe, 1990; Quiring, 1995; Urmson & Ree, 1989). From this perspective, the existence of an organization is determined from past processes that cannot be changed. However, its present and future are determined not only by the past but also by how it chooses to exercise its freedom, creativity, and responsibility. It can choose to serve only the intermediate needs of humankind if it wishes, but it can also choose to contribute to humankind's ultimate ends (Cobb, 1995; Moore, 1995; Quiring, 1995).

Maslow (1962) had a tremendous influence on bringing spiritual fulfillment into the workplace. He broke with the dominant Freudian and Skinnerian models of psychology, espousing the idea that humans were different from their animal brethren in that they needed *self-actualization,* which he describes as a spiritually fulfilling life achieved through self-expression and creativity (Capra, 1982). Interestingly, a strategic manager named Ernest Bader, founder in the 1930s of the Scott Bader Company in the United Kingdom, practiced what Maslow would preach some 30 years later. He believed that the key to a successful enterprise was to design work around meeting the higher-level needs of employees. He says, " 'Increases in wages or better conditions of work can be no moral equivalent for pride in craftsmanship, social recognition and acclaim, opportunities for advancement, and for the free expression of personality and initiative' " (quoted in Hoe, 1978, p. 80).

As with the other instrumental values we have discussed, valuing spiritual fulfillment has both economic and ecological benefits. Halal (1986), Senge (1990), Freeman and Gilbert (1988), and Handy (1989) have all presented convincing arguments that long-term economic success in today's turbulent business environment requires that organizations know their role in the larger society, contribute to the quality of life rather than simply the quantity of consumption, and provide learning frameworks that allow employees to creatively express their inner spirit. Schumacher (1973, 1979), Daly and Cobb (1989, 1994) and Starik and Rands (1995) present convincing arguments that organizations that contribute to the quality of life and human spiritual fulfillment, basing their existence on enhancing humankind's ultimate ends, will naturally consume less, waste less, think smaller, and foster these same values in their employees, customers, and communities.

Conclusions

Following strategic managers through their economic success versus ecosystem viability dilemma leads to the realization
that the answers lie neither to the left nor to the right. The
answers lie in front, in finding the middle way—the path to a
sustainable balance between the seemingly polar opposites of
economic and ecological survival.

Solving the dilemma begins with instilling a set of values
in business organizations that will transcend this divergent
problem, values that will help strategic managers recognize
that business success and the natural environment are not mor-
tal enemies. Sustainability forms the core of this value system
because it provides a foundation upon which to make economic
decisions compatible with the carrying capacity of the planet.
Instrumental values such as wholeness, posterity, smallness,
quality, community, and spiritual fulfillment can then serve as
the pathways through which sustainability is achieved because
they help to focus managers' attention on alternative solutions
that transcend their dilemma.

PART III

Managing on a
Small Planet

Our goal in this final part of the book is to equip strategic managers with the management concepts and tools they will need to integrate sustainability into their strategic decisions. We begin by establishing that the Earth is a stakeholder of significant power and import in organizations, and that it is represented by a wide array of representatives in the immediate business environment. We then present several concepts, including ecocentric management, enterprise strategy, sustainability strategies, industrial ecosystems, learning organizations, and fundamental change processes, which, when taken as a whole, constitute a conceptual framework for sustainable strategic management. Next, we discuss several tools and processes that strategic managers can apply in order to establish effective environmental management systems. In the last chapter in the book, we delve deeper into the concept of sustainability in an effort to explore more fully what it will take for humankind to succeed in its quest for a sustainable world.

Chapter 8

Nature's Stake in Organizations

The field of management emerged during the second half of the 19th century as industrialization captured the attention of the world. As is true with all the disciplines that emerged at that time, management's beginnings were heavily rooted in the mechanistic model. The mental prototype of the business organization during most of the 20th century has been one of a manufacturing firm with long, impersonal assembly lines manned by workers performing narrow, mindless tasks, led by managers relying on formal authority, precise procedures, and unbending rules in directing workers.

Adam Smith shaped the economic thought from which these mechanistic structures appeared. He espoused the concept of division of labor based on the mechanical view that a person's on-the-job behavior would be more efficient if it were broken down into small, standardized parts. The field of management emerged when Max Weber's bureaucracy and Frederick Taylor's scientific management provided the organizational structure and job engineering techniques necessary to make division of labor an operational concept that could be meaningfully applied in large-scale manufacturing organizations.

Thus, with Taylor and Weber, the mechanistic management paradigm was born. Within this paradigm, organizations were viewed as goal-directed entities made of coordinated parts, the parts being people. The job of the manager was to make these parts work more efficiently together, cutting labor costs and improving profits. Hierarchical authority was bestowed so that knowledgeable managers could give orders and expect compliance. Middle management levels swelled as the need to pass information and orders within the hierarchy grew. Workers were seen almost exclusively as means to ends, hired for their hands and not their minds.

However, as we discussed in Chapter 5, the scientific paradigm has changed. Relativity and quantum physics have dispelled the belief that the universe is a deterministic machine. A new scientific paradigm has emerged that sees the universe as an interconnected whole. Reality is seen as relative, depending on the perspective of the observer. The management paradigm is beginning to adapt to this new worldview. In the emerging management paradigm, organizations are viewed as interconnected networks of employees, suppliers, customers, and communities that strive for human and social fulfillment as well as for economic goal accomplishment. Their structures resemble "fluid tangles of individuals and units going their own way in a larger web of societal connections" (Halal, 1986, p. 151). These structures "show how it's possible to grow large while staying small, [to] control and create accountability while giving space . . . , [to] unleash organic growth through local processes and self-organization . . . , [and to] keep in touch with the demands of many local environments" (Morgan, 1993, p. 88). The internal and external boundaries of these organizations almost disappear, allowing for open flows of information and interaction with all other salient strands in the organization's web (Morgan, 1986).

Stakeholder Management:
Attending to the Strands in the Web

These other salient strands in the organization's web are often referred to as its *stakeholders*, "Persons or groups that can affect or are affected by the achievement of the organization's objectives" (Freeman, 1984, p. 46). Stakeholders include customers, shareholders, employees, regulators, suppliers, competitors, activist and advocacy groups, and so on, all of whom have an interest in the practices of the corporation (Freeman, 1984). *Stakeholder management* essentially refers to serving the varied, often conflicting, needs of these multiple stakeholders.

Stakeholder management requires giving weight to the ethical, social, and political dimensions of a situation along with the economic dimensions, bringing ethical considerations to the forefront of strategic decision making (Ansoff, 1979; Carroll, 1995; Clarkson, 1995; Donaldson & Preston, 1995; Freeman, 1984; Freeman & Gilbert, 1988; Hosmer, 1994; Jones, 1995). Freeman and Gilbert (1988) point out that all business strategies have an ethical foundation regardless of whether management is aware of it. They believe that organizations should apply ethical reasoning to their strategic decision-making processes, analyzing who is affected by the decisions, how they are affected, what rights the parties have, and so on. Thus, stakeholder management reveals that the narrow economic niche in which business organizations once resided has expanded into a much broader societal niche (Zenisek, 1979). It helps make it clear that organizations that serve the needs of the greater society are more likely to prosper.

Earth: The Ultimate Stakeholder

It should be clear from the previous seven chapters that it is necessary for the natural environment to achieve its proper place in the management paradigm, something it has yet to do (Shrivastava, 1994). How do strategic managers weigh the environment? How much consideration does it deserve? We believe that properly representing the planet in management theory and practice begins with the recognition that the Earth is a stakeholder of significant import for business organizations. Recognizing the significance of the Earth as a stakeholder is critical in integrating sustainability into the ethical core of organizations, thus allowing organizations to recognize that the long-term survival of business and the long-term survival of the Earth are intricately interconnected. This belief is shared by others, such as Jim Post (1991) and Mark Starik (1995); however, some have criticized this notion. Some have said that including the natural environment as a stakeholder changes the definition of the term too drastically; other criticisms have been in the form of tongue-in-cheek questions about how the Earth can sit on boards of directors (Seligman, 1995).

In a narrow sense, the definitional criticisms have some merit. Freeman (1984) says that a stakeholder is "a person or group" (p. 46), which the Earth certainly is not. From a broader perspective, however, the Earth includes and supports all of humankind within its sphere, giving it a significant "person or group" dimension. Further, the Earth clearly meets the rest of the definition of a stakeholder as set out by Freeman (1984): It "can affect or be affected by the achievement of the organization's objectives" (p. 46). The Earth is the geographical location of all business activity, the source of the resources and energy necessary to make the economic engine purr, and the sink into which the wastes of economic activity are poured; it is what humankind is ultimately risking in its 350-year experiment called the Industrial Revolution (Post, 1991; Starik, 1995; Shrivastava, 1995a). From this perspective, the Earth is the ultimate stakeholder in business organizations. As Jim Post (1991) says, "As global natural resources are depleted, the survival potential of the planet is itself at stake. Never before has Earth itself become a stakeholder of such significance to corporations and managerial decision making" (p. 34).

The Green Stakeholders

As to the criticism that the planet doesn't sit on boards of directors: It may not be sitting in the chair, but some of its powerful human friends likely are. And these friends don't just confine themselves to boardrooms. They are also in the stores, the financial markets, the courtrooms, the media, the halls of government, and the organizations themselves. Nature has a large cadre of stakeholders representing her interests in the immediate business environment, including consumers, investors, employees, legislators, regulators, litigators, interest groups, lenders and insurers, and environmental-standards setters (Starik, 1990, 1995; Throop, Starik, & Rands, 1993; Welford & Gouldson, 1993; Williams, Medhurst, & Drew, 1993). The prospects for both short-term and long-term organizational success being directly tied to satisfying the needs of these *green stakeholders* give the planet plenty of clout in the marketplace. Below, we examine in more detail some of the Earth's green stakeholders.

Regulators

Government regulation has been aimed at environmental ills for many years. Teddy Roosevelt made conservation a popular political issue at the turn of this century. The courts have long held business organizations liable for employee health problems resulting from exposure to dangerous substances, such as asbestos and coal dust, and the Environmental Protection Agency (EPA) has existed for over two decades in the United States. More recently, the greening of government got a big boost in Europe in 1983, when 27 members of West Germany's Green Party were elected to seats in the National Assembly (the Bundestag), calling for a society that was nonviolent and non-exploitive in relation to Nature (Spretnak & Capra, 1986). Today, the Green Party is on the verge of replacing the Free Democratic Party as Germany's third political party (Templeman, 1995).

In the United States, a conglomeration of federal agencies, led by the EPA, is responsible for generating and enforcing environmental regulation. The Department of Energy (DOE), the Department of Justice (DOJ), the Occupational Safety and Health Administration (OSHA), the Federal Trade Commission (FTC), the National Forest Service, the Bureau of Land Management (BLM), and the Fish and Wildlife Service are some of the other U.S. federal agencies that have responsibility for environmental regulation.

More than 60 U.S. federal laws mandate environmental regulations. Many focus on specific environmental problems, such as air pollution, water pollution, asbestos use, and species protection. Others focus on specific industries, such as agriculture and utilities, and some focus on regions or habitats, such as coastal zones, forests, and wetlands. Still others focus on specific organizational practices, such as the accuracy of environmental claims made in advertising. Of these 60 or so laws, 6 are generally considered to constitute the primary core of U.S. environmental regulation: the Clean Air Act (CAA); the Comprehensive Environmental Response, Compensation and Liability Act, as amended by the Superfund Amendment and Reauthorization Act (CERCLA/SARA—better known as the Superfund law); the Clean Water Act (CWA); the Resource Conservation and Recovery Act (RCRA); the Safe Drinking Water Act (SDWA); and the Toxic Substances Control Act (TSCA) (Wilson, 1991).

Individual states also have significant influences on the environmental behaviors of business organizations. For example, California has the toughest air pollution standards in the nation, and the California Air Resources Board has instituted automobile emission standards that get progressively tighter over a 12-year period. By 1996, many cars in that state will have to run on alternative fuels, and by 1998, 2% of the cars sold in the state will be required to emit no pollutants at all; many states in the eastern United States have adopted some version of this California Law (Woodruff, Peterson, & Lowery, 1991). Other states have focused on other issues; for example, Maine and Massachusetts have instituted strict packaging laws (Stipp, 1991b).

Regulators in the United States generally have teeth. Firms can find themselves paying large penalties, spending millions on cleanups and restoration, and in some cases, having their executives thrown in jail. The EPA is increasing the number of special agents under provisions of the Pollution Prosecution Act of 1990. It collected approximately $200 million in fines and penalties during the 3-year period from 1989 to 1991, and it collected another $135 million in penalties in 1992 (Bureau of

National Affairs, 1993b). The DOJ has also gotten more concerned with breaches of environmental law; it is shifting a significant number of lawyers to its Environmental Crimes Section (Bureau of National Affairs, 1993a). This increased enforcement activity has created real concerns for business executives because of the shift up the corporate chain for responsibility for environmental violations (Taylor, 1994). Two important cases involving RCRA violations, *United States v. Dean* (1992) and *United States v. Hoflin* (1989), upheld that executives may be criminally liable for the environmental crimes of subordinates, and it will likely become increasingly commonplace to find corporate officers being prosecuted, and possibly incarcerated, for environmental crimes.

Environmental regulation certainly goes beyond the U.S. border. Germany has adopted some of the toughest and most creative environmental laws and policies in the world. Of special interest is the German Packaging Legislation (*Verpackungsverordnung*), a law that is "a radical departure from historical methods of setting recycling and reuse quotas on packaging material" (Arnold & Long, 1994, p. 840). Under the law, organizations are required to accept used packaging from consumers and recycle it unless technically infeasible to do so (Arnold & Long, 1994; Young, 1991). In the two-phase implementation strategy for *Verpackungsverordnung*, an infrastructure was first created for materials retrieval and processing, and then quotas and targets were set by the Ministry of the Environment. The most significant aspect of the infrastructure being established is the Duales System Deutschland (DSD). DSD is a nonprofit corporation supported by firms in the packaging industry that will coordinate and implement a recycling program throughout Germany, at an estimated cost of $10 billion. At the heart of DSD's program is the *green dot* system for identifying and processing recyclable packaging (Arnold & Long, 1994).

In July 1994, Germany passed another landmark environmental law, the Closed Substance Cycle and Waste Management Act (*Kreislaufwirtschafts und Abfallgesetz*), which essentially extends the idea of the closed-loop management of packaging established by the *Verpackungsverordnung* to include all types of wastes generated in the German economy. The Closed Substance Cycle and Waste Management Act is scheduled to go into effect in October, 1996. Wastes, according to this law, are broadly defined as anything unrelated to the original intent of a product that arise as a result of production, processing, or consumption. This definition encompasses everything from toxic by-products of production to used cars and old newspapers. Based on the philosophy that there is an implicit intergenerational contract that mandates that people living today have no right to unload their environmental problems on future generations, the law essentially mandates a "life-cycle economy." The law specifies that it is no longer economically or ecologically viable to maintain a dual system in which industry produces wastes and then leaves it up to the public to find ways to dispose of it. Rather, the law is based on the polluter-pays principle, which says that those responsible for generating wastes are responsible for finding ways to avoid, recycle, reuse, or safely dispose of them, in that order (Kirchgeorg, 1994).

Most other European nations are also taking environmental issues seriously. For example, the United Kingdom completely restructured its environmental regulatory policies and processes with the 1990 Environmental Protection Act. The act brings U.K. environmental regulations and enforcement procedures into line with the requirements of the European Community (EC), and it also puts the United Kingdom out in front of its fellow EC members in some areas. For example, the EC's Integrated Pollution Prevention and Control Directive was crafted after the U.K. legislation (Welford & Gouldson, 1993).

The natural environment has been a central theme in European Community policy, and it is tied directly to the EC's economic strategy (Hull, 1990). There was an explicit environmental mandate in the Single European Act of 1987, establishing that the EC's "level playing field" principle supported the right of all EC citizens to a clean environment (Welford & Gouldson, 1993). One example of EC environmental regulation is the European Eco-Management and Audit Scheme (EMAS). EMAS became EC regulation in 1992, providing a framework for firms to assess their environmental impacts and plan future actions. Although currently voluntary, the EMAS regulations have become models for EC member nations' compulsory regulations, and they will likely become compulsory in the entire EC over time (Welford & Gouldson, 1993).

After much debate and renegotiation, the North American Free Trade Agreement (NAFTA) was finally passed with its environmental side agreement. This puts into place an environmental philosophy in NAFTA similar to that in the EC. Officially known as the North American Agreement on Environmental Cooperation (September 13, 1993), the NAFTA environmental side agreement affirms that "conservation, protection and enhancement of the environment" in Canada, Mexico, and the United States are important and that the three nations will cooperate "in achieving sustainable development for the well-being of present and future generations" (p. 1). The agreement sets out 10 objectives designed to accomplish this, including strengthening cooperative efforts among the three nations to develop and improve "environmental laws, regulations, procedures, policies and practices" (p. 2). However, it remains to be seen whether NAFTA's lofty environmental philosophies and goals can be achieved; some are skeptical at this point (Husted, 1994; Kelly, 1993).

Many other international treaties have been negotiated to regulate environmental problems across borders. In 1992, the highly publicized United Nations Conference on the Environment and Development, the Earth Summit, was held in Rio de Janeiro, resulting in nations of the world signing agreements committing themselves to developing regulations and incentive programs that address a wide variety of the planet's environmental ills (Post, 1994). In fact, Arnold and Long (1994) say the United States is a party to some 170 environmental agreements. They say that 17 of these agreements use trade measures as a basis, dating back to the Convention Relative to the Preservation of Fauna and Flora in Their Natural State, signed in 1933. One of the most recent and far-reaching of these international agreements is the Montreal Protocol. Signed in 1987 and revised in 1990 by dozens of industrialized nations (including the United States), the Montreal Protocol set standards for protecting the ozone layer, including the phasing out of the production of CFCs (Arnold & Long, 1994; Buchholz, 1993).

We could go on with this discussion, but by now the point should be clear. Environmental regulation is everywhere business is done: At the state level, at the national level, at the trade alliance level, and at the global level. Much ado is being made in the press these days about how the conservative political trends in the United States spell doom for environmental regulation (Dowd, 1994; Thompson, 1995). However, the brief discussion above provides ample evidence that environmental regulation is entrenched and pervasive throughout the world. It will continue to be a significant influence on how business is practiced regardless of the waffling political winds that change directions constantly inside Washington, D.C.'s, beltway.

In fact, the pervasiveness of environmental regulation across boundaries is one factor contributing to what most strategic managers believe is the most serious problem related to environmental regulation: its complexity and resulting high costs. Much of the discussion between environmental executives and academics at Georgetown University's Conference on Environmental Ethics in October 1994 centered on the fact that organizations today are faced with an alphabet soup of often conflicting command-and-control regulations that cost them time and money, and, in many cases, restrict them from taking more effective actions to improve their environmental performance. The executives expressed a great deal of frustration with what they believed to be myriad petty, irrelevant, expensive regulations, and they complained about the commando-style regulators who are more interested in citing them and fining them than in helping to solve environmental problems.

At the conference, Tom Jorling (1994), vice president of environmental affairs at International Paper, presented a very convincing picture of what he called the "compliance funnel," to illustrate the overbearing, hodgepodge regulatory environment of his industry. He listed over 30 different laws, regulatory agencies, and permitting processes related to environmental management in the paper industry, and he pointed specifically to the irrationality and complexity of many of them. For example, he pointed to several cases where water quality regulations were such that the firm's waste water often had to be returned to its source more chemical-free than it was before it entered the factory.

Porter and van der Linde (1995) discuss this issue at length by comparing and contrasting the regulatory environments of U.S. and Scandinavian pulp-and-paper industries. They point out that the lack of sufficient phase-in periods and technological flexibility in U.S. regulations meant that pulp-and-paper industries were required to rapidly adopt expensive end-of-pipe technologies without the opportunity to develop any innovative process improvements that would have allowed for more economically feasible pollution-prevention approaches. In Scandinavia, on the other hand, the regulations did not restrict technologies and included phase-in periods; this led to the development of innovative pollution prevention technologies in pulping and bleaching. The result has been that the Scandinavian pulp-and-paper industry is now the global leader in such technologies.

This example provides a look at what the future of environmental regulation likely holds. It is important to realize that, despite the criticisms from industry, strict environmental regulation has been a very effective tool for ensuring improvements in the environmental performance of business organizations. The important issue, according to Porter and van der Linde (1995), is not regulatory strictness; it is regulatory structure. They say that strict regulations are necessary because they protect the natural environment and provide competitive advantages for organizations. However, they believe that regulations should be structured so that they promote product and process innovations that give firms first-mover advantages in the global marketplace, which is what Scandinavian pulp-and-paper firms now enjoy. They define good environmental regulations as being strict, focusing on outcomes rather than technologies, allowing phase-in periods, and using market incentives rather than penalties. They believe that regulatory processes need to be more predictable and less costly, involving more industry participation and more technically capable regulators who can be helpful to industry.

Many others are echoing Porter and van der Linde (1995). The consensus is that there is a need for strict environmental regulation but what regulation needs to be is more consistent, less intimidating, and more economically feasible for business organizations. It needs to be less punishment based and more incentive based, and it needs to give organizations some discretion to use their own creative processes to find ways to effectively improve environmental performance. Regulators need to be more supportive, giving financial and technical support when necessary; they need to take on the role of educators, communicators, and consultants (Clair, Milliman, & Mitroff, 1995; Feyerherm, 1995; Henriques & Sadorsky, 1995; Jones & Baldwin, 1994; Lawrence & Morell, 1995; Portney, 1993; Stead & Stead, 1995; Turcotte, 1995; Winn, 1995). Regulators in the United States seem to be taking conclusions such as these to heart. Recent U.S. regulatory efforts have been more incentive based, setting targets instead of requiring specific technologies, and so forth. Also, U.S. regulatory agencies are making efforts to be more supportive and open to outside suggestions; for example, the DOE has sponsored environmental auditing seminars for its contractors designed to help them to comply, and the EPA has begun to use more systematic community and industry input when making decisions about how to alleviate environmental problems.

Green Consumers

According to Faye Rice (1990) of *Fortune* magazine, consumers in the United States are becoming "demanding, inquisitive, [and] discriminating. They are insisting on high-quality goods that save time, energy, and calories; preserve the environment; and come from a manufacturer they think is socially responsible" (p. 38). A basic element of this consumer revolution is green consumerism. Many have predicted that addressing the concerns of green consumers will be one of the most important issues business organizations will face in the 1990s (Coddington, 1993; Kirkpatrick, 1990; Ottman, 1992).

Essentially, *green consumers* are people who buy green products, use them as long as possible, and recycle the wastes. *Green products* are those that are of high quality, durable, made with nontoxic materials, produced and delivered using energy efficient processes, packaged in small amounts of recyclable material, not tested on animals, and/or not derived from threatened species (Elkington, Hailes, & Makower, 1988; McClosky, Smith, & Graves, 1993; Ottman, 1992). Green products fall into a category referred to as *high-involvement* products. Products of this type serve as personal statements about the values of the consumers who purchase them (Etzioni, 1988; Kotler, 1990; McClosky et al., 1993; Ottman, 1992). As such, green products are not bought simply for their utility; they are purchased because they send a message from the consumers to the manufacturers about their products. According to Ottman (1992), green consumers are sending the message that they want "quality over quantity, long-term over short-term, and we over me" (p. 21).

Green consumerism is reportedly a growing trend (Coddington, 1993; Ottman, 1992). Surveys in both North America and Western Europe have indicated that a majority of consumers say they are concerned about the impact that products have on the environment, are more likely to buy products in recyclable or degradable packages, are willing to pay extra for such packaging, and have declined to buy products because of their environmental impacts. Many say it is even worth accepting a lower standard of living if it means protecting the environment (McClosky et al., 1993; Ottman, 1992; "Research Alert," 1991; Schorsch, 1990).

However, research on actual buying patterns of green consumers and their influences on organizational strategies tell a different story (Makower, 1995; Ottman, 1992; Roper Organization, 1992; Stead & Stead, 1995). The Roper Organization (1992) found serious differences between the premiums North Americans said they were willing to pay for green products and the premiums they were actually willing to pay. For example, people said they would pay a 4.7% premium for a more environmentally friendly automobile but were actually willing to pay only a .5% premium, and results were very similar for other products, such as detergents, gasoline, and aerosols. Also, strategic managers in industrial organizations in the United States reported feeling only modest pressures for product and process improvement from green consumers (Stead & Stead, 1995).

Most speculation about the reasons for the discrepancies between the rather loud voices and quiet behaviors of green consumers centers on the varying shades of green found among the consumer population. As Ginny Carroll (1991) states, "Green comes in more shades than an Irish hillside, from sickly chartreuse to deepest emerald" (p. 24). Surveys have categorized the various shades of green in many ways, including true-blue greens, premium greens, greenback greens, greener than greens, light greens, maybe greens, no-cost ecologists, sprouts, privileged bystanders, browns, ungreens, hard core browns, hostile conservatives, and on and on (Coddington, 1993; Ottman, 1992). Generally, in the United States, these many shades break down into three categories: (a) About 25% of the population are active environmentalists and hard-core green consumers, willing to put their money and their actions where their sentiments lie; (b) about 31% fit into a swing group who talk a good environmental game but often let economic and convenience issues outweigh their environmental concerns in the marketplace; and (c) about 44% are either not concerned about or hostile to environmental concerns (Ottman, 1992).

Another reason why green consumer buying patterns and influences may be less than expected is that consumers often do not trust the information they get from organizations about the environmental benefits of their products and services. Many consumers believe that the environmental claims of business organizations are little more than marketing gimmicks (Makower, 1995; Ottman, 1992; Schwartz, Springen, & Hager, 1990). Thus, being green becomes filled with choices that are not only complicated but that have to be made with data that are confusing, incomplete, and misleading. According to Denis Hayes (1990), the father of Earth Day,

People want to buy the right things, but they don't trust most of
the information that they get. . . . If you walk into a supermarket
today, you tend to think that, "My God, we've reached environmental
nirvana." Everything seems to be Earth-friendly, environment-
friendly, ozone-friendly, degradable, biodegradable, photode-
gradable, natural, organic, recycled, recyclable—and it doesn't
mean anything. People know it doesn't mean anything. (p. 18)

According to Joel Makower (1995, p. 52), "Thanks largely
to some outright fraudulent green-marketing campaigns early
on [like biodegradable plastic garbage bags], most people are
still unclear about some basic concepts." There are many prominent examples of how misleading claims about the environmental benefits of products have backfired, often leaving egg
on the faces of organizations. For example, Westley and Vredenburg (1991) discuss how Loblaw, Inc., of Canada launched
its G.R.E.E.N. line of products in 1989, only to have both the
greenness of the products and the accuracy of the advertisements questioned by environmental and consumer groups.

Ottman (1992) says that problems such as this lead consumers away from organizations for their information on the environmental impacts of products and services. Instead, they seek
information from sources in the environmental community.
These are often the very sources that firms criticize for an
antibusiness, proenvironmental bias in the information they
distribute. To alleviate this problem, Ottman (1992) and Makower (1995) believe that firms have to be willing to provide
accurate, honest information about the environmental performance of their operations and products.

This sense of confusion about green claims has led to calls
for organized, independent efforts to consolidate information
and help simplify the choices for green consumers. These concerns have spurred the development of several programs in
which independent organizations test the environmental safety
of products and apply their seals of approval (sometimes called
eco-labels) to those products that pass these tests. In general,
eco-labels are awarded after a cradle-to-grave life-cycle analysis certifies that the products use fewer resources; emit less
harmful emissions when they are produced; use biodegradable,

recyclable, and/or recycled inputs; have longer product lives; can be reused or recycled, and so on (Beck & Howett, 1992; Dadd & Carothers, 1990; Green Seal, 1990; Schorsch, 1990; Weber, 1990). The Blue Angel program in Germany was the first eco-labeling program, beginning operation in 1977; Blue Angel labels are now affixed to over 3,100 products in 57 different product categories (Ottman, 1992). Canada instituted its Environmental Choice program in 1989. Japan's Eco-Mark program, which provides labels for advertising as well as products, began in 1990. In the United States, eco-labeling efforts have been instituted by private concerns, including some individual organizations such as Wal-Mart. The two most visible eco-labeling efforts in the United States have been Green Seal, Inc., and Scientific Certification Systems (SCS—originally known as Green Cross). Home Depot now offers building materials made from forest products harvested in sustainable ways, and the firm has contracted with SCS to certify that these environmental claims are valid (Lober & Eisen, 1995).

Organizations have been rushing to capture the hearts and dollars of green consumers for several years now. Only one half of 1% of the products introduced in 1985 claimed to be green; by 1991, that rate had jumped to 13.4%, approximately 26 times higher. About a quarter of the new household products introduced in 1990 claimed to be some shade of green (Frierman, 1991), and nearly 70% of all marketers are making environmental improvements in packaging (Ottman, 1992).

As good as the news of green consumerism is for the planet, a couple of words of caution are necessary here. First, identifying green products is no easy task. Life-cycle analysis and eco-labeling, for all their good intentions, cannot guarantee that products will be environmentally safe (Dadd & Carothers, 1990; Stipp, 1991a). Second, not all of the so-called green products on the market are all that green; consumers need some way to separate truly green products from mere green marketing schemes. Greenness can't simply be another marketing gimmick; it requires a true commitment based on values for a small planet. Third, as Ottman (1992) points out, the term green consumer is, in a sense, an oxymoron. True greenness goes beyond simply buying more Earth-friendly products; it also involves a willingness to consume less.

Individual customers are not the only ones acting as green consumers in today's marketplace. Organizations themselves are using purchasing agreements to ensure that the components, packaging materials, and so on that they get from their vendors and suppliers are more environmentally friendly. For example, certain telecommunications firms, computer manufacturers, and fast-food restaurants have negotiated purchase contracts with vendors and suppliers that require the use of more recycled materials and less CFCs, heavy metals, and toxins in their components and packaging (Dillon & Baram, 1993).

Ethical Investors

As Amy Domini and Peter Kinder (1986) say, "Every investment . . . has an ethical dimension" (p. xi). The idea of using investment power for social as well as financial returns dates back to the 1920s, when various religious groups demanded that their money not be invested in *sin stocks* (liquor, tobacco, and gambling). The Pioneer Fund of Boston began eliminating from its portfolios companies that had operations in any of these three areas in 1928. Since then, many funds have emerged that screen their portfolios along numerous ethical, social, and environmental lines. Religious organizations have continued to be major influences in the ethical investing movement; for example, the Christian Scientists began the Foursquare Fund in 1962, and in 1968 the United Methodist Church withdrew its $10 million portfolio from First National City Bank (now Citibank) because of the bank's investments in South Africa. The Interfaith Center on Corporate Responsibility invests funds totaling over $25 billion from the pension funds of 220 Roman Catholic orders and 22 Protestant denominations (Council on Economic Priorities [CEP], 1991).

The social turmoil experienced in the United States in the 1960s was the catalyst for rapid growth in ethical investing. Social activist Saul Alinsky garnered support from hundreds of Eastman Kodak shareholders in 1966 (the group controlled almost 40,000 shares of voting stock), demanding that the firm hire 600 additional minority employees; civil rights leaders lobbied Chase Manhattan and Citibank to stop them from investing in South Africa; stockholders of both Honeywell and Dow Chemical used annual meetings as public forums to air their objections to the antipersonnel weapons and napalm these firms were producing for use in the Vietnam War.

In 1968, a Jewish synagogue requested that Alice Tepper Marlin, a securities analyst in Boston, develop a *peace portfolio* for it. When she had developed the portfolio, Marlin convinced her firm to run a newspaper advertisement offering the fund to other investors; some 600 investors responded to the ad. This interest in the peace portfolio eventually led to the formation of the Council on Economic Priorities (CEP) in 1969, which provides social performance ratings for individual companies. CEP evaluates corporations on criteria such as environmental performance, charitable contributions, advancement of women and minorities, animal testing, community outreach, and family benefits (CEP, 1991).

As the above examples suggest, there are two basic approaches to ethical investing. The first involves investing in firms or mutual funds that demonstrate a sincere effort to be socially and environmentally responsible. Implicit in this approach is that firms with poor social or environmental records should be avoided or withdrawn from investment portfolios. There has been a tremendous increase in the amount of money invested in this way. What was a $40 billion market in 1984 now exceeds $625 billion, and it is expected to continue to expand (Brill & Reder, 1992; Rauber, 1990; Rose, 1990).

Ethical investments are designed to be good for the investors' wallets as well as their consciences. However, returns on mutual funds that focus specifically on environmental performance have been mixed. Some of these funds have performed reasonably well, and a few, such as Germany's HCM EcoTech fund, have performed very well (Brill & Reder, 1992; CEP, 1991; White, 1995). However, White (1995) reports that the overall performance of environmental mutual funds has been weak in both the United States and Germany. One market that shows strong promise for ethical investors in the future is recycling. Although recycling operations have essentially been losers over the past decade, with high handling and processing costs and very restricted markets, these trends have finally reversed themselves, and the future looks very bright. Browning-Ferris, the industry leader in recycled materials processing, is experiencing double-digit growth in its recycling business, and the other large firms in waste management are having similar results (Williams, 1995).

Like information on green products, information on ethical investing opportunities is fraught with pitfalls. As we have mentioned, there are many shades of green, and there is no way for a firm to be 100% environmentally safe. Investors need to carefully investigate potential eco-investment opportunities for both their economic return potential and the truth of their environmental claims. There are organizations that try to make the job easier for both institutional and individual investors, including Switzerland's Eco Rating International and the Investor Responsibility Research Center (IRRC) in the United States (Harrison, 1993). The IRRC is a nonprofit organization funded by subscription fees from investment institutions and corporations. It publishes the *Corporate Environmental Profiles Directory* and the bimonthly *Investors' Environmental Report* (Investor Responsibility Research Center, 1992; Investor Responsibility Research Center & Global Environmental Management Initiative, 1992).

The second approach to ethical investing involves the use of proxy rights and annual shareholder meetings to initiate changes in the social and environmental practices of corporations. The shareholder actions at Eastman Kodak, Honeywell, and Dow Chemical mentioned above began a flood of such activities on behalf of the environment and other social causes. Two shareholder resolutions were presented at the 1970 General Motors annual meeting that resulted in the company appointing the first black to GM's board, Lewis Sullivan (author of the famed Sullivan principles, guidelines for companies doing business in South Africa). From that point, the number of ethical proxy proposals at GM shareholder meetings increased exponentially; there were 111 such proposals presented at the 1983 meeting (CEP, 1991).

Ironically, probably the greatest impetus for the growth and maturity of proxy proposals related to improving environmental performance is also one of the most serious environmental disasters of all time—the *Exxon Valdez* oil spill. Exxon's lax attitude toward the spill and its cleanup resulted in the formation of the Coalition for Environmentally Responsible Economies (CERES), a consortium of environmental groups (including the Sierra Club, Friends of the Earth, the National Wildlife Federation, the National Audubon Society, and the Wilderness Society) and social investment funds (including the Calvert Fund, Parnassus Fund, Working Assets Fund, and Franklin Research and Development Corporation). The purpose of CERES is to "set forth broad standards for evaluating activities by corporations that directly or indirectly impact the Earth's biosphere" (CERES, 1990, p. 7).

CERES has chosen proxy proposals as its primary vehicle for accomplishing its purpose. It has developed the CERES Principles (originally the Valdez Principles), a set of broad principles designed to provide an environmental responsibility signpost for investors to follow when they choose among investment opportunities. The 10 principles deal with biosphere protection, resource sustainability, risk reduction, product safety, damage compensation, disclosure of environmental mishaps, appointment of environmentalists to boards of directors and management positions, and annual self-audits of environmental activities. CERES is asking companies to sign these principles in order to signify their long-term commitments to the process of achieving environmental sustainability. Early proxy proposals to adopt the CERES Principles attained more support than CERES ever dreamed possible (CERES, 1990; Harrison, 1993). Today, there are over 60 CERES signatories, including Fortune 500 firms such as General Motors, Polaroid, H. B. Fuller, and Sun Company (Scott, 1995).

Employees

As we discussed in Chapter 2, employees are often the first to be affected by the environmental management practices of the firm. Freeman (1984) says, "The basic element of any framework for organizations must include the central building block of the firm, its people" (p. 245). Freeman and Gilbert (1988) believe that individual worth should be the value that forms the foundation of an organization's principles. Their basic premise is that an individual "has the basic right to pursue his or her own projects . . . free from coercion and interference from others. . . . Individuals are ends and never mere means to someone else's ends" (p. 82). They refer to this as a *personal project enterprise strategy*.

Further, as Freeman (1984) points out, a firm's employees are a diverse group of people whose interests and activities generally extend beyond their jobs. They are members of activist groups, they serve on community boards, they are involved in political activities, they are members of professional, trade, and service organizations, and so on. Also, employees are often owners and/or stockholders of the firms that employ them. As such, employees often have an influence on the organization that goes well beyond their performance at work. Halal (1986) says that the growth of employee stock ownership plans (ESOPs) is indicative of the move toward more intricate relationships between organizations and their employees.

One of the first people to practice stakeholder management was Ernest Bader, introduced in Chapter 7. In 1945, he said, " 'The classes of persons entitled to their . . . satisfactions are the owners, the customers of the products or services and the workers. Between these three is a constant jostling' " (quoted in Hoe, 1978, p. 80). Of these three, Bader was a strong proponent of the employee as the most important stakeholder. He said, " 'The stakes of owners and customers in a business are temporary, transient and partial, but the employee normally . . . seeks in and through [the organization] a much wider personal satisfaction' " (quoted in Hoe, 1978, p. 80).

Bader proved his overriding commitment to his employees in 1951, when he gave them the company, making the Scott Bader Commonwealth the first employee-owned firm in the United Kingdom. This unique organization still operates successfully today. Its operation is based on a code that (a) stresses the organization as a working community; (b) measures success of the organization in terms of technical, social, and political as well as economic dimensions; (c) makes it the express duty of managers to make all jobs personally fulfilling for employees; (d) mandates that decisions in the firm be made by consensus; and (e) states that all employees are responsible and accountable for making decisions about their jobs. Further, the code includes commitments to produce only beneficial products, to protect the natural environment, and to question any activities that appear to waste the Earth's resources.

E. F. Schumacher (1979) was a friend and confidant of Ernest Bader, helping Bader to transfer the Scott Bader Company to its employees and serving on the company's board until Schumacher's death (Hoe, 1978; Wood, 1984). Schumacher (1979) also believed that employees were important stakeholders: "Business is not there simply to produce goods, it also produces people" (p. 73). According to Schumacher, organizations have the responsibility to provide *good work* for employees: work that is enjoyable and that satisfies the creative and spiritual needs of employees. Schumacher (1979) was very passionate in his descriptions of good and bad work, saying, "[Employees] should be taught that work is the joy of life and is needed for development, but that meaningless work is an abomination" (pp. 118-119).

Schumacher (1979) believed that the lack of available good work in our bureaucratized, mass production society was a primary contributor to economic and ecological ills. He felt that when there is no intrinsic fulfillment from the job, the natural tendency is for employees to focus on getting more money and more things, which contributes to both inflation and environmental degradation. He believed that a key to achieving sustainability was to create organizations structured around the principles of good work (Schumacher, 1973, 1979).

Environmental Interest Groups

Private citizens have brought significant environmental pressures to bear on business organizations for years through the activities of environmental interest groups (Starik, 1990, 1995; Welford & Gouldson, 1993). Three very prominent and very different examples of efforts to protect the natural environment by environmental interest groups are the Sierra Club Legal Defense Fund's efforts to protect the northern spotted owl, the Environmental Defense Fund's efforts to convince McDonald's to reduce solid wastes, and Greenpeace's campaign to stop Shell Oil UK from sinking the Brent Spar oil platform in the North Sea.

The Sierra Club Legal Defense Fund has used the courtroom as its platform to restrict logging in the old-growth forests of the northwestern United States on the grounds that such logging violates the Endangered Species Act by threatening the habitat of the northern spotted owl (Turner, 1991). By contrast, the Environmental Defense Fund developed a cooperative alliance with McDonald's that eventually resulted in a major overhaul of the fast-food giant's packaging and waste-management practices (Allen, 1991; Eisenhart, 1990). On the other hand, Greenpeace's efforts against Shell were directly confrontational; Greenpeace activists physically boarded and chained themselves to the Brent Spar platform and refused to leave, and Greenpeace ships, loaded with both activists and journalists, followed and harassed the Shell tug boats as they tried to move Brent Spar 120 miles to the dump site ("North Sea Victory Over Shell," 1995).

Recent research by Clair, Milliman, and Mitroff (1995) gives an excellent picture of the differences among the various environmental interest groups that attempt to influence business organizations. They found that these groups differ along four continuums. First, they have different ecological philosophies, ranging from those with "emotional, intuitive, and spiritual" (p. 173) philosophies to those with technological, scientific, rational, data-oriented philosophies. Second, interest groups differ in their methods of advocacy; at one end of this

continuum are groups that are direct, confrontational, and per-
sistent, and at the other end are groups that are indirect, low-
key, and willing to cooperate. Third, environmental interest
groups differ according to their desired end states—that is,
their beliefs about what segment or segments of society need
changing, how much they need changing, and how urgent the
need for change is. Finally, environmental groups differ along
structural dimensions, including professionalism, size, and complexity. Of these four, Clair et al. (1995) believe that the method
of advocacy dimension is key, and they advocate a willingness-
to-cooperate mode of operation for environmental groups. "Cooperation between environmental and business organizations
has led to mutual learning and to environmentally benign products, processes, and services" (p. 164).

Turcotte (1995) found that the nature of the relationship
between business organizations and environmental groups dif-
fers based on whether the environmental group's approach is
one of conflict or collaboration and based on whether the business organization is accepting or resistant to the demands of the
environmental groups. She found that relationships between
environmental groups and business organizations existed all
along these dimensions. She concluded that managers should
understand the diverse approaches of environmental groups,
and that they should develop cooperative relationships with
these groups based on a mutual search for sustainability.

Lenders and Insurers

Environmental problems bring with them the potential for
legal liability, financial liability, property damage, and property loss (Greeno, 1994; Kolluru, 1994). Environmental cleanup
costs alone are about $500 million annually and increasing in
the United States (Wade, 1992). Aetna Life and Casualty took a
$750 million charge in July 1995, doubling the size of its liability
fund, in order to cover future liabilities from pollution and toxic
waste disposal (reported on *CNN Business Morning*, July 12,
1995). This means that environmental problems are concerns

for the financial institutions that extend credit and insurance to business organizations. For this reason, lenders and insurers today regularly require environmental audits, and they are less and less willing to finance and insure environmentally risky projects, especially in the wake of court decisions that make current owners responsible for environmental problems, even if they were created by previous owners (Wade, 1992).

Global warming has become an especially problematic issue for the insurance industry. As discussed in Chapter 2, some of the predictions of the impacts of global warming, such as the rising water temperatures and the rising sea levels, are coming true. These trends could mean a 20-day extension in the hurricane season and a 33% increase in the number of hurricanes that make it to land, with as much as a 30% increase in catastrophic losses. Such losses would completely deplete insurance company catastrophe reserve funds (E. Linden, 1994). Franklin Nutter of the Reinsurance Association of America said, " 'The insurance industry is first in line to be affected by climate change. It is clear that global warming could bankrupt the industry' " (quoted in E. Linden, 1994, p. 79).

The fact that lenders and insurers are stakeholders with tremendous influence on organizations goes without question. Lack of either financial backing or insurance spells doom for most new business activities. Thus, business ventures today can't really be considered feasible unless the potential financial liabilities related to property damage, personal injury, disaster cleanup, and natural resource costs are carefully considered (Teets, Kuhnke, Bradley, & Bridegan, 1994). Although insurance companies are beginning to offer environmental remediation insurance (ERI), these policies are quite limited in terms of losses covered, maximum payouts, and length of coverage (Wade, 1992).

Environmental Standards Setters

A number of standard-setting initiatives focusing on improved environmental performance are coming from trade associations, quality associations, and other groups. In general, the approach of these groups is to establish environmental standards that, although voluntary, are required for group membership, certification, and so on. Six such initiatives are having especially strong influences on industry environmental standards (Cahill & Kane, 1994). We have already mentioned two of these influential initiatives in other contexts, the CERES Principles and the European Community's Eco-Management and Audit Scheme. The other four are the Chemical Manufacturers Association's Responsible Care Guidelines, the International Chamber of Commerce's Charter for Sustainable Development, the British Standards Institution's Standard 7750, and the International Standards Organization 14,000 standards (known as ISO 14,000).

In March 1990, the members of the Chemical Manufacturers' Association (CMA) agreed to enact a set of guidelines designed to significantly improve the way firms in the industry managed the environmental aspects of the chemical manufacturing process. The CMA calls these guidelines Responsible Care, and they are modeled after similar guidelines enacted by chemical manufacturers in Canada (Buzzelli, 1994). There are nine Responsible Care guidelines:

1. To safely develop, produce, transport, use, and dispose of chemicals
2. To make health, safety, and the environment priority considerations in planning for both current and new products
3. To promptly report any chemical or health hazards and to be prepared to deal with them if they occur
4. To inform customers how to safely transport, store, and use chemicals
5. To always operate plants in a safe manner
6. To support research on the environmental impacts of products, processes, and wastes
7. To contribute significant efforts to resolve problems caused by past practices
8. To participate with the government to develop laws and regulations that promote a safer, more environmentally sound industry
9. To share environmental management experiences and information with other firms in the industry (Stratton, 1991)

The CMA has established good-faith efforts to implement these guidelines as a requirement for membership, and in fact, some organizations have withdrawn from the CMA because of their unwillingness to pursue Responsible Care (Buzzelli, 1994).

The International Chamber of Commerce (ICC) adopted the Business Charter for Sustainable Development in November 1990. The charter was developed in a cooperative effort involving the United Nations Environmental Programme, the International Environmental Bureau, and the Global Environmental Management Initiative (GEMI), along with the ICC (Kelly, 1991). In the charter, the ICC calls on " 'enterprises and associations to follow [a set of 16] principles' " with the objective of encouraging " 'a wide range of enterprises to commit themselves to improving their environmental performance in accordance with these principles' " (quoted in North, 1992, p. 182). The 16 principles of the charter are summarized in Table 8.1.

One association that took the ICC charter to heart immediately was GEMI (which, as mentioned above, helped to craft the charter). GEMI, which grew out of an environmental management group formed by the Business Roundtable in 1989, is an organization whose membership includes environmental management professionals from large international corporations, public utilities, and so on. GEMI's basic aim is to promote environmental excellence through total quality management within the global business community (Kelly, 1991). One of GEMI's primary projects has been to develop and implement among its membership an Environmental Self-Assessment Program (ESAP), a detailed environmental self-auditing process designed to integrate the 16 ICC principles into the strategic processes of the organization (ESAP is discussed more thoroughly in Chapter 10).

The British Standard Institution's BS 7750 environmental management standards are probably the most comprehensive and specific to date. BS 7750 is essentially an internal environmental management system that includes processes for establishing environmental objectives, implementing those objectives, and measuring and reporting on the firm's progress

TABLE 8.1

Principles of the Business Charter for Sustainable Development

Principle 1	Make environmental management a corporate priority.
Principle 2	Integrate environmental management into all corporation levels and functions.
Principle 3	Improve organizational processes to be more environmentally friendly.
Principle 4	Educate, train, and motivate for improved environmental performance on the part of employees.
Principle 5	Assess environmental impacts of the firm's past, present, and future operations.
Principle 6	Improve the environmental sensitivity of products and services.
Principle 7	Educate customers, suppliers, and the public about the environmental impacts of the firm's products and services.
Principle 8	Develop and operate facilities in order to improve efficiency, increase the use of renewables and recyclables, and the like.
Principle 9	Support research on the environmental impacts of raw materials, emissions, wastes, products, production processes, and the like.
Principle 10	Use the precautionary principle as a basis for decision making about environmental performance.
Principle 11	Promote the adoption of these principles among the firm's contractors and suppliers.
Principle 12	Be fully prepared to protect health, safety, and the ecosystem in environmental emergencies.
Principle 13	Make public and transfer environmentally sound technologies and management methods.
Principle 14	Contribute to the development of public policy and educational initiatives that enhance the public's environmental awareness.
Principle 15	Foster open dialogue with employees and the public about their environmental concerns.
Principle 16	Regularly audit environmental performance and report the results to key stakeholders.

SOURCE: North (1992).

toward accomplishing those objectives (Drobney, 1994). Although meeting the requirements of BS 7750 is technically voluntary, firms wishing to do business in the United Kingdom will likely feel pressure from their customers and clients there to comply with it, just as they have with the BS 5750 quality management standards (Carty, 1993).

The BS 7750 standards are currently serving as models for the development of the new ISO 14,000 standards, which will constitute the closest thing yet to a set of truly global environmental management standards (Chynoweth & Kirschner, 1993). The ISO 9000 quality standards have always had an environmental component, but ISO 14,000 will focus exclusively on environmental management. These new ISO standards are expected to be in place perhaps as early as 1996; when they are, ISO 14,000 certification will become a requirement in many European markets, just as ISO 9000 certification is today. Although ISO 14,000 certification will be expensive initially, it could help organizations reduce environmental costs in the long run by standardizing environmental labeling, permits, and inspections throughout Europe, and it could act to deter individual nations from instituting more costly command-and-control regulations (Cascio, 1994; "Progress on ISO 14,000," 1994).

Conclusions

Organizations are viewed today as organic, value-driven, information-processing networks with permeable internal and external boundaries. They are smart, and they are motivated by enlightened self-interest that bases profits on the organization's ability to serve its stakeholders. Fully integrating the Earth into the decision-making frameworks of strategic managers means accepting the Earth as a key stakeholder in organizations, one that encompasses all of society, including the organizations themselves.

We have tried to demonstrate in this chapter that the Earth is a legitimate and important stakeholder in business organizations, one with significant scope (Judge & Krishnan, 1994; Meznar, Chrisman, & Carroll, 1990) and power (Freeman, 1984; Freeman & Gilbert, 1988). The scope of the Earth is very wide, encompassing all present human inhabitants of the planet, the future generations of human beings and the other species that exist on the planet, and the planet's biophysical systems (the biosphere, hydrosphere, atmosphere, and geosphere). Further, the Earth's representatives in the economy, including regulators, green consumers, ethical investors, employees, interest groups, lenders and insurers, and environmental standards setters, have a great deal of power, especially in a collective sense. We believe that the enormous scope of the Earth, the power of its green stakeholders to influence organizations, and the fact that the planet has its own weapons for dealing with out-of-control systems (natural disasters, drought, disease, and so on), make the Earth a stakeholder with which to be reckoned.

Chapter 9

Strategic Management for a Small Planet

We demonstrated in the last chapter that the Earth is a stakeholder with growing power and influence. Not only is it the ultimate source of natural capital and the ultimate receiver of wastes, it is represented in the immediate business environment by a growing cadre of green stakeholders. These stakeholders want less pollution and fewer wastes; they want more recycling; they want more renewable energy sources; they want products that are safer for the ecosystem, and so on. They are telling firms in a variety of ways that their ability to prosper in the future means finding economically feasible ways to operate within the biophysical limits of the planet.

Given this, strategic managers are faced with effectively implementing what we call *sustainable strategic management,* a broad term that encompasses all the processes necessary to integrate sustainability into the strategic core of organizations. Sustainable strategic management refers to internal cognitive, strategic, structural, and operational processes that are important for organizations wishing to function in sustainable ways. Further, as Throop, Starik, and Rands (1993) say, "Strategies promoting ecological sustainability . . . [must] recognize the interconnectedness of all firms and individuals in the global commons" (p. 75); therefore, sustainable strategic management also refers to myriad internal and external alliances, networks, and relationships that are important for organizations wishing to function in sustainable ways. Starik and Rands (1995) describe these alliances and networks as "a web of . . . sustainability relationships with individuals, other organizations, political-economic entities, and social-cultural entities" (p. 917).

Copious research in strategic management has pointed to the fact that successfully implementing long-term strategic efforts of any type requires that the core philosophies and value systems of the organization be consistent with the strategic initiative (see Chapter 5), and that the organization create the appropriate strategies, technologies, structures, and processes necessary to support the strategic effort over the long term (Banks & Wheelwright, 1979; Galbraith & Kazanjian, 1986; Hrebiniak & Joyce, 1984; Kerr, 1985; Kerr & Slocum, 1987; Noar, 1977; Salter, 1973; Stonich, 1981). Successfully implementing sustainable strategic management initiatives requires that organizations pay attention to these same factors. Further, because there are normally wide philosophical, ethical, operational, and structural differences between strategic initiatives based on hard growth and strategic initiatives that are based on sustainability, successfully instituting sustainable strategic management efforts in organizations often requires fundamental cultural change efforts (Post & Altman, 1992, 1994; Stead & Stead, 1994a; Throop et al., 1993). Shrivastava (1992) refers to the wide variety of cultural and process changes necessary for effective sustainable strategic management as *corporate self-greenewal.*

In this chapter, we discuss several concepts that are important for focusing the attention and actions of strategic managers on the broad spectrum of processes related to integrating sustainability into their strategic decisions. When tied together, we believe that these concepts provide a sound framework for guiding strategic managers in their efforts to develop the philosophical and ethical underpinnings, strategies, production and operations systems, structures, and change processes necessary to support sustainable strategic management initiatives in organizations.

Ecocentric Management: A Philosophy of Sustainability

In building a conceptual framework for successful sustainable strategic management, a very good place to begin is with Paul Shrivastava's (1995a) *ecocentric management paradigm*. Central to the ecocentric management paradigm is the assumption that the Earth is the ultimate stakeholder. In this regard, Shrivastava (1995a) says, "If organizations are to effectively address the ecological degradation inherent in risk societies, then they must use a new management orientation [that centers on] . . . the stakeholder that bears the most risks from industrial activities: Nature!" (p. 127).

The ecocentric management paradigm has embedded in it two fundamental concepts: industrial ecosystems, which are discussed at some length later in this chapter, and ecocentric management (Shrivastava, 1995a). Ecocentric management is essentially a philosophical ideal that Shrivastava (1995a) says is necessary for aligning the management processes of business organizations with the biophysical processes of the natural environment. According to Shrivastava (1995a), this means taking very different perspectives on at least seven organizational elements. He says that under the tenets of ecocentric management, compared with current organizational practices, the following should be true:

1. Organizational goals should emphasize "sustainability, quality of life, and stakeholder welfare" (p. 131).
2. Organizational values should reflect the importance of the central role of Nature as well as the importance of intuition and understanding.
3. Organizational products should be designed to be more ecologically sensitive.
4. Organizational production systems should use less energy and fewer resources and produce fewer wastes.

5. Organizational structures should be less hierarchical, more participative and decentralized, with lower income differentials between managers and the workforce.
6. Organizational environments should be interpreted to reflect the finite nature of the Earth's ability to provide energy and resources and to absorb wastes.
7. The basic organizational business functions of marketing, finance, accounting, and human resource management should reflect consumer education, long-term ecologically sustainable growth, accounting for full environmental costs, and a safe, healthful, and fulfilling work environment.

Shrivastava (1995a) says that the vision and mission of organizations applying ecocentric management should include commitments to "minimizing virgin-material and nonrenewable-energy use, eliminating emissions, effluents and accidents, and minimizing the life-cycle cost of products and services" (p. 131). He says that the input, throughput, and output processes of the firm should be designed to fulfill these commitments, with the ultimate goal of "closing the loop of output and input processes" (p. 133).

Many argue that the shift in the focus of management from anthropocentric to ecocentric would improperly emphasize Nature over humankind. At the root of such arguments is the Cartesian assumption that humankind is separate from and superior to Nature. However, as we demonstrated in earlier chapters, humankind is neither separate from nor superior to Nature. Instead, humankind and Nature are integrally intertwined, with the survival of each dependent on the other. Thus, ecocentric management is not designed to emphasize Nature over humankind. Rather, it is designed to emphasize Nature with humankind. As such, it provides an excellent philosophical view from which to set the processes of sustainable strategic management in motion. In this regard, Shrivastava (1995a) says,

This [ecocentric] view of the firm suggests revising management's basic concepts of organizational objectives and strategy.
. . . This new concept of strategy deals with the co-alignment of an organization with its environment. . . . This strategy must . . .

address issues of impact of the firm's activities on the natural and social environments, and it must provide avenues for renewal of environmental resources that the organization uses. (p. 134)

Enterprise Strategy: Standing for Sustainability

Enterprise strategy provides an excellent framework for developing organizational strategic processes that reflect the philosophies of ecocentric management. *Enterprise strategy* is an overarching level of strategy that allows firms to explicitly integrate ethical considerations into economic decisions. According to Ed Freeman (1984), enterprise strategy is designed to answer the question, "What do we stand for?" (p. 90). Thus, enterprise strategy reflects a firm's responsibilities to the larger society in its strategic decision-making processes (Ansoff, 1979; Freeman, 1984; Schendel & Hofer, 1979).

The roots of enterprise strategy lie within the confines of stakeholder theory, which, as mentioned in Chapter 8, has a strong ethical base. In this regard, Freeman (1984), Freeman and Gilbert (1988), and Hosmer (1994) all make cases that the true strength of enterprise strategy is that it provides a framework in which ethical concerns can be effectively incorporated into strategic management processes. They say that enterprise strategy specifically addresses the value systems of managers and stakeholders in concrete terms, focusing attention on what the firm *should* do.

At the heart of enterprise strategy formulation is *stakeholder analysis*. Stakeholder analysis identifies the firm's stakeholders along with the "stakes" that each has in the firm (economic, technological, social, etc.). This helps the firm to understand the roles that its various stakeholders play and to identify the interconnections between the stakeholders. Analyzing *stakeholder power*, that is, examining the scope and breadth of a stakeholder (discussed briefly in the previous chapter), is a critical component of stakeholder analysis. Such an analysis makes it possible to understand the "trump cards" held by each of the firm's stakeholders (Freeman & Gilbert, 1988). Also critical for stakeholder analysis is understanding the firm's *stakeholder management capability*—that is, its ability to meet the needs of stakeholders now and in the future (Freeman, 1984). Assessing stakeholder management capability involves comparing the firm's stakeholder maps with its standard operating procedures and the way it allocates resources and interacts with its stakeholders. Such an assessment provides an understanding of how well organizational processes fit with the external environment, and it provides a better understanding of how the firm's moral obligations to its stakeholders really come into play (Carroll, 1995).

According to Freeman (1984), analyzing a firm's enterprise strategy requires integrating the results of stakeholder analysis with an analysis of the firm's values and an analysis of the societal issues it faces. *Values analysis* brings the ethical system of the firm to the surface, making it an explicit part of the strategy formulation process. Societal issues analysis allows the firm to incorporate the social context of the organization into strategy formulation. This stakeholders × values × issues analysis is very helpful in a firm's understanding of its enterprise strategy because it reveals "different moral views and different answers to the question, What do we stand for?" (Freeman, 1984, p. 101).

Thus, this analysis results in a clearer understanding of the type of enterprise strategy a firm is pursuing. Freeman (1984) and Freeman and Gilbert (1988) suggest several types of enterprise strategies, each based on different moral views and different assumptions about who the most important stakeholders are (the ones that hold the trump cards). For example, stockholder enterprise strategies reflect an overriding commitment to shareholders; managerial prerogative enterprise strategies reflect the dominant position of senior managers in the firm's hierarchy of stakeholders; and personal projects enterprise strategies reflect the firm's prevailing moral commitment to its employees as the most important stakeholders.

Once a firm includes the Earth as the ultimate stakeholder, stakeholders × values × issues analysis allows the firm to more thoroughly identify the scope, breadth, and power of the planet as a stakeholder in the organization, including the strength of its various green representatives in the immediate business arena. It also allows the firm to more clearly assess the degree to which sustainability has emerged as a core value in the firm, and it allows the firm to clarify the impacts of its operations on the Earth's resources, species, and systems. This analysis allows the firm to integrate the Earth as a trump card into the organization's strategic thinking processes. Thus, from this process a new genre of enterprise strategy emerges in which the organization *stands for sustainability.*

Sustainability Strategies: Fulfilling Green Visions

Shrivastava (1996) says that a strategic vision "reflects a corporation's fundamental assumptions about itself, the very foundations on which it stands" (p. 174). In this regard, a firm's strategic vision is a reflection of its enterprise strategy. A strategic vision is an image that both guides and limits the firm's decision-making processes at all levels (Senge, 1990; Shrivastava, 1996). The vision serves as the foundation for developing the firm's mission, goals, objectives, and strategic actions. It also serves as a basis for determining what information the organization considers important and the ways the organization measures its success. Thus, a strategic vision provides the mold through which a firm's strategic actions can begin to take shape out of its enterprise strategy.

According to Hart (1995) and Shrivastava (1995a, 1996), instituting sustainable strategic management in organizations begins with a strategic vision based on sustainability. Such a vision provides the foundation for making decisions that support a new definition of long-term organizational prosperity, one that integrates the need to earn a profit with responsibility to protect the environment. Like a sailing craft in a race, the individual firm would see that the key to being competitive is the efficient and effective use of renewable resources and energy, the ability to be light and maneuverable, and the ability to leave no trace of operations in its wake.

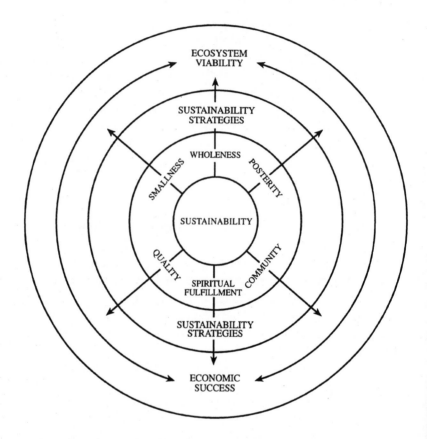

Figure 9.1. Envisioning Sustainability Strategies

As can be seen in Figure 9.1, such a vision demonstrates the interconnectedness between economic success and the health of the ecosystem; the organization would see itself as a part of a greater society and natural environment to which its survival is tied. Thus, this vision would serve as an excellent foundation for sustainable strategic management processes based on instrumental values such as wholeness, posterity, smallness, community, and spiritual fulfillment.

A vision based on sustainability "must be in place before complete corporate greening can be possible" (Shrivastava,

1996, p. 175). Once in place, operating within such a vision leads naturally to the development of competitive strategies designed to simultaneously enhance the quality of the ecosystem and the long-term survivability of the firm (Hart, 1995; Kiernan, 1992; Shrivastava, 1995a, 1996). We refer to these strategies as *sustainability strategies*. Sustainability strategies are not compromise strategies; they are not designed merely to earn a profit while doing as little damage as possible to the ecosystem. Rather, they are integrative strategies; they provide competitive advantages to organizations by simultaneously enhancing the quality of the ecosystem and the long-term survivability of the firm. As Art Kleiner (1991b) says, "In the long run, the principles of economic growth and environmental quality reinforce each other" (p. 38). Michael Porter (1991) reiterates this point, saying, "The conflict between environmental protection and economic competitiveness is a false dichotomy" (p. 168).

Sustainability strategies can be classified according to the nature of the competitive advantages they provide—that is, advantages based on lowering costs or providing opportunities for market differentiation (Hart, 1995; Porter, 1985; Shrivastava, 1996). *Process-driven sustainability strategies* are the first type. Economically, process-driven sustainability strategies are designed to provide firms with cost advantages through improved environmental efficiency (Hart, 1995; Shrivastava, 1995a, 1996; Stead & Stead, 1995). Ecologically, these strategies serve to reduce resource depletion, materials use, energy consumption, emissions, and effluents. Examples of activities often included in process-driven sustainability strategies include (a) redesigning pollution and waste control systems, (b) redesigning production processes to be more environmentally sensitive, (c) using recycled materials from production processes and / or outside sources, and (d) using renewable energy sources (Stead & Stead, 1995).

The second type are *market-driven sustainability strategies*. Economically, market-driven sustainability strategies are designed to provide firms with competitive advantages by allowing them to ecologically differentiate their products from their competitors in the marketplace (Shrivastava, 1996; Stead &

Stead, 1995). Ecologically, these strategies reflect *product stewardship* (Hart, 1995), the idea that environmental hazards and life-cycle costs should be minimized in products or services. Some of the activities that can make up market-driven sustainability strategies are (a) entering new environmental markets or market segments, (b) introducing new environmentally oriented products, (c) redesigning products to be more environmentally sensitive, (d) advertising the environmental benefits of products, (e) redesigning product packaging, and (f) selling scrap once discarded as wastes (Stead & Stead, 1995).

Research reveals that sustainability strategy implementation has become pervasive in industry throughout the United States, Canada, and the European Community as firms seek to improve their environmental performance, enhance their competitiveness, and respond to pressures from green stakeholders such as regulators and consumers (Dillon & Fischer, 1992; Schot & Fisher, 1993; Stead & Stead, 1995; Throop et al., 1993; Williams, Medhurst, & Drew, 1993). Research also reveals that both market-driven and process-driven sustainability strategies can be economically feasible, even lucrative, for firms. Investments and payback periods are generally reasonable, and financial outcomes, including revenue enhancement, return on assets, return on investment, and return on equity, are often quite positive (Hart & Ahuja, 1994; Stead & Stead, 1995; Williams et al., 1993).

Stuart Hart (1995), in his natural-resource-based theory of the firm, greatly enriches the understanding of sustainability strategy formulation and implementation. He argues effectively that the natural environment offers firms some of the most important competitive advantages now and in the future. He develops a three-stage sustainability strategy progression: The first stage, which he refers to as *pollution prevention strategies*, essentially involves implementing process-driven strategies in order to simultaneously conserve resources and reduce costs. Because of the increasing demands for external scrutiny of environmental operations, Hart argues that pollution prevention strategies not only provide firms with competitive advantages, they also provide firms with opportunities to establish social legitimacy in the greater community.

In the next stage, which Hart (1995) calls *product stewardship*, firms evolve from a pollution prevention focus to a focus on the complete life-cycle impacts of their products and processes. Product stewardship strategies are market driven in that they provide sustained opportunities for firms to differentiate themselves from their competitors, but they go well beyond this. Basing product stewardship strategies on life-cycle analysis means that this differentiation is achieved by attending to both process and market factors in strategy formulation and implementation. Further, total product stewardship is best achieved by involving all of the firm's external stakeholders— including suppliers, environmentalists, regulators, and the community—in its product development processes.

The third stage described by Hart (1995) is the development of *sustainable development strategies*. These are strategies that include the cost-saving, market differentiation, and social legitimacy dimensions of pollution prevention and product stewardship. However, they are a radical departure from these strategies because they shift the firm's focus from markets in developed nations of the world to markets in the developing world, primarily south of the equator (Hart, 1994, 1995). Hart says that the competitive advantages related to sustainable development strategies are garnered from the firm's keen sense of commitment to Nature and society. He says that a firm's long-term vision of sustainability must be the driving force behind sustainable development strategies. Formulating and implementing such strategies requires a willingness to make long-term commitments of organizational resources to the development of technologies that have low environmental impacts and serve the unique needs of customers in the developing nations of the world.

Hart (1995) points out that these three types of strategies are interconnected at a variety of levels. As implied in the discussion above, they are, to a large degree, cumulative and sequential. Pollution prevention strategies are both a beneficial avenue to product stewardship strategies and an important part of product stewardship strategies. Product stewardship strategies are both helpful paths to and significant parts of sustainable development strategies. However, Hart points out that the interconnections between these three strategies flow in the other direction as well. He says that a strong vision of sustainable development is the most powerful foundation a firm can have for facilitating the formulation and implementation of pollution prevention and product stewardship strategies.

Hart's (1995) natural-resource-based theory of the firm is very valuable in explaining in some depth how sustainability strategies provide firms with sustained competitive advantages in developed markets across the globe. However, we believe that the theory's most important contribution may be that it opens an ecologically sensitive theoretical door through which firms can establish long-term niches in the rapidly growing markets of the developing world. Sustainable-development strategies as described by Hart are designed not only to bring economic success to organizations that are willing to make the long-term commitments necessary to compete in the developing world; these strategies also are designed to account for the unique social and environmental problems facing developing nations. Within this framework, Hart provides some economically feasible strategic pathways by which organizations can meaningfully contribute to the alleviation of the serious ecological and social problems plaguing the developing world—problems that must be faced if society is to truly achieve sustainability.

In essence, then, sustainability strategies are what organizations that *stand for sustainability* do: It is through sustainability strategies that the philosophies and ethics of sustainable strategic management become tangible. Sustainability strategies are thus excellent vehicles for operationally integrating the biophysical constraints of Nature into strategic decision-making processes. In short, sustainability strategies provide valuable avenues for bringing both the ecological and economic dimensions of an organization's green vision to life.

Industrial Ecosystems: Aligning Production With Nature

We mentioned in the introduction of this chapter that sustainable strategic management requires that organizations operate within ecologically based networks with other firms and stakeholders. These networks are commonly referred to as *industrial ecosystems* because they model their production and market processes on the characteristics of mature natural systems (Richards, Allenby, & Frosch, 1994; Shrivastava, 1995a, 1995b). According to Shrivastava (1995a), "Conceptually, [an industrial ecosystem] consists of organizations that jointly seek to minimize environmental degradation by using each other's waste and by-products and by sharing and minimizing the use of natural resources" (p. 128). Richards et al. (1994) say, "In an industrial ecology, unit processes and industries are interacting systems rather than isolated components. . . . The focus changes from merely minimizing wastes from a particular process or facility, commonly known as pollution prevention, to minimizing waste produced by the larger system as a whole" (p. 3).

E. F. Schumacher's concept of "appropriate technology" (which he originally called "intermediate technology") is an important historical forerunner to the development of the concept of industrial ecosystems. In the mid-1950s, while working as an economic adviser to the British National Coal Board, Schumacher came to the conclusion that industrial technology was taking an irreparable toll on the natural environment because of its overuse of coal and other fossil fuels. In 1954, he warned that our current economic activities were creating dire problems because of technologies that relied on massive amounts of nonrenewable energy and resources (Wood, 1984). Even though his warnings fell on deaf ears during the industrial expansion of the 1950s, this realization was a personal breakthrough for Schumacher. From that point on, it was abundantly clear to him that the technologies of the industrial age were built on dreams no more real than puffs of smoke (Wood, 1984). He saw these technologies as being inhuman, favoring the rich over the poor, and destroying the very Earth on which they existed. He realized that if society did not develop technologies more sensitive to human and environmental concerns, its days on this planet would be numbered (Schumacher, 1973).

From these concerns, Schumacher (1979) began to develop his ideas of appropriate technology. He describes appropriate technology using terminology very similar to that used later to define industrial ecosystems: He says that appropriate technology provides for "production which respects ecological principles and strives to work with Nature" (p. 57). He bases the development of appropriate technology on three assumptions: (a) It is possible to make things smaller; (b) it is possible to do things simpler; and (c) it is possible to do things cheaper. He says that production technologies based on these assumptions stress low-cost methods and equipment that are available to most people, can be used on a small scale, and are compatible with humankind's creative needs. By "low-cost technologies," Schumacher means total costs, measured not only in financial terms but also in terms of the depletion of the Earth's natural capital (Schumacher, 1973).

According to Richards et al. (1994), achieving an industrial ecosystem that is truly in concert with Nature's biophysical processes requires transcending three progressively difficult stages of industrial evolution. The first stage, the Type I industrial ecosystem, is the classical industrial model. In this stage, the global production and distribution systems operate on straight linear processes in which virgin raw materials and energy are converted into goods and services. The by-products of these processes are heat and material wastes that either dissipate into or must be disposed of in the natural environment. The second stage of industrial evolution, a Type II industrial ecosystem, involves some recycling of materials and energy in production processes but still requires the linear transformation of virgin inputs and energy into products and wastes that must be absorbed by Nature. The third stage of evolution is to a Type III industrial ecosystem in which the only inputs are renewable energy, and operations are totally closed-looped with virtually total materials reuse and recycling. Type

III industrial ecosystems export only heat into the external environment. These Type III systems mimic mature natural ecosystems, which are generally quite stable, operating on minimal amounts of entropy.

From the above description, it is clear that humankind is still in the early stages of industrial ecosystem evolution. Currently, most efforts seem geared largely toward moving from Type I to Type II. The use of recycled materials and renewable energy are certainly on the rise in industry, and efforts such as pollution prevention and total quality environmental management (TQEM, discussed in the next chapter) have been particularly valuable in helping individual firms to improve their environmental management processes. However, at this point, Type III, closed-loop, interconnected networks of firms operating only on renewable energy and exporting only absorbable heat remain largely an ideal to be pursued. Nevertheless, simple Type III systems involving a few interacting firms are beginning to appear. Shrivastava (1995a) discusses such a system located in Kalundborg, Denmark, in which the management of raw materials, by-products, energy, water, and wastes is coordinated among six local organizations and several farms. The system has facilitated significant water savings, waste minimization, resource conservation, and energy conservation in Kalundborg. There are also ongoing efforts in the United States to promote the development of industrial ecosystems; an industrial-ecology park is being developed in upstate New York, and the city of Chattanooga, Tennessee, is attempting to develop industrial ecosystems as part of its efforts to become a "green city."

Though not yet a reality on a wide scale, Type III industrial ecosystems provide an excellent ideal upon which to design the production and operations management systems of firms seeking to implement sustainable strategic management processes. This ideal encourages firms to seek production methods that model Nature, using minimal resources and energy, generating minimal amounts of wastes, and developing ecologically symbiotic relationships with other organizations and stakeholders.

Learning Organizations: Structures for Sustainability

It has long been recognized that increasing environmental turbulence and advancing technology dictate the need for more flexible, dynamic organizational structures that are flatter and that rely on more informal, knowledge-based decision-making processes (Burns & Stalker, 1961; Emery & Trist, 1965, 1973; Woodward, 1965). It has also long been recognized (although not always acknowledged) that interactions between business and the natural environment are significant features of this environmental turbulence (Emery & Trist, 1973; Schumacher, 1973, 1979).

Probably the first person to actually combine these two facts in a structural framework explicitly designed for organizations pursuing sustainable strategic management was (again) E. F. Schumacher (1973). He believed that large organizations inhibit freedom, creativity, and human dignity and that they damage the ecosystem. He believed that the only way to reverse the negative effects of vast organizations is to "achieve small-ness within the large organization" (p. 242). It was on this premise that he based his theory of large-scale organization.

The theory consists of five principles. The first says that large organizations should be divided into *quasi firms,* which are small, autonomous teams designed to foster high levels of entrepreneurial spirit. The second principle says that account-ability of the quasi firms to higher management should be based on a few items related to profitability. Decisions are made by the team members in ad hoc fashion without interference from upper management; upper management steps in only if the profitability goals are not being met. Third, the quasi firms should maintain their own economic identity; they should be allowed to have their own names and keep their own records. Their financial performance should not be merged with other units. Fourth, motivation for lower-level workers can be achieved only if the job is intellectually and spiritually fulfilling with ample opportunities to participate in decisions (that is, good work). Schumacher says that this can be achieved in two ways: One is to base the organization's structure on small, autonomous work teams; the other is to allow for more employee ownership and participation at the strategic level. The fifth principle of the theory of large-scale organization, the principle of the middle axiom, says that top management can transcend the divergent problem of balancing the need for employee freedom with the need for organizational control by setting broad, strategic directions and allowing the quasi firms to make their own decisions within these broad directions (Schumacher, 1973).

Schumacher (1979) says that firms organized around these principles would be structured "like Nature with little cells" (p. 83). He says that such organizations would resemble a helium balloon vendor at a carnival with a large number of balloons for sale. The vendor (who represents top management) holds the balloons from below rather than lording over them from above. Each balloon represents an autonomous unit that shifts and sways on its own within the broad limits defined by the vendor.

As was the case with appropriate technology, many are now echoing Schumacher's sentiments. There is a growing consensus that achieving sustainable strategic management is most likely to occur in organizations that are driven by green visions and that have flat, informal, team-based, knowledge-based structures that allow for more control by employees (Halal, 1986; Hart, 1995; Post & Altman, 1992; Shrivastava, 1995a, 1996; Stead & Stead, 1994a). Post and Altman (1992) have probably explored the structural dimensions of corporate greening in as much depth as anyone, and they believe that the most appropriate structural form for successful sustainable strategic management is the learning organization.

Learning organizations are holistic, interconnected structures that can successfully define their own futures through double-loop learning processes that allow them to question and change the foundation values, visions, and assumptions that underlie the way they think and behave. In the words of Beckhard and Pritchard (1992), learning organizations are structured to reach to "the very essence of organizations—their basic purposes, their identities, and their relationships" (p. 1). Learning organizations require vision-driven leadership that focuses on designing, teaching, and stewarding the organizational vision (Beck-hard & Pritchard, 1992; Handy, 1989; Senge, 1990).

Peter Senge (1990) has probably contributed more than anyone to the development of learning organizations. He de-scribes five interrelated *learning disciplines* that constitute the framework of learning organizations. The central discipline is systems thinking, which focuses on identifying points of lever-age within circular, archetypical models that represent the long-term interrelationships between key variables (see Chap-ter 5). The other four disciplines include personal mastery, or allowing for the pursuit of personal visions within the context of the organization; a shared organizational vision, which col-lectively and synergistically represents the employees' per-sonal visions; a willingness to question mental models, that is, to examine basic values and assumptions that underlie organ-izational actions; and team learning processes, which empha-size double-loop learning and continuous, honest reflection and dialogue designed to bring the firm's underlying mental models to the surface as legitimate points of discussion and change.

Learning organizations provide a framework for a more intrinsic, spiritual view of the purpose of organizational life (Handy, 1989; Harman, 1988, 1991; Ray, 1991; Senge, 1990). Senge (1990) says that in learning organizations there is "a more sacred view of work" (p. 5) and that allowing employees the opportunity to be creative and self-directed in the pursuit of their personal visions is the "spiritual foundation" of learning organizations (p. 7). Ray (1991) says that adopting learning structures "is a move to the spirit, to inner qualities such as intuition, will, joy, strength, and compassion . . . , [and] to the power of inner wisdom and authority and the connection and wholeness in humanity" (p. 37).

Learning organizations are designed to continuously focus on and question the underlying values and assumptions that guide the firm. They bring a holistic, spiritual dimension into the psyche of organizations, and they are vision driven, team oriented, knowledge based, open, and free-flowing, allowing for increased employee participation in strategic decisions. In short, learning organizations are ideal structures for integrating sustainability into organizational values and visions, and they are ideal structures for facilitating the translation of these green values and visions into organizational strategic actions that are in concert with both the economic success of the firm and the processes of Nature.

Fundamental Change: Creating Sustainability Cultures

Thus, in sum, sustainable strategic management involves the following:

1. Adopting ecocentric management as the philosophical umbrella under which the firm's visions, missions, goals, inputs, throughputs, and outputs are developed
2. Integrating sustainability and related instrumental values into the core of the firm's enterprise strategy, creating an overarching organizational ethical system that encourages the firm to "stand for sustainability"
3. Translating this stance into a green vision and formulating and implementing sustainability strategies that provide the firm with competitive advantages in the pursuit of that vision
4. Designing production and operations systems around the notion of Type III industrial ecosystems, which, like Nature, operate on a minimum of resource use, energy consumption, and waste generation
5. Creating and maintaining learning structures that provide the organizational frameworks necessary for tying together economic success, human spiritual fulfillment, and a vision of sustainability

If this summary clarifies anything, it is that most firms have an arduous journey ahead of them in their efforts to implement sustainable strategic management. If sustainable strategic management is to be successfully implemented in business organizations, it will likely require that organizations change their cultures in very fundamental ways (Post & Altman, 1992, 1994; Stead & Stead, 1994a; Throop et al., 1993). Cultural change is a very difficult task that requires examining and redefining the core assumptions and values of the organization, the nature of the work, and the roles of the employees. Changing cultures generally involves developing new knowledge, skills, objectives, performance measures, reward systems, and training programs, as well as informal structures that support the new culture (Schein, 1985).

William Ruckelshaus (1991) uses an excellent analogy to explain the magnitude of the philosophical changes necessary for developing a culture to support sustainable strategic management. He points out that, whereas all organizations in capitalistic nations have a deep understanding and appreciation of the concept of profit, this concept had absolutely no meaning in old communist-bloc nations. He says that sustainability is as foreign a concept for strategic managers in capitalistic nations as profits used to be for communist managers. He says, "Sustainability has to be made the bones and belly of corporate life, to join the intrinsic concepts like profit and loss, debt and equity, capital and cost, that make our system work" (p. 7).

Jeffrey Heilpern and Terry Limpert (1991) of the Delta Consulting Group use the implementation of TQEM to illustrate the degree of change in organizational assumptions necessary to implement sustainable strategic management. They say that a basic problem with assisting firms in implementing basic total quality management (TQM) is that the firms usually are founded on "quality-hostile" assumptions, such as the idea that profits are all that really matter and that the organization is a lot smarter than its customers. Before TQM can be implemented, the firms must replace these with "quality-friendly" assumptions, such as the idea that quality is defined by the customer and that profits result from high quality. Adding the environmental (E) dimension to TQM presents an even more difficult cultural dilemma. Firms must not only adopt quality-friendly assumptions, they also must adopt the environment-friendly assumptions that form the basis of sustainability.

The research of Post and Altman (1992) supports the contention of Ruckelshaus and the others that significant cultural change is generally necessary for implementing sustainable strategic management. Post and Altman (1992) conclude that successful adoption of sustainable strategic management generally requires organizations to achieve a *third-order* change, involving the development of new values, new objectives, new structures, new reward systems, and new norms. They say that "internal paradigm shifts and transformational change are necessary as companies attempt to adjust to the rapidly changing world of green politics and markets" (p. 13).

Third-order change is quite different from both first-order change (developing new ways to reinforce current objectives, values, norms, structures, etc.) and second-order change (purposefully modifying current objectives, values, norms, structures, etc.). Third-order change is discontinuous, requiring that organizations achieve and perpetuate an entirely different qualitative state (Bartunek & Moch, 1987). Organizations attempting third-order change cannot expect to be successful by taking the slow linear steps associated with lesser degrees of organizational change. Rather, third-order change requires fundamental efforts designed to completely shift the consciousness of the firm to a different level. Such efforts require the creation and stewardship of a new organizational vision until it is accepted as the very essence of the organization; this can be accomplished only by simultaneously changing all the systems and processes of the organization to support the new culture (Beckhard & Pritchard, 1992).

Research results are mixed regarding the adequacy of current organizational efforts to make the fundamental changes necessary to institute sustainable strategic management. Of the three firms Post and Altman (1992) studied, only one had made the cultural changes necessary to fully implement sustainable strategic management. Other research points to the fact that organizations are beginning to "talk the talk" of the environment very well, but their efforts to "walk the walk" are lagging behind their rhetoric. Firms are espousing Earth-friendly values and developing Earth-friendly policies, and they are appointing specialists, gathering information, and implementing programs related to these values and policies (Henriques & Sadorsky, 1995; Stead, Stead, Wilcox, & Zimmerer, 1994). However, their efforts to take the difficult steps necessary to actually fundamentally transform their organizational cultures so that sustainable strategic management will be perpetuated over the long run, such as redesigning structures and recrafting performance, control, reward, and reporting systems, have been less than spectacular up to this point (Stead et al., 1994).

Although the third-order changes needed to achieve sustainable strategic management certainly pose some serious challenges for organizations, they can be overcome. Business organizations have proven time after time that they can successfully adapt their cultures to new environmental conditions when necessary. As ecological concerns continue to move into the forefront of the strategic issues facing business, organizations that adopt sustainability as the basis of their cultures will be prepared to develop the philosophies, strategies, technologies, structures, and management systems necessary to support the sustainable strategic management initiatives they will need to survive.

Conclusions

In a nutshell, sustainable strategic management is achievable when organizations can manage to institute the internal and external processes that will allow them to function as parts of larger networks of ecologically interconnected firms and stakeholders, all of whom are stressing the processes of Nature, the common good of the human community, and the fulfillment of spiritual as well as economic needs as the proper paths to long-term economic success. This is no doubt an idealistic, utopian image—a dream, if you will. Yet it has been well documented that organizations that ascend to leadership positions often do so by committing themselves to the long-term pursuit of dreams that seem unattainable to others (Hamel & Prahalad, 1989; Hart, 1995). Yes, sustainable strategic management is indeed a dream, but it is a dream whose time has come. Firms who pursue it have the potential to succeed in the long term by integrating themselves with Nature.

Chapter 10

Creating Environmental Management Systems

Satisfying the stakeholder demands of the Earth and its many green representatives has become very important to organizations, and as a result firms are beginning to take sustainable strategic management seriously. To quote Ladd Greeno (1994) of Arthur D. Little, "Environmental management . . . is becoming one of the most important strategic matters to develop in decades . . . as corporations have discovered [that] the strategic, regulatory, liability, and competitive issues are all entangled and will become even more so" (p. 44). In this chapter, we will examine in some detail the environmental management systems that are beginning to emerge as business organizations try to effectively deal with this web of strategic environmental issues.

Environmental Management Systems: Closing the Value Chain

Firms are rapidly discovering that effectively dealing with the strategic complexities of the relationship between them-

selves and the Earth requires that they go beyond single programs or approaches. Firms have learned (some the hard way)
that their environmental accidents, damages, and clean-up
costs increase, and their reputations are damaged, when a complete system of environmental management is not in place
(Welford & Gouldson, 1993). Thus, at the heart of implementing
sustainable strategic management in organizations is the development of an integrated environmental management system
(EMS), sometimes referred to as an environmental health and
safety management system (EHS).

The Europeans are making concerted efforts to create some
EMS standardization. For example, both the European Community's Eco-Management and Audit Scheme (EMAS) and the
British Standard (BS) 7750 (discussed in Chapter 8) establish
clear requirements for an EMS. Under BS 7750, firms are required to set and communicate policies; clearly define management and employee environmental responsibilities; establish
environmental education and training programs; develop plans
to accomplish environmental objectives; establish review processes of environmental impacts, legal requirements, and stated
goals and targets; and develop appropriate record keeping and
control mechanisms to ensure compliance with the firm's plans
(Welford & Gouldson, 1993).

Even with these efforts in place, environmental management systems vary both in terms of what elements are included
in them and the relative importance of each element. However,
there is general agreement on some of the important elements
of an EMS: At the heart of an effective EMS is strong commitment to improved environmental performance at the board and
senior management levels of the organization. An effective
EMS also requires developing and communicating throughout
the organization clear environmental goals along with specific
objectives and targets to support these goals. Critical to any
EMS is the development of sustainability strategies designed to
achieve the outcomes outlined in the firm's environmental
goals, objectives, and targets. Systematic reviews of environmental performance measured against these stated goals, objectives, and targets as well as against the firm's past environ-

mental performance and legal requirements are also necessary elements of an EMS. Further, these reviews can be carried out only if effective environmental information and environmental reporting systems are established. Of course, none of this will take place unless human resource processes, including training, employee performance standards, performance appraisal systems, and reward systems, are brought into line with the firm's environmental performance goals. All of this requires participative, empowerment-based structures that encourage all employees to take direct responsibility for environmental improvements as basic parts of their jobs (Greeno, 1993; Shrivastava, 1996; Welford & Gouldson, 1993).

A key to establishing an effective EMS is to ensure that it is comprehensive (Greeno, 1993; Welford & Gouldson, 1993). Michael Porter's (1985) *value chain* can provide an excellent conceptual framework for establishing a comprehensive EMS, if it is extended to include the natural environment. Porter (1985) argues that each of a firm's activities—from physical creation through manufacture to the consumer—can be analyzed in order to better understand the firm's sources of costs and market differentiation. From this, the firm can focus on adding value to its activities by finding ways to reduce costs and/or improve products at each stage of the value chain. He says that the value chain includes primary activities, which are those related to manufacturing and marketing a product, and support activities, such as human resource management, information systems, auditing, and so on. Although Porter limits his discussion of the value chain to the closed circular-flow economy, applying the value chain to sustainable strategic management dictates that it be extended to include resources in Nature and waste disposal after consumption. Meffert and Kirchgeorg (1994) refer to this as the *closed-loop value chain approach.*

For the remainder of this chapter, we will use the closed-loop value chain as a framework for discussing a plethora of processes and tools that we believe are important for establishing an effective, comprehensive EMS. We will begin by discussing life-cycle analysis (LCA) because it is a pervasive framework and a tool that permeates all of the primary and support closed-loop value chain activities. We will then discuss how the primary closed-loop value chain can be managed in more environmentally sensitive ways. In this regard, we will first discuss the implementation of process-driven sustainability strategies; we will present some examples of these strategies, and we will discuss the roles of total quality environmental management (TQEM) and design for environment (DFE) in implementing these strategies. Second, we will focus on the implementation of market-driven sustainability strategies; we will present some examples of these strategies, and we will discuss the concept of environmental marketing in some depth as it relates to these strategies. Following the discussion of primary closed-loop value chain activities, we will present four support closed-loop value chain activities that are necessary for effective environmental management systems, including environmental auditing, full-cost accounting, environmental management information systems (EMIS), and environmental reporting. Finally, we will discuss how achieving sustainability will require that organizations go beyond individually implementing closed-loop value chain activities; it will require that they participate in sustainability partnerships with diverse arrays of other organizations at the economic, social, cultural, and ecological levels.

Life-Cycle Analysis:
Foundation for Cradle-to-Grave Management

"The most far-reaching implication of integrating environmental concerns in the economic decisions of companies is the need to take a life-cycle approach to environmental analysis" (Richards, Allenby, & Frosch, 1994, p. 13). *Life-cycle analysis* (LCA) is a total-systems approach designed to provide a cradle-to-grave appraisal of the ecological impacts of products and processes. LCA involves analyzing resources, emissions, energy, and environmental effects all along the closed-loop value chain (Gladwin, Levin, & Ehrenfeld, 1994; Makower, 1993).

Through LCA, not only do organizations have a tool that can give them solid data on how to improve their environmental performance, they also have a tool that can help them to extend the life of their products, making them more competitive in the marketplace (Meffert & Kirchgeorg, 1994; Sullivan & Ehrenfeld, 1994).

LCA begins in Nature. That is, in the first stage of LCA, an analysis of the ecological impacts of acquiring the raw materials and energy that serve as inputs into the firm's products and processes is performed. In the second stage, the ecological impacts of the manufacturing process are assessed. This includes examining component manufacturing processes as well as final product manufacturing processes and product assembly processes. Third, the transportation and distribution systems related to delivering the product to market are analyzed in terms of distribution modes, distances, fuel consumption, and so forth. Fourth, the environmental consequences of how the product is used are analyzed, including assessments of product durability, energy requirements, polluting potential, and the like. Fifth, the product's potential for reuse and/or recyclability is analyzed. The sixth stage of LCA is to examine the product's ultimate disposal in terms of its toxicity, volume, biodegradability, and so on (Dillon, 1994; Sullivan & Ehrenfeld, 1994).

Business organizations, governmental agencies, and certification organizations all over the world are making concerted efforts to base their environmental actions on effective LCA. The result has been a mushrooming of LCA tools and techniques, such as LCA databases, expert systems, and software (Gladwin et al., 1994). One firm that is working toward integrating LCA into its environmental management processes is AT&T, which recently introduced what it calls Green Product Realization, designed to minimize the life-cycle impacts of its products (Gladwin et al., 1994; Sekutowski, 1994). AT&T chose a relatively simple project as the first Green Product Realization undertaking: greening the telephone. In this project, the design, manufacture, use, and end-of-life environmental impacts were all considered in an effort to make the telephone more resource and energy efficient, less toxic, longer lasting, and more recyclable (Sekutowski, 1994).

As good as all of this may sound, it is important to understand that LCA is extremely complex and nowhere close to being fully developed (Richards et al., 1994). AT&T chose its simplest product for its first Green Product Realization project precisely because LCA methodologies "are not very rigorous at this time" (Sekutowski, 1994). LCA outcomes are easily skewed by the assumptions of those doing the analysis, and LCA seldom provides clear-cut answers concerning the greenness of products and processes. It is difficult at this time to use LCA to make environmental distinctions among simple items such as paper products, and it is not currently possible to conduct LCA on products that are very complex in terms of materials, components, and design (Richards et al., 1994).

Regardless of the current rudimentary state of LCA methodology, it is absolutely essential to forge ahead with its development and improvement. According to Ayres (1994), without LCA, the laws of thermodynamics are effectively eliminated from consideration in product and process development. Even though the methodological limitations of LCA mean that organizations cannot currently get all the answers they need about their relationship with the planet, at least LCA is philosophically consistent with searching for and eventually finding those answers (Ayres, 1994).

Process-Driven Sustainability Strategies: Preventing Pollution Before It Happens

As we discussed in the previous chapter, process-driven sustainability strategies are designed to provide competitive cost advantages to firms through process improvements designed to save energy, materials, and resources and to reduce emissions, effluents, and so on. Recall that process-driven strategies are essentially what Hart (1995) refers to as pollution prevention, the first level of sustainability strategies designed to improve environmental performance during the manufacturing process.

Process-Driven Sustainability Strategies in Action

In 1975, 3M (one of the world's largest polluters and waste generators at the time) began its Pollution Prevention Pays (3P) program. The program was designed to switch the focus of pollution prevention at 3M from the output end to the input end of the firm's production processes. Executives were convinced that preventing pollution before it occurred made a great deal of economic sense when compared with the high costs and inherent inefficiencies of scrubbing it, treating it, storing it, burning it, transporting it, and burying it after it had been generated (Bringer & Benforado, 1994; Gold, 1990; North, 1992; Shrivastava, 1996). The 3P program was established on six basic principles:

1. 3M is responsible for solving its own environmental problems.
2. Pollution should be prevented at the source.
3. Natural resources should be conserved and/or reclaimed.
4. Products should have minimal negative environmental impacts.
5. All facilities should always be in regulatory compliance.
6. 3M should assist government agencies responsible for environmental protection. (Bringer & Benforado, 1994)

One of the unique features of the 3P program at 3M is its bottom-up, project approach. Rather than creating a centralized pollution prevention department responsible for generating the majority of pollution prevention ideas, 3M allows any technical employee or group of employees to propose pollution prevention projects. The project proposals are peer reviewed by a panel with members from each of the technical groups, known as the 3P Coordinating Committee, and those that are approved are then implemented in the various operational units of the firm. In order to keep the 3P project ideas flowing, recognition and awards are given for those who directly contribute in measurable ways to the projects, including the 3P Project Awards and the Chairman's Environmental Leadership Award. Also, 3M has created information exchange networks about pollution prevention, and it conducts regular workshops and seminars on various aspects of pollution prevention (Bringer & Benforado, 1994; North, 1992).

In the first 17 years of the 3P program, there were some 3,500 3P projects carried out at 3M. The firm is reportedly saving about $550 million per year because of these 3P projects. These savings come from an annual reduction of 575,000 tons in air pollution, water pollution, sludge, and solid wastes as well as a reduction of 1.6 billion gallons per year in wastewater generation. Further, the firm has implemented an energy conservation program that has saved it $650 million, and it spent $170 million between 1990 and 1993 to install thermal oxidizers to further control air pollution (Bringer & Benforado, 1994; Gold, 1990). 3M's efforts have not gone unnoticed. It won the World Environment Center's first Gold Medal in 1985, and it was awarded the Council on Economic Priorities' Corporate Conscience Award in 1988 (Gold, 1990).

The 3P program at 3M has evolved over the years into what the firm now refers to as 3P Plus. 3P Plus includes all of the original dimensions of the 3P program, but it has broadened the program to focus more on long-term environmental management plans, product responsibility, energy management, internal compliance auditing, environmental marketing, resource recovery, and ozone-depleting chemical phaseout. 3P Plus includes the Challenge 95 program, with a target to reduce energy use by 20% and waste generation by 35% during the period from 1990 to 1995. Also included in 3P Plus are the Year 2000 Goals, with targets of a 90% reduction in air, water, and land emissions and a 50% reduction in waste generation from 1987 levels by 2000 (Bringer & Benforado, 1994).

As mentioned earlier, Dow Chemical is earning a 53% return from its investments in pollution prevention (Buzzelli, 1994). Dow is a firm that has been much maligned over the years for its environmental performance, primarily because it produced both napalm and Agent Orange during the Vietnam War. However, Dow has emerged as a leader in pollution prevention (Hart, 1995). It has instituted a program called WRAP (Waste Reduction Always Pays). Examples of WRAP decisions at Dow include redesigning catalytic converters, installing pipes that are more resistant to corrosion, and ensuring that suppliers provide purer raw materials. The installation of the corrosion-resistant pipes has resulted in an annual savings of $890,000 to the firm while eliminating the discharge of the hydrochloric-caustic cleansers used to remove corrosion from the old pipes. Dow cut its toxic emissions in half between 1984 and 1988, and it is on target to cut these emissions in half again by 1995 (Kleiner, 1991a; Shrivastava, 1996). Also, Dow has reduced its organic releases into the water by 95% since 1980 (Shrivastava, 1996).

Similar to 3M's 3P program and Dow's WRAP program is Chevron's SMART program (Save Money and Reduce Toxics). This program has been singled out as one of the best pollution-prevention programs in the United States by the EPA. Since the program began in 1986, the firm has reduced pollution by 50% and hazardous wastes by 60%. Although the SMART program requires significant up-front investment, such as $22 million in a new storm-water treatment system, Chevron has also gleaned significant cost savings from SMART, such as $10 million in reduced hazardous waste disposal costs (Shrivastava, 1996).

Located in Greeneville, Tennessee, the Alltrista Zinc Products Corporation (formerly the Ball Zinc Products Division) produces 95% of the penny blanks in the United States, as well as zinc battery casings. In the late 1980s, the firm implemented a waste-reduction strategy that led to a 38% reduction in the 18,000 pounds of toxic sludge generated daily at the plant. The installation of a new wastewater treatment system in July 1990 permitted the firm to reduce its sludge generation by an additional 52%. The firm had cut its sludge to only 2,600 pounds per day, and it was recycling 800 pounds of this. Thus, it was shipping only 10% (1,800 pounds per day) of its original discharge to off-site dumps. The cost of these process improvements was $750,000, and the investment paid off handsomely for Alltrista; the Earth was spared 16,200 pounds of toxins per day, and the firm realized an annual cost savings of $500,000. In 1993, Alltrista finally reduced its sludge shipment costs to zero. The firm made other process improvements that reduced its sludge discharges below 1990 levels, and the remaining sludge (which contains primarily copper) is now being recycled. The copper recycler pays the freight costs to ship all of Alltrista's sludge from Tennessee to Arizona.

Alltrista was awarded the 1992 Tennessee Governor's Award for Excellence in Hazardous Waste Management, along with Great Dane Trailers of Memphis.[1] In 1987, Great Dane was emitting 224,000 pounds of toxic chemicals into the air annually and was shipping 123,000 pounds of toxic wastes from paint-related materials to off-site dumps each year. In February 1990, the firm instituted process changes that have led to a 90% reduction in air emissions and a 100% reduction in paint-related wastes. The paint wastes are now completely recycled into a superior-quality undercoat for the trailers, a product that was previously purchased from an outside supplier. For its efforts, the firm and the planet are both reaping the benefits; Great Dane saves about $135,400 annually in waste disposal costs.

Recent research has revealed that examples like the ones above are not exceptions. According to survey results, process-driven sustainability strategies are being widely implemented in industry (Lent & Wells, 1994; Stead & Stead, 1995). In a survey of 167 firms in 4 of the most polluting industries (chemicals, pulp and paper, metals, and utilities) it was found that, although front-end investments in process-driven sustainability strategies were generally reported to be high, the majority of the respondents reported that they expected to recoup these investments in less than 6 years. Further, the respondents reported that making these investments had positive impacts on their bottom lines (Stead & Stead, 1995).

Total Quality Environmental Management (TQEM)

We discussed in Chapter 7 that quality is an important instrumental value for supporting strategic management systems based on sustainability. In fact, quality has been one of the central concepts in the field of management for the past decade, and environmental management is no exception to this. TQEM is being widely implemented in industry today. In their survey of 41 Fortune 200 nonservice firms, Lent and Wells (1994) found that 60% of the respondents were implementing TQEM. No doubt, TQEM currently represents the leading edge of approaches for implementing process-driven sustainability strategies.

Total quality management (TQM) programs involve implementing organizational structures and processes that ensure that a firm consistently provides high-quality goods and services to its customers. The core principles of TQM are as follows (Bhushan & MacKenzie, 1994; Bringer & Benforado, 1994; Heilpern, 1990; Shetty, 1994; Welford & Gouldson, 1993):

1. Quality is a strategic issue that requires the strong commitment of top management.
2. Effective relationships with customers and suppliers are central in defining and maintaining quality.
3. A firm's core work processes should be capable of consistently satisfying customers' perceptions of quality.
4. Effective quality management requires increased use of measurable data and less reliance on instinct and experience.
5. Effective quality management requires an organizational system that has a continuous focus on problem solving.
6. Higher quality translates into higher financial returns for the firm.
7. Quality is everyone's job and can be achieved only through total participation and teamwork.

TQEM is "an approach for continuously improving the environmental quality of processes and products through the participation of all levels and functions in an organization" (Nash, Nutt, Maxwell, & Ehrenfeld, 1994, pp. 217-218). TQEM has emerged as one of the most useful and widely implemented frameworks for developing environmental management systems because it provides firms with a framework for accounting for the ecological impacts of products and processes all along the primary closed-loop value chain (Bemowski, 1991; Hart, 1995; North, 1992; Shrivastava, 1995b, 1996; Welford & Gouldson, 1993; Willig, 1994). By incorporating Nature into the TQM formula, firms are able to achieve high levels of top management commitment and employee involvement in pollution prevention, waste reduction, and so forth (Bringer & Benforado, 1994; Hart, 1995; Lent & Wells, 1994; Shrivastava, 1995b, 1996).

Achieving sustainability is the long-term goal of TQEM (Bringer & Benforado, 1994). By making total quality the primary objective of a firm's EMS, TQEM helps to dispel several misconceptions about the relationship between quality and environmental protection: (a) that quality and the environment have nothing in common; (b) that environmental problems are the bailiwick of environmental professionals, not line employees involved in producing the products; (c) that measuring wastes means trouble for employees because the results can only hurt, not help, an employee's performance appraisal; (d) that wastes that do not exceed regulatory standards are unimportant; and (e) that tighter environmental regulations automatically translate into lower profits (Bemowski, 1991).

The greatest impetus for the development and implementation of TQEM has been the Global Environmental Management Initiative (GEMI). GEMI's membership includes about 30 international corporations, including Allied Signal, Amoco, AT&T, Boeing, Bristol-Myers Squibb, Digital, Dow, Apple Computer, Eastman Kodak, DuPont, Merck, Procter & Gamble, the Southern Company, and several others. According to George Carpenter (1991) of Procter & Gamble, GEMI's first chairman, GEMI is committed to TQEM because

> environmental quality and total quality are complementary and synergistic concepts. . . . When businesses apply total quality to environmental management, they reap three basic benefits: an alignment with business strategy, continuous improvement with measurable results, and a customer and supplier alignment. (pp. 2-3)

GEMI held its first conference in January 1991, attracting over 250 participants from many international companies, government agencies, and consulting firms. Since that time, GEMI has held conferences annually. As mentioned in Chapter 8, GEMI was one of the major players in the development of the International Chamber of Commerce's Business Charter for Sustainable Development. In 1992, GEMI introduced its Environmental Self-Assessment Program (ESAP), which is designed to help firms assess their effectiveness in implementing TQEM in order to fulfill the 16 principles of the ICC charter (see Chapter 8 for a summary of these principles).

Completing an ESAP involves a thorough and tedious process of examining, modifying, and institutionalizing organizational policies, systems, and procedures, instituting training and educational efforts; and developing monitoring and reporting systems in the context of each of the ICC principles. ESAP works by dividing each ICC principle into several basic performance elements. For example, the first principle, "recognizing environmental management as the highest corporate priority" (GEMI, 1992, p. 17), is broken down into six elements: scope of corporate policy, management involvement, resources, communications, implementation, and accountability. The firm scores itself on a scale of 0 to 4 on each element, with 0 meaning that the element is not applicable, 1 meaning that the firm is complying with regulations, 2 meaning that the firm is in the systems development phase, 3 meaning that the environment is actually being integrated into the firm's general business functions, and 4 meaning that the firm has achieved a total quality approach with regard to that element. Next, the firm determines what weight to assign each element based on the element's importance to the firm's operation. Then the firm determines its final score by combining the element scores with the element weights (GEMI, 1992).

One of the firms that served as a driving force behind the formation of GEMI was Procter & Gamble (P&G). P&G formally established its TQEM program in 1989, when it first issued its environmental quality policy and mission statement; however, its commitment to improved environmental performance actually has its roots in P&G's long-standing commitment to corporate social responsibility (Shrivastava, 1996). The environmental quality statement of P&G reads in part, " 'Procter & Gamble continually strives to improve the environmental quality of its products, packaging, and operations around the world' " (quoted in Shrivastava, 1996, p. 92). With a highly decentralized organizational structure already in place, P&G was well prepared to develop the broad commitment and involvement at all levels necessary to make TQEM work. In fact, the impetus for P&G's environmental quality policy originated with rank-and-file employees and middle managers. Further, P&G has made concerted efforts to bring its external stakeholders, including customers, suppliers, and regulators, into its TQEM process (Shrivastava, 1996).

Shrivastava (1996) says that P&G's TQEM program is, in fact, a total systems approach that focuses on improving the firm's environmental performance from inputs to throughputs to outputs. At the input end, P&G stresses the need to conserve resources and energy and to use environmentally safe materials in its products and packaging if they are available. For example, P&G instituted forest management programs, established co-generation processes in which wood-pulp wastes from paper mills are used as fuel, and substituted a gel for the bulky wood pulp it once used as the absorbing element in its disposable diapers. The throughput processes at P&G have also been greened. TQEM is being used as a foundation for continuous production process improvement, and P&G has made the transfer of its environmental best practices to all of its production facilities a basic part of its environmental quality program. The outputs of P&G, its products, have been the subject of serious environmental scrutiny as the firm has worked to reduce packaging and to improve product environmental safety. However, the firm's efforts to improve its environmental performance at the output end have evolved beyond focusing on specific products to focusing on more general aspects of waste management, such as composting and source reduction.

AT&T is another prominent GEMI member that is energetically implementing TQEM. In 1990, Bob Allen, chairman of the AT&T board of directors, announced that the firm intended to vigorously incorporate environmental concerns into all of its business activities. TQEM was chosen as the primary vehicle for accomplishing this goal because it gets everyone in the company involved in satisfying its environmental stakeholders (Stratton, 1991). The environmental goals AT&T set for itself were very ambitious. It planned a 50% reduction in CFC use by 1991 and total elimination of CFCs from its processes by 1994. AT&T also set for itself a goal of 50% reduction in toxic air

emissions by 1993, a 95% reduction by 1995, and total elimination by 2000. Also, the firm wanted to achieve a 25% decrease
in total manufacturing process wastes, a 35% increase in the
amount of paper recycled, and a 15% decrease in the amount of
paper used by 1994 (Bringer & Benforado, 1994; Stratton, 1991).

AT&T's TQEM efforts have led to some innovative solutions, such as the development of BIOACT, a citrus fruit deriva-
tive that AT&T has substituted for the toxic solvents it used to
clean electronic equipment. AT&T also developed its low solid
fluxer, which allowed the firm to stop using CFCs in the manufacture of circuit boards (Bringer & Benforado, 1994). Strategic
managers at AT&T want to make it clear that the firm's commitment to TQEM is more than a simple public relations trick.
As AT&T's Art Soderberg told the participants at the first GEMI
conference in 1991, " 'It's not just for public relations; it's for the
sake of the environment we live in and our children' " (quoted
in Stratton, 1991, p. 19).

Design for Environment (DFE)

In Japan, the Ministry of International Trade and Industry
(MITI) has established the development of the "ecofactory" as
a top priority for the next decade (Ettlie, 1994). In the United
States, General Motors, Chrysler, and Ford have jointly invested
in the Vehicle Recycling Development Center (Bylinsky, 1995).
These efforts are indicative of "the next step in the renaissance
of product development" (Lent & Wells, 1994, p. 21): *design for
environment* (DFE). DFE is a critical tool for implementing process-driven sustainability strategies because it allows the blend-
ing of ecological concerns, market trends, technology trends,
and regulatory requirements into the features of a firm's products (Lent & Wells, 1994). Some 60% of the firms surveyed by
Lent and Wells (1994) indicated that DFE is very important for
improving environmental performance in organizations.

According to Allenby (1994), "The idea behind DFE is to
ensure that all relevant and ascertainable environmental considerations and constraints are integrated into a firm's product

design processes" (p. 139). The goal of DFE is to implement environmentally sound production processes and to produce environmentally sound products while remaining competitive in terms of product performance and price (Allenby, 1994). There are a wide range of dimensions that encompass DFE, including design for disassembly, refurbishment, component recyclability, and materials recyclability (Allenby, 1994); material substitution; source reduction and waste reduction of energy and toxic substances; product life extension; remanufacturing; and energy and materials recovery (Gladwin et al., 1994).

Implementing DFE requires that organizations engage in two broad categories of activities. The first category involves an array of comprehensive and cross-functional endeavors. These include reviewing internal documents to determine what unnecessary environmental damage is being caused by the firm's product components and processes, reviewing specification requests from customers to ascertain whether or not they may be ecologically unsound, and identifying unnecessary production process steps. Also included in this category of broad, cross-functional DFE activities is the analysis of downstream wastes (King, 1994). According to Andrew King (1994), analyzing wastes downstream from their source allows organizations to *learn from waste.* Similar to using urinalysis to detect health problems, learning from waste refers to the feedback process in which wastes are analyzed after they are generated in order to uncover problems related to the manufacturing process. For example, leaks or improper storage procedures that occurred earlier in the production process can be detected by analyzing the chemical content of wastes (King, 1994).

The second category of DFE activities are those aimed at analyzing specific design options, products, processes, or inputs. These analyses begin with life-cycle analysis, and they generally require three analytical stages. In the first stage, called scoping, the target design option, product, process, or input is identified and the depth of the analysis necessary to complete the DFE is determined. In the second stage, data gathering takes place using life-cycle analysis. In the third stage, the data are carefully translated so that they can be used by design teams (Allenby, 1994).

One industry that is taking DFE to heart is the automobile industry (Bylinsky, 1995; Klimisch, 1994). A fact not generally recognized is that automobiles are already among the most completely recycled products on the market; on the basis of weight, 75% of the materials in scrapped automobiles are currently being recycled, including virtually all of their metallic content. The primary DFE challenge for the automobile industry is to find ways to deal more effectively with the nonmetallic content of automobiles. Progress has certainly been made in this regard, especially with lead in batteries, CFCs in air-conditioning systems, and coolants in engines. Also, significant progress is beginning to be made in recycling motor oil and tires. The primary DFE focus in the auto industry is now on recycling nonmetallic components of the auto body and power train; this is the main thrust of what is currently happening at the Vehicle Recycling Development Center mentioned above (Klimisch, 1994). BMW is one automobile manufacturer that is taking recycling seriously. BMW is replacing solder and glue with fasteners on its bumpers so that they can be easily removed and recycled, and it is replacing the synthetic materials in its instrument panels with materials that allow them to be recycled in one piece. Over 80% of the weight of BMWs is already recyclable, and the firm has set a goal of 95% (Bylinsky, 1995).

Market-Driven Sustainability Strategies: Differentiation Through Product Stewardship

We discussed in Chapter 9 that market-driven sustainability strategies are those designed to reap competitive advantages by ecologically differentiating a firm's products and services from its competitors. As will become clear in the ensuing discussion, market-driven sustainability strategies are risky if they are not based on real environmental improvements. Otherwise, these strategies may be seen as little more than inflated marketing claims. In other words, market-driven sustainability strategies should reflect what Hart (1995) calls product stewardship, which involves ecological vigilance all along the closed-loop value chain.

Market-Driven Sustainability Strategies in Action

Loblaw International Merchants, Ltd. is Canada's largest food distributor. Over the years, Loblaw has proven to be one of the most astute firms in its industry at differentiating its products in the marketplace. In 1988, a core of strategic managers at Loblaw began discussions about the emerging strategic importance of environmental issues, and about the fact that these issues presented Loblaw with serious questions regarding its competitiveness as well as its responsibilities as a corporate citizen. The result of these discussions was the introduction of Loblaw's G.R.E.E.N. President's Choice line of products in June 1989. Originally included in this line were fertilizer, topsoil, disposable diapers, recycled motor oil, phosphate-free laundry and dishwasher detergents, and sanitary napkins (Westley & Vredenburg, 1991). The line has since been expanded to include unbleached and recycled paper products, nontoxic cleaning supplies, child-safe products, pesticide-free juices, all natural foods, and so on. In the first month after introduction, G.R.E.E.N. sales were 50% above projections, and Loblaw currently reaps more than $100 million in revenues from its over 100 G.R.E.E.N. products (Carson & Moulden, 1991; Shrivastava, 1996; Westley & Vredenburg, 1991).

As successful as Loblaw's G.R.E.E.N. line has been, its introduction was certainly not without controversy. Westley and Vredenburg (1991) tell how strategic managers at Loblaw decided that it would be to the firm's advantage if they could find an environmental interest group to endorse its G.R.E.E.N. line. The Loblaw executives approached two groups, Friends of the Earth and Pollution Probe, and entered into discussions with them. Pollution Probe eventually agreed to endorse the G.R.E.E.N. line if it could independently verify the ingredients of the products. Loblaw agreed to pay royalties to Pollution

Probe in return for its endorsement. All of this would have been well and good except that another environmental group, Greenpeace, held a press conference to denounce the G.R.E.E.N. fertilizer because of its dioxin content, demanding that Pollution Probe withdraw its endorsement. Following on the heels of the Greenpeace denouncement was a charge by the Consumers Association of Canada that Loblaw's advertisements about the environmental friendliness of the G.R.E.E.N. line were misleading.

Another firm that can attribute a great deal of its success in the marketplace to its Earth-friendly policies and products is Patagonia. Patagonia, an outdoor clothing company, has had a strong social bent since its founding in the 1960s. Early in the 1980s, the firm began donating a portion of pretax profits to small grassroots environmental groups, largely because of the strong environmental values of its founder and president. Since then, Patagonia has made concerted efforts to evaluate the environmental costs of its products at every stage of the closed-loop value chain (Winn, 1995). Patagonia has also introduced a line of clothing made entirely of recycled plastic pop bottles. According to Monika Winn (1995), who has studied Patagonia closely, "The creative combination of appealing to consumer concerns about the environment and consumer preferences for high-quality products illustrates an effective integration of personal values and targeted marketing [at Patagonia]" (p. 141).

The Body Shop International has been one of the most successful green retail firms ever. The Body Shop is a chain of franchises, supplemented with catalog sales, that sells personal-care products. Founded by self-described antibusiness radical Anita Roddick, The Body Shop sees itself as a vehicle for social and environmental change. The firm doesn't even mention its products in its mission statement; rather, it focuses the statement on its core values. According to Anita Roddick (1995), "Values are the DNA of our company."

The Body Shop markets its products as biodegradable, environmentally friendly, and never tested on animals. The products come in refillable and/or recyclable packaging, and the firm pays its employees to donate a half day a week to some social cause. Also, the firm uses simple, small-scale technologies, and it has recently installed wind turbines in order to provide a renewable energy source to power its production processes. The firm applies what it calls "trade not aid" in establishing economic and cultural links with indigenous people in developing nations across the globe (Roddick, 1995; Shrivastava, 1996). From its beginning in 1976 until 1990, The Body Shop's annual sales grew between 40% and 50% a year (Greengard, 1990).

The Body Shop has come under severe criticism recently, and much of that criticism has been aimed directly at Anita Roddick and her husband, Gordon. Many charges have been launched against the firm's claims of natural ingredients, no animal testing, charitable activities, and so forth, and the personal integrity of the Roddicks has been questioned (Entine, 1994). Other criticisms of the firm have been aimed at the often radical approaches The Body Shop takes in making its social points, and still others have charged that the firm's products are both unnecessary and too expensive (Shrivastava, 1996). However, there is no question that The Body Shop has had a profound influence on the environmental and social responsibility of the firms in its industry. Since The Body Shop burst onto the scene, virtually every cosmetics and personal-care firm has made efforts to emulate it in some way.

Another renowned example of a firm that has been successful with its market-driven sustainability strategies is Ben & Jerry's Homemade Ice Creams. Ben & Jerry's was founded in 1978 by Ben Cohen and Jerry Greenfield, who, like Anita Roddick, were strongly influenced by the social activism of the 1960s (Shrivastava, 1996). Also, like The Body Shop, Ben & Jerry's makes it clear in its vision, values, mission, and actions that it stands for sustainability. Paul Shrivastava (1996) had the opportunity to go to Ben & Jerry's headquarters in Waterbury, Vermont, and observe the environmental management processes of the firm firsthand. He describes the environmental management practices of Ben & Jerry's as "organic." He says, "Environmental efforts occur naturally and effortlessly within the company. Environmental tasks are not separated from operating functions. They are an integral part of everyday activities. Everyone in the company participates" (Shrivastava, 1996, p. 120).

One of Ben & Jerry's primary means of implementing its socially and ecologically sensitive values is through the ingredients in its products. It purchases all of the blueberries that it uses in its Wild Maine Blueberry Ice Cream from Native Americans in Maine. It buys its Brazil nuts and cashews from native tribes in the rain forests of the Amazon, and it buys its candy from a firm that donates profits to preserve the rain forests. Also, Ben & Jerry's focuses on its entire product life-cycle in efforts to continuously improve its environmental performance. Pollution prevention, energy conservation, resource conservation, and waste management are all integral to the firm's operations (Shrivastava, 1996).

Like The Body Shop, Ben & Jerry's is not without its critics. Some say that its claims of social and environmental performance are inflated, designed more to create an effective marketing image than to protect Nature. For example, the firm has admitted that only 5% of the nuts it has used in its Rainforest Crunch Ice Cream were actually purchased from indigenous tribes (Kurschner, 1995). Another serious reservation about the social responsibility of Ben & Jerry's revolves around the fat content in its ice cream, which is among the highest in the industry. Heart specialist Dean Cornish, one of the pioneers in the treatment of heart disease through diet and exercise rather than surgery, says that, from his perspective, Ben & Jerry's is one of the most socially irresponsible firms (Cornish, 1993). The CEO of Ben & Jerry's, Robert Holland, responds to such criticism by pointing out that Ben & Jerry's has never suggested that its products should be eaten as dietary staples. He suggested that people eat whole grains, fruits, and vegetables all day and treat themselves to a bowl of Ben & Jerry's in the evening as a reward. People who follow this advice will likely never have to see the inside of Cornish's office.

Market-driven sustainability strategies have been very prominent in the catalog sales segment of the retail market. One of the pioneer firms in this regard is Smith & Hawken, which describes itself as "a catalog for gardeners." Founded in 1977,

Smith & Hawken actually emerged from a nonprofit environmental group, Ecology Action, that wanted to promote old European organic gardening methods in the United States. The group had run into a problem because these methods required higher-quality gardening tools than those available in the United States. That's when one of Ecology Action's board members, successful entrepreneur and author, Paul Hawken, reluctantly stepped in and agreed to start a catalog company to sell high-quality British gardening tools. Hawken, food-cooperative manager, Dave Smith, international consultant and futurist, Peter Schwartz, and others put up $25,000, and Hawken went off to England to arrange for the firm's initial inventory purchase. Smith & Hawken's rise from that point was almost meteoric. It sold $200,000 worth of garden tools the first year, and sales reached $1 million in 3 years and $10 million in 5 years. Smith & Hawken's sales currently exceed $50 million annually (Schwartz, 1991), and its catalog has expanded from its original line of organic gardening tools to include items such as outdoor furniture made from sustainably harvested wood.

Another successful environmentally oriented catalog sales firm is Seventh Generation, which began in 1988. The firm offers some 300 products, including recycled paper products, energy efficient lightbulbs, water-saving devices, and environment-friendly cleaning items. Seventh Generation has essentially followed an environmental education strategy. Throughout its catalog are information boxes that provide insights on a wide variety of environmental issues and practices, and Seventh Generation publishes a monthly newsletter and operates a green-consumer hotline (Ottman, 1992). Seventh Generation currently has sales exceeding $10 million annually. However, founders Jeffrey Hollender and Alan Newman are as proud of the firm's environmental success as they are of its economic success. They say that in 1990 alone, Seventh Generation customers saved about 249 million gallons of water and 15,000 trees and avoided putting 41 million pounds of pollutants into the air by purchasing the firm's products (Seventh Generation, Inc., 1991).

The number of catalog sales companies that specialize in ecologically sensitive products has certainly proliferated over the past few years. Other popular firms in this market segment include Real Goods, the Natural Choice, Sundance, and Earth Care. One of the most interesting developments in catalog sales, however, has been the entrance of environmental interest groups into the market. The Sierra Club, the World Wildlife Fund, and Friends of the Earth are among the many environmental groups that have added catalog sales to their repertoire of activities.

Like process-driven strategies, the anecdotal evidence that market-driven strategies are economically rewarding ways for firms to differentiate themselves from their competitors is supported by research. Almost 60% of the 167 industrial firms responding to the sustainability-strategy implementation survey mentioned earlier said that the market-driven strategies they had implemented were having positive impacts on their revenues, while only 8% of the respondents said that these strategies were having a negative effect on their bottom lines (Stead & Stead, 1995).

Environmental Marketing

Of course, a key to successful market-driven sustainability strategies is environmental marketing. *Environmental marketing* refers to engaging in activities that put product stewardship at the center of an organization's development responsibilities and business growth opportunities (Coddington, 1993; Frankel & Coddington, 1994). According to Jackie Ottman (1992), environmental marketing has two important objectives: (a) to develop green products that effectively balance performance, price, convenience, and environmental compatibility and (b) to project an image to consumers that these products are both high quality and environmentally sensitive (Ottman, 1992). Meffert and Kirchgeorg (1994) set an even more challenging objective for environmental marketing. They say that environmental marketing is "an essential prerequisite for transforming the consumer society into a sustainable society" (p. 2).

Ottman (1992) outlines five challenges for environmental marketing. The first is to define the term *green* with all the complexities, methodological issues, and pitfalls it implies. The second challenge is to find ways to convince consumers about the need for lifestyle changes that emphasize greener behaviors and products. Third, environmental marketing needs to focus on educating consumers about the true nature of environmental problems and how they relate to the products they consume. Fourth, environmental marketers must find legitimate, nonmisleading ways to communicate the environmental features and benefits of products. The fifth challenge for environmental marketing is to gain credibility for the idea that business interests do not necessarily conflict with environmental responsibility.

Ottman (1992) says that "green [is] the new value-added" (p. 9). Meffert and Kirchgeorg (1994) make it clear that how and to what degree value is added via environmental marketing depends on the interaction between the price and/or opportunity costs of the product and the environmental benefits of the product. They say that if a green product provides environmental benefits at a lower price and/or opportunity cost to consumers, then the added value occurs because the green product offers the firm both traditional competitive advantages and environmental advantages. If, as so often happens, a green product is recognized by the consumer to be environmentally beneficial but the product is more expensive, harder to find, or both, then the value added is achieved only through the product's greenness. If the greenness of a product is not perceived to be environmentally beneficial to the consumer and the product's price/opportunity costs exceed those of competing nongreen products, then added value can be achieved only by changing consumer attitudes or providing regulatory structures to support the green product.

Of course, adding value via environmental marketing ultimately means developing effective environmental marketing strategies. Frankel and Coddington (1994) and Ottman (1992) both suggest several principles that they say are important for effective environmental marketing strategies. These principles may be summarized as follows:

1. Environmental marketing strategies should be based on a clear understanding of the environmental, social, economic, and political issues that affect the organization.
2. Environmental marketing strategies should be supported by strong organizational commitment, beginning with top management and permeating all levels of the firm.
3. Environmental marketing strategies should be completely honest and nondeceptive; Frankel and Coddington (1994) say, "Sell soft, not hard" (p. 665), and Ottman (1992) says, "Underpromise and overdeliver on your marketing claims" (p. 152).
4. Environmental marketing strategies should be developed in close consultation with external stakeholders, including regulators, the media, environmental interest groups, suppliers, and retailers.
5. Environmental marketing strategies should have built in, whenever possible, favorable prices, quality, convenience, and market-niche factors.
6. Environmental marketing strategies should emphasize education, especially for suppliers, retailers, and consumers.
7. Environmental marketing strategies should emphasize environmental symbols, such as natural beauty, biodiversity, and outdoor activities.
8. Environmental marketing strategies should minimize the environmental impacts of the strategies themselves by using recycled paper and the like.

The one factor that cannot be overemphasized when discussing effective environmental marketing is honesty and integrity. We discussed at some length in Chapter 8 the fact that consumers are often bombarded with unsubstantiated claims of biodegradability, recyclability, natural ingredients, and so forth. We pointed out earlier in this chapter that firms such as Loblaw, The Body Shop, and Ben & Jerry's have had their reputations in the market tarnished by claims about the environmental benefits of their products that some have said are inflated and misleading. As Frankel and Coddington (1994) say, "A company should not represent itself as being more environmentally responsible than it is; it is the environmental marketer's job to help ensure that the company's deeds match its words" (p. 645).

Supporting the Closed-Loop Value Chain

As discussed above, the value chain includes activities that support the primary value chain activities. One activity critical for supporting the closed-loop value chain is the development of human resource management systems, including perform-ance measurement, reporting, appraisal, and reward systems, that will reinforce a sustainability culture in the organization. We discussed this at some length in the Chapter 9. Also, none of the primary closed-loop value chain activities discussed above can be implemented with any degree of success without adequate information systems for gathering, processing, as-sessing, storing, retrieving, and reporting on environmental performance. Below, we briefly present four interrelated infor-mation-processing activities designed to provide the critical information necessary for effective life-cycle analysis, sustain-ability strategy implementation, total quality environmental man-agement, design for environment, and environmental marketing.

Environmental Auditing

According to the International Chamber of Commerce, *en-vironmental auditing* is a "systematic, documented, periodic, and objective evaluation" about the performance of a firm's environ-mental management systems and equipment (Makower, 1993). Environmental audits provide strategic managers with valu-able information for establishing environmental control loops in the firm. This means that they can help firms in their efforts to assess progress on environmental objectives, meet regulatory requirements, avoid financial liabilities related to environmental performance, track the benefits and costs of the firm's environ-mental management programs, establish accountability for en-vironmental performance all along the closed-loop value chain, and know how well it is serving the greater community (Cal-lenbach, Capra, Goldman, Lutz, & Marburg, 1993; Ledgerwood, Street, & Therivel, 1992; Makower, 1993).

Environmental audits are not substitutes for but, rather, are additions to, financial audits. In fact, Callenbach et al. (1993)

say that effective environmental auditing requires a blend of quantitative and qualitative elements. Environmental indicators necessary for measuring specific amounts and types of pollution and wastes are one important element of environmental audits. Three other important elements are environmental impact assessments, materials assessments, and energy assessments. Together, these allow the firm to understand how and to what degree it is affecting the natural environment by converting low-entropy inputs into high-entropy outputs. Full-cost accounting (discussed in more detail below), cost-benefit analysis, and economic feasibility calculations are three important environmental-auditing elements that help to quantify the economic and ecological consequences of a firm's environmental operations. Other important elements of environmental auditing are technological assessments and consumer surveys, which can provide the firm with valuable information on the social, political, and market implications of its environmental performance. Further, no environmental auditing system can function effectively without a supporting environmental management information system (discussed in more detail below) (Callenbach et al., 1993).

Full-Cost Accounting

The generally accepted managerial accounting practices of today do take certain environmental costs into account. The Financial Accounting Standards Board (FASB), in its Issue 90-8, says that the costs of treating contamination, including the costs of problem analysis, the costs of toxic substance removal and neutralization, and the costs of preventing future contamination, should be charged as expenses to firms (Roussey, 1992). Also, FASB Opinion No. 5, Accounting for Contingencies, requires that firms record a potential environmental loss if it can reasonably be assumed that the environmental loss will actually occur in the future and the costs of the loss can be reasonably estimated (Roussey, 1992; Surma & Petracca, 1993).

However, these standards are related only to present and future financial liabilities, and they have limited value in supporting the management of the closed-loop value chain (Todd, 1994). As Todd (1994) says, "Simply put, you can't manage what you never see, and with today's managerial accounting systems, managers don't see most environmental costs" (p. 191). Adequately supporting the closed-loop value chain will mean evolving from these limited accounting standards and practices to *full-cost accounting systems* that account for all the environmental costs associated with doing business, including the costs of externalities incurred by society and the planet (Beaumont, Pedersen, & Whitaker, 1993; Todd, 1994). For example, the full costs of an automobile would include all of the traditional costs associated with acquiring the materials, building the car, and delivering it to the customer, but they would also include the costs of potential air pollution, health problems, resource depletion, traffic congestion, death and injury, and blight (Elkins, Hillman, & Hutchinson, 1992).

Developing full-cost accounting processes, procedures, and systems presents myriad complex problems. First of all, because there is no economic market for a cubic meter of clean air or the aesthetic beauty of the countryside, pricing environmental costs is subjective at best. Second, the time scales related to environmental issues render traditional discounting methods virtually useless. This makes it very difficult to assign any kind of meaningful cost figures to the intragenerational and intergenerational welfare and ethical issues related to full-cost accounting (Beaumont et al., 1993).

Nonetheless, efforts are being made to develop and apply full-cost accounting. Dow Chemical has developed a financial management system that allocates environmental costs directly to the units that generate them rather than spreading them out throughout the company as overhead (Buzzelli, 1994). Also, the EPA is currently engaged in developing full-cost accounting practices in its Environmental Accounting Project, the American Institute for Certified Public Accountants is sponsoring workshops on full-cost accounting methods, and GEMI has published a primer on the subject.

Environmental Management Information Systems

As mentioned above, an adequate *environmental management information system* (EMIS) for storing, processing, and retrieving information related to environmental performance is a critical closed-loop value chain support activity. According to Johannson (1994), the most appropriate framework for an effective EMIS is what she calls the "ecology, quality and information-technology triad" (p. 332). The result of basing an EMIS on the interactions of these three concepts is an information system capable of providing a firm with meaningful data about the continuous improvement of its environmental performance (Johannson, 1994).

At the heart of any effective information system is accurate data, and an EMIS is no exception. A number of databases can provide valuable information on things such as environmental conditions, industry and government standards, pollution thresholds, environmental publications, and the like. UMPLIS (a general environmental information database), AWIDAT (a waste management database), and DABAWAS (a water pollution database) are three that are widely used (Callenbach et al., 1993). Under the provisions of SARA and RCRA, the government publishes three environmental databases: the Toxic Release Inventory (TRI); the biennial survey of waste treatment, storage, and disposal facilities; and the National Hazardous Waste Survey (Allen & Behmanesh, 1994). The number of environmental databases is proliferating rapidly (Gladwin et al., 1994).

Besides databases, there are several other elements necessary for an effective EMIS. For example, information management technology is necessary in order to store, retrieve, and process data. LEXIS and Hypertext are two data and document management systems useful in this regard (Spedding, Jones, & Dering, 1993). Further, systems dynamics (SD) are important in order that a firm be able to electronically simulate the complex relationships between economic and ecological performance (Callenbach et al., 1993). Of course, an effective EMIS is more than just a sophisticated computer system. It involves maintaining and continuously updating environmental management checklists (which can be computerized) that serve to guide organizations through the maze of procedures and matters that must be attended to in managing environmental performance (Callenbach et al., 1993; Spedding et al., 1993). It also involves building scenarios about future environmental issues and performance and using decision trees to analyze the potential consequences and trade-offs of environmental actions (Callenbach et al. 1993).

Environmental Reporting

It is generally agreed that accurately and fully reporting on a firm's environmental actions and performance to its stakeholders is a critical environmental management activity. In the United States, the TRI reporting requirements established by the EPA mean that the public now has access to vast amounts of environmental performance data on organizations that was heretofore unavailable. The European Community's EMAS program will likely have similar effects on *environmental reporting* in Europe. Further, many firms are finding that they can reap several advantages by being more proactive and voluntary in their environmental reporting activities. Doing so can improve their communication with stakeholders, establish publicly that they are committed to the environment, and show how that commitment has been translated into specific environmental management programs and improved environmental performance in the firm (GEMI, 1994).

There are important considerations that should be taken into account in preparing and disseminating environmental reports. First of all, the audience for environmental reports must be selected. GEMI (1994) suggests that employees, shareholders, financial institutions, customers, local communities, interest groups, the media, and regulators should all be included. Second, the information to be included in reports needs to be determined. This information should be derived directly from the firm's internal environmental audit in order to ensure completeness and accuracy (GEMI, 1994), and it should include information on environmental problems as well as progress (Buzzelli, 1994). Several organizations have developed guidelines for corporate environmental reporting, including the Public Environmental Reporting Initiative (PERI), the Investor Responsibility Research Center (IRRC), and CERES, among others. These guidelines can help firms to select what needs to be reported (GEMI, 1994).

Seeking Sustainability Beyond the Closed-Loop Value Chain

A critical point that we have made at several junctures in this book is that the world community must function as an integrated whole within the biophysical limits of the planet if sustainability is to be achieved. This means that achieving sustainability will ultimately require that organizations focus beyond the internal, individual dimensions of sustainable strategic management. They will have to participate in sustainability partnerships with other business organizations, political and regulatory organizations, environmental activist groups, educational institutions, and so on (King, 1995; Starik & Rands, 1995; Throop, Starik, & Rands, 1993). This is critical for organizations if they are, in Hart's (1995) terms, to evolve from product stewardship to sustainable development.

In their multilevel analysis of *ecologically sustainable organizations* (ESOs), Starik and Rands (1995) present an excellent discussion of this point. Similar to our portrayal of the relationship between business and the ecosystem in Figure 1.1, Starik and Rands (1995) say that ESOs cannot exist unless they are willing to engage in activities that promote sustainability at many levels, including the individual level, the organizational level, the political-economic level, the social-cultural level, and the ecological level. Of course, one of the keys to achieving sustainability at these levels is to implement the primary and support closed-loop value chain activities discussed thus far in this chapter. However, these activities are not sufficient by themselves to allow firms to function sustainably at all of these levels.

Starik and Rands (1995) say that, in addition to initiating the previously discussed closed-loop value chain activities, ESOs need to develop environmental partnerships with entities at all levels. They need to develop industrial-ecosystem partnerships with ecologically complementary organizations in order to minimize wastes and conserve resources. Also, they need to develop partnerships with environmental interest groups, lawmakers, regulators, and other business organizations in order to promote legislation, public policy, and industry standards related to improved environmental performance. Finally, they need to develop partnerships with the media, religious institutions, educational institutions, political institutions, and diverse peoples throughout the globe in order to precipitate the social and cultural changes necessary for long-term sustainability.

Examples of partnerships like these are numerous. Firms such as The Body Shop, Ben & Jerry's, and Shaman Pharmaceuticals have developed partnerships for ingredients and the like with indigenous people. The partnership between the Environmental Defense Fund and McDonald's, which led to major waste-reduction efforts at the fast-food giant, has been widely reported. Further, we have mentioned numerous other partnerships committed to promoting sustainability throughout this book, including the Global Environmental Management Initiative, the Chemical Manufacturers' Association's Responsible Care Program, the Coalition for Environmentally Responsible Economies, and the International Chamber of Commerce.

One of the most far-reaching and ambitious sustainability partnerships to date in the United States has been the creation of the President's Council on Sustainable Development (PCSD). The PCSD is composed of "25 individuals representing business, labor, environmental, civil rights, tribal and local leaders along with members of the President's Cabinet [charged with developing] a national sustainable development action strategy that will foster economic vitality while protecting our natural and cultural resources" (PCSD, 1995, p. 1). The specific goals of the PCSD include ensuring a healthy natural environment; sustaining economic prosperity; promoting social justice, equity, and well-being; conserving resources and biodiversity;

creating an ethic of stewardship in all institutions and individuals; developing sustainable communities; encouraging civic responsibilities; stabilizing the U.S. population; promoting education that stresses sustainability and the quality of life; and
taking a leadership role in fostering these goals throughout the
global community (PCSD, 1995).

Conclusions

In sum, firms that *stand for sustainability* are faced with
developing environmental management systems that account
for Nature at all stages of the closed-loop value chain. In this
chapter, we have briefly outlined what that means. It means
making life-cycle analysis a central feature in everything the
firm does, from cradle to grave. It means instituting TQEM,
DFE, and environmental marketing processes that make the
implementation of process-driven and market-driven sustainability strategies possible. It means restructuring human resource systems to support sustainability as the core of the
organization's culture, and it means establishing information
systems that will allow the organization to accurately, completely, and honestly gather, process, account for, assess, store,
retrieve, and report on environmental performance. Finally, it
means that firms must go beyond these closed-loop value chain
activities and enter into meaningful sustainability partnerships
that form the strands of an economic, political, social, cultural,
and ecological web to ensure that the commons can be sustained for posterity.

Note

1. Information on Alltrista Zinc Products Corporation and Great Dane
Trailers of Tennessee came from the nomination letters to the selection committee for the Governor's Award for Excellence in Hazardous Waste Management.
Further information on Alltrista was received from Mr. Roy Robinson, Alltrista's Chief Engineer.

Chapter 11
_____

Changing the Myth

As we come to the end of the book, we want to visit the concept of sustainability one last time. We have made a concerted effort throughout the book to develop an in-depth understanding of sustainability. We began by providing managers with both a theoretical and a practical understanding of what happens when business interfaces with the natural environment. From this, we presented ideas from the collective wisdom of the field that strongly suggest the following interrelated requirements for achieving sustainability: stabilizing and/or reducing population, developing low-entropy industrial systems and processes, creating more social and economic equity between the developed and developing nations of the world, and creating community-based decision-making structures to protect the commons.

We also presented ethical, cognitive, and economic faces of sustainability in an effort to provide managers with some basic models for reframing their interactions with Nature. We discussed the need to include Nature in humankind's ethical sphere, the need to think in more systematic and long-term ways, the need to couch economic assumptions within the evolutionary processes of the planet, and the need to develop value systems with sustainability at their core. Finally, we presented a wide range of concepts and tools that we believe can be very helpful for managers pursuing long-term strategic visions based on sustainability. These concepts and tools can guide managers as they seek to efficiently and effectively account for the Earth as the ultimate stakeholder.

All of this has been designed to present a single message: Business organizations can be managed in ways that will allow the global economic system to flourish within the ecological limits of Nature. We have not suggested that achieving this state will be easy; but we have suggested that it is possible, and we have suggested some ways to do it. We have made the case that economic gain and ecological responsibility can exist on the same side of the coin.

However, it is important to understand that we really do not have a clear picture of what it will take for humankind to achieve sustainability, nor does anyone else. Many believe that there will never be an answer except in retrospect. As Denis Collins (1995) writes, "The ultimate judge on continued human existence is not the individual, it is the natural environment" (p. 374). Gladwin, Kennelly, and Krause (1995) echo this same sentiment, saying, "Sustainability, in the end, may lie beyond or after the fact" (p. 878).

Thus, it is important for the readers to understand that no one knows for sure what will have to happen for humankind to achieve sustainability. There is certainly a lot of conjecture and some rudimentary empirical evidence, but there are still no clear answers to questions about the survival chances for this marriage that we and others are trying to create between business organizations and the natural environment. Will this relationship flourish, grow, and mature over time, becoming stronger as it deals with the many issues that are bound to challenge its sovereignty? Or will this relationship unravel in the face of hard decisions that dictate dichotomous choices between Nature and economic success?

There are many who are skeptical. Many scholars in this field who are passionately pursing solutions to the sustainability puzzle in their public lives will confide privately that they do not see much chance for humankind to come into sustainable balance with its ecosystem without Mother Nature herself providing the means for change. Their scenarios of food shortages, increased natural disasters, and the like are not pretty. Many say that the dream of neatly tying economic gain and ecological protection together and presenting them as this generation's gift to posterity may be just a pipe dream.

Even those who are making concerted efforts to put sustainability into practice in their organizations do not seem convinced that they have found sustainability's magic bullet. In her address to the Academy of Management in Vancouver, British Columbia, in August 1995, The Body Shop founder, Anita Roddick, admitted openly that her firm is not yet environmentally responsible, a statement supported by the investigative work of Jon Entine (1994). For all its efforts, The Body Shop still has some very serious questions to answer in its quest for sustainability, including the most basic of all: Are its products necessary? Paul Hawken (1993a, 1993b), founder of Smith & Hawken and, like Roddick, a successful entrepreneur committed to sustainability, has probably expressed these sentiments as poignantly as anyone:

> If every company on the planet were to adopt the environmental and social practices of the best companies—of, say, The Body Shop, Patagonia, and Ben & Jerry's—the world would still be moving toward environmental degradation and collapse. . . . Today there is a contradiction inherent in the premise of the socially responsible corporation: to wit, that a company can make the world better, can grow, and can increase profits by meeting social and environmental needs. It is a have-your-cake-and-eat-it fantasy that cannot come true. (1993a, p. 55)

In fact, assuming that the formula for ecologically sustainable business organizations presented in this book is valid, then sustainability is achievable only in an economy where virtually every enterprise across the globe adopts value systems and visions based on sustainability, develops ecocentric management systems, becomes a part of industrial ecosystems, formulates and implements sustainability strategies, and develops the learning structures and fundamental change processes necessary to maintain and improve their environmental performance for posterity. The complexities involved in seeing such a system actually evolve are enormous.

There are many barriers to achieving sustainability, and they are complex, incredibly intertwined, serious, and, some say, overwhelming. At the biophysical level, the entropy law provides the absolute physical wall beyond which human activity on Earth will not be possible. Gladwin et al. (1995), ask, "Quite simply, how many organizations could exist in the absence of oxygen production, fresh water supply, or fertile soil?" (p. 875). In order to bring the economic system into sync with the Earth's natural entropic processes, humankind must find ways to slow down the high-entropy energy, resource, and waste processes that result from the current level of business activities. This means bridging several biophysical barriers, including refining the methodologies of life-cycle analysis; finding safe and/or plentiful substitutes for the nonrenewable resources and toxic chemicals now in use; developing the efficient use of clean, renewable energy sources; developing better processes for recovering, recycling, and disposing of wastes; developing more efficient production processes; and developing closed-loop networks of industrial ecosystems throughout the globe.

Further, sustainability is not just a biophysical problem. If it were, then maybe it would be easier to confront. However, as Gladwin et al. (1995) point out, sustainability is a human development problem, with all of the ethical, cultural, social, religious, political, civil, and legal implications that entails. For example, reducing birthrates to sustainable levels means addressing an array of issues, including gender equity, economic equity, health care, education, birth control, social mores, and religious principles. Slash-and-burn destruction of the rain forests in countries such as Indonesia, Brazil, and Cameroon will not stop without facing issues such as democracy, human rights, property rights, and international trade. Solving the problems of the unsustainable megalopolises around the globe means facing all these same issues and many others, such as how to finance sustainable public transportation systems and how to find employment for the millions of poor who migrate to these cities every year.

These are not just the problems of this generation, they are the problems of those not yet living. They are the problems of the children and the children's children: They are the problems of the seventh generation. They are also the problems of the other species on the planet, both current and future. Gladwin et al. (1995) capture the essence of what achieving sustainability really means when they say that it is "intergenerational, intragenerational, and interspecies. . . . Sustainability embraces both environmental and human systems, both near and far, both the present and the future" (p. 878).

Honestly, when viewed from the lens of rational thought and scientific inquiry that has dominated the way humans have viewed the universe for the last 350 years or so, the odds of coming up with solutions to the problems related to the interface between business and the natural environment do not seem very good to us. The idea that *economic man* will ever willingly surrender his quest for castles and gold so that people he will never know can have a comfortable place to live in a safe society with clean air to breath, adequate soil for food, clean water to drink, and the opportunity for creative self-expression is essentially ludicrous within the current framework of the materialistic, ego-centered, growth-oriented, mechanical, mental models that are currently driving human thought processes.

In short, we believe that achieving sustainability is not about changing how humans do things; it is about changing how humans view things. If humans are ever to see the light of sustainability, it will not be because they are rational, logical, and scientific; it will be because they are able to change the underlying myths, archetypes, and paradigms that guide the way they see the planet and their place on it.

Myths, Archetypes, and Paradigms:
Spiritual Guides From the Unconscious

Joseph Campbell (1988) says, "The images of myth are reflections of the spiritual potentialities of every one of us. Through contemplating these, we evoke their powers in our own lives" (p. 207). Campbell says that *myths* essentially do three things: They guide individuals through the processes of growing up, maturing, and dying; they provide ethical instruction concerning how individuals should relate to society; and they instruct individuals and societies about how to relate to Nature and the greater consciousness of the universe. Campbell describes myths as universal spiritual themes that are disguised in multicultural clothing. Myths portray different gods, different story lines, different heroes, and different circumstances, all of which are tied to a particular culture. However, at their core, Campbell (1988) says that myths are "songs of the universe" (p. xvi), subconscious guides that cross all cultural and ethical bounds.

In today's society, the word *myth* generally invokes the perception of falsehood, a story that is not true. However, Campbell (1988) says that this is a mistaken interpretation of the word. He says that the myth's truth lies not in its story line but in its metaphors. At their essence, myths are beyond truth or falsehood: They are the metaphysical frameworks within which people determine truth and falsehood. In this sense, myths are true when they guide individuals and societies on paths of living that are in harmony with themselves, with other humans, and with Nature. They are false when their guidance leads to conflicting, confrontational relationships with themselves, other humans, and Nature.

Campbell says that myths evoke what Carl Jung calls *archetypes* of the collective unconscious. Archetypes are derived from the Greek word *arche* and they are central to the philosophies of Plato and Aristotle. *Arche* is generally translated as "first principle," "ultimate principle," and "unmoved principle." In this sense, an arche is the general underlying form of things, and an archetype serves to remind the soul of this underlying form whenever humans attempt to interpret experience (Wheelwright, 1935). Thus, like myths, archetypes do not guide people in the conscious sense, like road signs, theories, or rule books; rather, their guidance is metaphorical, invisible, enduring, and most of all, spiritual.

Myths are also related to what Thomas Kuhn (1962) calls *paradigms,* the underlying assumptions through which humans view their world. Like myths and archetypes, paradigms are not truth; they define the boundaries of the search for truth. Kuhn (1962) says that questioning dominant paradigms is a risky business that must be pursued as an act of faith in the face of significant resistance from those tied to the old paradigm. According to Lewis Mumford (1956), such changes require the adoption of new metaphysical and ideological foundations. Kuhn (1962) says that these changes must come from the edges of society, are generally more tacit than explicit, and must come clothed in new, unfamiliar language patterns. Mumford (1956) says that the metaphysical nature of paradigms makes fundamental paradigm shifts quite rare, occurring only a few times in all of human history.

Thus, although some may quibble over definitional specifics, myths, archetypes, and paradigms are synonymous concepts in their essential form. They are the basic forms and frameworks upon which humankind bases its interpretations of truth. Reality is true or false to the degree that it fits with the dominant myth, archetype, and paradigm. They are the underlying patterns that define how humans instruct their young; how humans are expected to mature; the roles humans are expected to play in society; the relationships among humans, society, and Nature; and the paths to human and societal spiritual fulfillment.

Toward the "Society of the Planet"

As we mentioned in Chapter 1, Campbell (1988) says that you can tell the dominant myth of a given society by examining the heights of its buildings. He says that the multistory seats of economic activity that define the skylines of our cities today demonstrate that humankind's most dominant current myth is that of economic wealth. Many argue that this myth grew out of the scientific revolution in the 17th century and has since come to dominate all of society's institutions, be they political, religious, educational, or economic (see, e.g., Berry, 1988; Capra, 1982; Gladwin et al., 1995; Harman, 1988; Schumacher, 1977). Gladwin et al. (1995) refer to this myth as the *technocentric paradigm.* Following is a summary of the underlying assumptions of this paradigm:

- The Earth is passive, inert, mechanical, infinitely divisible, and legitimately exploitable.
- Humans are separate from and superior to their natural environment.
- The Earth has infinite space with an inexhaustible supply of resources.
- Science is the proper framework within which to manage humankind's relationship with Nature.
- Cost-benefit analysis is the appropriate tool for making decisions about the potential for human suffering and environmental harm.
- Humans will always be able to find technological solutions to their problems.
- Natural capital is a perfect substitute for other forms of capital.
- The economy is a closed circular flow of goods and services between households and organizations and is isolated from Nature.
- Humans are self-serving, one-dimensional beings who pursue fulfillment solely by attempting to satisfy their unlimited, secular material wants.
- Social welfare is most easily improved through unlimited economic growth that allows for the continuous trickling down of wealth to the masses, meaning that poverty will eventually disappear if the rich can just get rich enough.

As we said above, true myths (or paradigms or archetypes) provide authentic subconscious frameworks within which humans can find knowledge, wisdom, higher meaning, joy, peace, and spiritual fulfillment in a harmonious relationship with society, Nature, and the universal oneness. The technocentric paradigm, the myth of economic wealth, is currently failing this acid test of truth. Population is growing out of control, poverty is increasing, violence and disease are running rampant, and the natural environment is becoming less tolerant of the human species. Gladwin et al. (1995) say that technocentrism falsely separates the economy from Nature; ignores thermodynamics; has no place for ecological scale; does not account for the holism and connectedness of phenomena; favors humans over Nature, men over women, rich over poor, and current generations over future generations; leads to imprudent calculations of cata- strophic risks; and is responsible for the agony currently exist- ing in the world.

Thus, the myth of economic wealth is failing as a spiritual guide. Thomas Berry (1988) says that economic wealth has evolved into a sort of "industrial-technological fundamental- ism" (p. 57) that is failing miserably as a religion. Berry (1988) says that humankind is in desperate need of a new story, a new myth, that will better address "how things came to be, how things came to be as they are, and how the future can be given some satisfying direction" (p. 124). He says that a transition to the new myth is necessary if humankind is to properly educate, heal, guide, and discipline itself in accordance with Nature in the future.

Gladwin et al. (1995) suggest the *sustaincentric paradigm* as the appropriate framework for humankind's new myth. They say that the sustaincentric paradigm assumes the following:

- The planet is home to humankind, and as such it should be kept clean, healthy, safe, and well managed.
- A healthy economy and a healthy ecosystem are intricately and irreversibly interconnected.
- Humans are both a part of Nature and, because of their superior intelligence, the chosen stewards of Nature.
- Humans have ethical responsibilities that are intragenerational, intergenerational, and interspecies.
- The ecosystem is finite with limited resources and limited regen- erative and assimilative powers.
- Irreplaceable parts of the natural capital, such as other species and the ozone layer, are nonsubstitutable.

- Ecosystem-economic system interactions are governed by the laws of thermodynamics, which dictate that unlimited growth is not possible forever.
- The precautionary principle is the appropriate tool for assessing the potential for human suffering and ecological catastrophe.
- Humans are multidimensional beings who can learn to appreciate aesthetic as well as economic value and can learn that wisdom, intellectual development, and spiritual fulfillment are as important as material well-being.
- The economic system should internalize all ecological and social externalities, such as energy/matter throughput and poverty.

In short, what we are trying to communicate here is exactly what Gladwin et al. (1995), Berry (1988), Schumacher (1977), Leopold (1949), Daly and Cobb (1989, 1994), and so many others we have drawn from throughout this book have been trying to tell humankind: It will never find sustainability solely through scientific logic and technological discovery. Finding sustainability is going to require a profound spiritual transformation. Whether it's given a fancy moniker like sustaincentrism or referred to simply as the land ethic, sustainability will have little influence until it becomes embedded in the mythological conscience that guides human thought and action. Joseph Campbell (1988) refers to this new mythological conscience as the *society of the planet*:

> If we will think of ourselves as coming out of the Earth, . . . we will see that we are the Earth, we are the consciousness of the Earth. These are the eyes of the Earth. And this is the voice of the Earth. . . . The only myth that is going to be worth thinking about in the immediate future is one that is talking about the society of the planet. . . . When you see the Earth from the moon, you don't see any divisions there of nations or states. That might be the symbol, really, for the mythology to come. That is the country we are going to be celebrating. And those are the people we are one with. (p. 32)

References

Acharya, A. (1995). Tropical forests vanishing. In L. Brown, N. Lenssen, & H. Kane (Eds.), *Vital signs 1995* (pp. 116-119). New York: Norton.

The acid rain report. (1989, February). *Congressional Digest*, pp. 38-39.

Allen, D., & Behmanesh, N. (1994). Wastes and raw materials. In B. R. Allenby & D. J. Richards (Eds.), *The greening of industrial ecosystems* (pp. 69-89). Washington, DC: National Academy Press.

Allen, F. E. (1991, April 17). McDonald's launches plan to cut waste. *Wall Street Journal*, pp. B1, B6.

Allenby, B. (1994). Integrating environment and technology: Design for environment. In B. R. Allenby & D. J. Richards (Eds.), *The greening of industrial ecosystems* (pp. 137-148). Washington, DC: National Academy Press.

Ansoff, I. (1979). The changing shape of the strategic problem. In D. Schendel & C. Hofer (Eds.), *Strategic management* (pp. 30-44). Boston, MA: Little, Brown.

Ansoff, I. (1980). *Corporate strategy: An analytical approach to business policy for growth and expansion.* New York: McGraw-Hill.

Argyris, C., & Schön, D. (1978). *Organizational learning: A theory of action perspective.* Reading, MA: Addison-Wesley.

Arnold, M., & Long, F. (1994). Trade and the environment: Challenges and opportunities. In R. V. Kolluru (Ed.), *Environmental strategies handbook* (pp. 797-849). New York: McGraw-Hill.

Ayres, R. U. (1989). Industrial metabolism. In J. H. Ausubel & H. E. Sladovich (Eds.), *Technology and environment* (pp. 23-49). Washington, DC: National Academy Press.

Ayres, R. U. (1994). Industrial metabolism: Theory and policy. In B. R. Allenby & D. J. Richards (Eds.), *The greening of industrial ecosystems* (pp. 23-37). Washington, DC: National Academy Press.

244

Banks, R., & Wheelwright, S. (1979). Operations vs. strategy: Trading tomorrow for today. *Harvard Business Review, 57*(3), 112-120.

Bartunek, J. M., & Moch, M. K. (1987). First-order, second-order, and third-order change and organization development interventions: A cognitive approach. *Journal of Applied Behavioral Science, 23,* 483-500.

Beaumont, J., Pedersen, L., & Whitaker, B. (1993). *Managing the environment.* Oxford, UK: Butterworth Heinemann.

Beck, T., & Howett, C. (1992). The green labeling phenomenon: Issues and trends in the regulation of environmentally friendly product claims. In T. F. P. Sullivan (Ed.), *The greening of American business* (pp. 309-345). Rockville, MD: Government Institutes.

Beckhard, R., & Pritchard, W. (1992). *Changing the essence.* San Francisco: Jossey-Bass.

Bemowski, K. (1991, April). Sorting fact from fiction. *Quality Progress,* pp. 21-25.

Berry, T. (1988). *The dream of the Earth.* San Francisco: Sierra Club Books.

Bhushan, A., & MacKenzie, J. (1994). Environmental leadership plus total quality management equals continuous improvement. In J. Willig (Ed.), *Environmental TQM* (pp. 43-49). New York: McGraw-Hill.

Boulding, K. E. (1956). General systems theory: The skeleton of science. *Management Science, 2*(3), 197-208.

Boulding, K. E. (1966). The economics of the coming spaceship Earth. In *Environmental quality in a growing economy* (pp. 3-14). Baltimore, MD: Johns Hopkins University Press.

Boulding, K. E. (1970). Fun and games with the gross national product: The role of misleading indicators in social policy. In H. W. Helfrich (Ed.), *The environmental crisis* (pp. 157-170). New Haven, CT: Yale University Press.

Bridbord, K., Decoufle, P., & Fraumeni, J. (1978). *Estimates of the fraction of cancer in the United States related to occupational factors.* Bethesda, MD: National Cancer Institute, National Institute of Health Sciences, Institute for Occupational Safety and Health.

Brill, J., & Reder, A. (1992). *Investing from the heart.* New York: Crown.

Bringer, R., & Benforado, D. (1994). Pollution prevention and total quality environmental management. In R. V. Kolluru (Ed.), *Environmental strategies handbook* (pp. 165-188). New York: McGraw-Hill.

Brown, L. R. (1992). Irrigation expansion slowing. In L. Brown, C. Flavin, & H. Kane (Eds.), *Vital signs 1992* (pp. 38-39). New York: Norton.

Brown, L. R. (1993). A new era unfolds. In *State of the world 1993* (pp. 3-21). New York: Norton.

Brown, L. R. (1994). Facing food insecurity. In *State of the world 1994* (pp. 177-197). New York: Norton.

Brown, L. R. (1995a). The acceleration of history. In L. Brown, N. Lenssen, & H. Kane (Eds.), *Vital signs 1995* (pp. 15-21). New York: Norton.

Brown, L. R. (1995b). Grainland shrinks. In L. Brown, N. Lenssen, & H. Kane (Eds.), *Vital signs 1995* (pp. 36-37). New York: Norton.

Brown, L. R. (1995c). World economy expanding faster. In L. Brown, N. Lenssen, & H. Kane (Eds.), *Vital signs 1995* (pp. 70-71). New York: Norton.

Brown, W. Y. (1990). Shaping and entering international markets. In *Proceedings of the Business Week symposium, The Environment: Corporate Stewardship and*

Business Opportunity in the Decade of Global Awakening (pp. 57-59). New York: Journal Graphics.

Buchholz, R. A. (1993). *Principles of environmental management.* Englewood Cliffs, NJ: Prentice Hall.

Bureau of National Affairs. (1993a, October 15). DOJ to focus on criminal enforcement of environmental laws, top official says. *Environment Reporter,* p. 1140.

Bureau of National Affairs. (1993b, January 6). Penalties largest on record. *Air and Water Pollution Control,* p. 2.

Burns, T., & Stalker, G. M. (1961). *The management of innovation.* London: Tavistock.

Buzzelli, D. (1994, March 9). *Toward sustainable development: Beware of environmental pit bulls.* Nathan Lecture, presented at the University of Michigan, Ann Arbor.

Bylinski, G. (1995, February 6). Manufacturing for reuse. *Fortune,* pp. 102-112.

Cahill, L. B., & Kane, R. W. (1994). Environmental management in the 1990s: More than just compliance. *Total Quality Environmental Management, 3*(4), 409-420.

Callenbach, E., Capra, F., Goldman, L., Lutz, R., & Marburg, S. (1993). *EcoManagement: The Elmwood guide to sustainable business.* San Francisco: Berrett-Koehler.

Campbell, J., with Moyers, B. (1988). *The power of myth.* Garden City, NY: Doubleday.

Capra, F. (1975). *The tao of physics.* Boulder, CO: Shambhala.

Capra, F. (1982). *The turning point.* New York: Bantam.

Capra, F., & Steindl-Rast, D. (1991). *Belonging to the universe.* San Francisco: HarperCollins.

Carpenter, G. D. (1991). GEMI and the total quality journey to environmental excellence. In *Proceedings, Corporate Quality/Environmental Management: The First Conference* (pp. 2-3). Washington, DC: Global Environmental Management Initiative.

Carroll, A. B. (1995). Stakeholder thinking in three models of management morality: A perspective with strategic implications. In J. Nasi (Ed.), *Understanding stakeholder thinking* (pp. 47-74). Helsinki, Finland: LSR.

Carroll, G. (1991, February/March). Green for sale. *National Wildlife,* pp. 24-27.

Carson, P., & Moulden, J. (1991). *Green is gold.* Toronto: Harper Business.

Carson, R. (1962). *Silent spring.* Boston: Houghton Mifflin.

Carty, P. (1993, May). Standard sets environmental goals. *Accountancy,* pp. 40-41.

Cascio, J. (1994, June). A primer on global environmental management standards. *Environment Today,* pp. 42-43.

Chiras, D. D. (1991). *Environmental science: Action for a sustainable future.* Redwood City, CA: Benjamin Cummings.

Christensen, C., Andrews, K., Bower, J., Hamermesh, R., & Porter, M. (1987). *Business policy: Text and cases* (6th ed.). Homewood, IL: Richard D. Irwin.

Chynoweth, E., & Kirschner, E. (1993). Environmental standards provide competitive advantages. *Chemical Week, 152*(16), 46-52.

Clair, J., Milliman, J., & Mitroff, I. (1995). Clash or cooperation? Understanding environmental organizations and their relationship to business. In D. Collins

& M. Starik (Eds.), *Research in corporate social performance and policy, Supplement 1* (pp. 163-193). Greenwich, CT: JAI.

Clark, W. C. (1989, September). Managing planet Earth. *Scientific American*, pp. 47-54.

Clarkson, M. B. E. (1995). A stakeholder framework for analyzing and evaluating corporate social performance. *Academy of Management Review, 20*(1), 92-117.

Coalition for Environmentally Responsible Economies. (1990). *The 1990 CERES guide to the Valdez Principles*. Boston, MA: Author.

Cobb, J. (1995, April). *Can Whitehead make a contribution to management theory?* Paper presented at the Conference on the New Paradigm in Business, Center for Process Studies, Claremont School of Theology, Claremont, CA.

Coddington, W. (1993). *Environmental marketing*. New York: McGraw-Hill.

Cole, P., & Goldman, M. (1975). Occupations. In J. Fraumeni (Ed.), *Persons at high risk of cancer* (pp. 167-184). New York: Academic Press.

Collins, D. (1995). The complexity of fresh air: Summary of findings and recommendations. In D. Collins & M. Starik (Eds.), *Research in corporate social performance and policy, Supplement 1* (pp. 369-381). Greenwich, CT: JAI.

Collins, D., & Barkdull, J. (1995). Capitalism, environmentalism, and mediating structures: From Adam Smith to stakeholder panels. *Environmental Ethics, 17*, 227-244.

Commoner, B. (1990). *Making peace with the planet*. New York: Pantheon.

Conte, L. (1995, January/February). The question of sustainable development. *Nature Conservancy*, p. 14.

Cornish, D. (1993, June). Keynote address delivered at the annual conference of the Institute of Noetic Sciences, Washington, DC.

Corson, W. H. (1994). Global environmental issues and sustainable resource management. In R. V. Kolluru (Ed.), *Environmental strategies handbook* (pp. 923-970). New York: McGraw-Hill.

Costanza, R. (1989). What is ecological economics? *Ecological Economics, 1*, 1-7.

Costanza, R. (Ed.). (1991). *Ecological economics: The science and management of sustainability*. New York: Columbia University Press.

Costanza, R., Daly, H. E., & Bartholomew, J. A. (1991). Goals, agenda, and policy recommendations for ecological economics. In R. Costanza (Ed.), *Ecological economics: The science and management of sustainability* (pp. 1-20). New York: Columbia University Press.

Council on Economic Priorities. (1991). *The better world investment guide*. Englewood Cliffs, NJ: Prentice Hall.

Crosson, P. R., & Rosenberg, N. J. (1989, September). Strategies for agriculture. *Scientific American*, pp. 128-135.

Dadd, D. L., & Carothers, A. (1990, May/June). A bill of goods? Green consuming in perspective. *Greenpeace*, pp. 8-12.

Daly, H. E. (1977). *Steady state economics*. San Francisco: Freeman.

Daly, H. E. (1986). Toward a new economic model. *Bulletin of the Atomic Scientists, 42*(4), 42-44.

Daly, H. E. (1991a). Elements of environmental macroeconomics. In R. Costanza (Ed.), *Ecological economics: The science and management of sustainability* (pp. 32-46). New York: Columbia University Press.

248   MANAGEMENT FOR A SMALL PLANET

Daly, H. E. (1991b). *Steady-state economics* (2nd ed.). Washington, DC: Island Press.

Daly, H. E. (1993, November). The perils of free trade. *Scientific American,* pp. 50-57.

Daly, H. E. (1995, January/February). The question of sustainable development. *Nature Conservancy,* p. 14.

Daly, H. E., & Cobb, J. B., Jr. (1989). *For the common good.* Boston, MA: Beacon.

Daly, H. E., & Cobb, J. B., Jr. (1994). *For the common good* (2nd ed.). Boston, MA: Beacon.

Davis, G. R. (1990, September). Energy for planet Earth. *Scientific American,* pp. 55-62.

de Larderel, J. A. (1994). *Aspirations in the Third World and realities in the First: Professional ethics and the environment.* Paper presented at the Environmental Ethics in Business Conference, Georgetown University School of Business and the Center for International Business Education and Research, Washington, DC.

Denisi, A., Cafferty, T., & Meglino, B. (1984). A cognitive view of the performance appraisal process: A model and research proposition. *Organizational Behavior and Human Performance, 33,* 360-396.

Dillon, P. (1994). Implications of industrial ecology in firms. In B. R. Allenby & D. J. Richards (Eds.), *The greening of industrial ecosystems* (pp. 201-207). Washington, DC: National Academy Press.

Dillon, P., & Baram, M. (1993). Forces shaping the development and use of product stewardship in the private sector. In K. Fischer & J. Schot (Eds.), *Environmental strategies for industry* (pp. 329-341). Washington, DC: Island Press.

Dillon, P., & Fischer, K. (1992). *Environmental management in corporations: Methods and motivations.* Medford, MA: Tufts University, Center for Environmental Management.

Domini, A. L., & Kinder, P. D. (1986). *Ethical investing.* Reading, MA: Addison Wesley.

Donaldson, T., & Preston, L. (1995). The stakeholder theory of the corporation: Concepts, evidence, and implications. *Academy of Management Review, 20*(1), 65-91.

Douglis, C. (1993, Fall). Images of home. *Wilderness,* pp. 12-22.

Dowd, A. R. (1994, September 19). Environmentalists are on the run. *Fortune,* pp. 91-96.

Drobney, N. L. (1994, August). Strategic environmental management: Competitive solutions for the 21st century. *Cost Engineering,* pp. 18-23.

Drucker, P. (1980, Spring). Toward the next economics. In The crisis in economic theory [Special issue]. *The Public Interest,* pp. 4-18.

Drucker, P. (1989). *The new realities.* New York: Harper & Row.

Durning, A. (1992). *How much is enough?* New York: Norton.

Durning, A. (1994). Redesigning the forest economy. In *State of the world 1994* (pp. 22-40). New York: Norton.

Dutton, J. E. (1986). Understanding strategic agenda building and its implications for managing change. *Scandinavian Journal of Management Sciences, 3,* 3-24.

Dutton, J. E., & Dukerich, J. M. (1991). Keeping an eye on the mirror: Image and identity in organizational adaptation. *Academy of Management Journal, 34,* 517-554.

Dutton, J. E., & Jackson, S. E. (1987). Categorizing strategic issues: Links to organizational action. *Academy of Management Review, 12,* 79-90.

Easterbrook, G. (1989, July 24). Cleaning up. *Newsweek,* pp. 26-29, 32-42.

Ehrlich, P. R., & Ehrlich, A. H. (1990). *The population explosion.* New York: Simon & Schuster.

Ehrlich, P. R., Ehrlich, A. H., & Holdren, J. P. (1977). *Ecoscience.* San Francisco: Freeman.

Eisenhart, T. (1990, November). McRecycle USA: Golden arches offers marketers a golden payoff. *Business Marketing,* pp. 25, 28.

Elkington, J., Hailes, J., & Makower, J. (1988). *The green consumer.* New York: Penguin.

Elkins, P., Hillman, M., & Hutchinson, R. (1992). *Wealth beyond measure.* London: Gaia.

Emery, F. E., & Trist, E. L. (1965). The causal texture of organizational environments. *Human Relations, 18,* 21-32.

Emery, F. E., & Trist, E. L. (1973). *Towards a social ecology: Contextual appreciations of the future in the present.* New York: Plenum.

Entine, J. (1994). Shattered image. *Business Ethics, 8*(5), 23-28.

Epstein, S. S. (1975). *The politics of cancer.* San Francisco: Sierra Club Books.

Ernst, K. R., & Baginski, R. M. (1989/1990). Visioning: The key to effective strategic planning. In H. E. Glass (Ed.), *Handbook of business strategy.* Boston, MA: Warren, Gorham & Lamont.

Ettlie, J. (1994, August). Green manufacturing. In *Proceedings of the IFSAM.*

Etzioni, A. (1988). *The moral dimension: Toward a new economics.* New York: Free Press.

Etzioni, A. (1991). What community, what responsiveness? *The Responsive Community, 2*(1), 5-8.

Faltermayer, E. R. (1989, July 17). Air: How clean is clean enough? *Fortune,* pp. 54-56, 58, 60.

Feyerherm, A. E. (1995). Changing and converging mindsets of participants during collaborative, environmental rule making: Two negotiated regulation case studies. In D. Collins & M. Starik (Eds.), *Research in corporate social performance and policy, Supplement 1* (pp. 231-257). Greenwich, CT: JAI.

Finney, M., & Mitroff, I. (1986). Strategic plan failures: The organization as its own worst enemy. In H. Sims & D. A. Gioia (Eds.), *The thinking organization* (pp. 317-335). San Francisco, CA: Jossey-Bass.

Flavin, C. (1995a). Oil production up. In L. Brown, N. Lenssen, & H. Kane (Eds.), *Vital signs 1995* (pp. 46-47). New York: Norton.

Flavin, C. (1995b). Wind power soars. In L. Brown, N. Lenssen, & H. Kane (Eds.), *Vital signs 1995* (pp. 54-55). New York: Norton.

Frankel, J., & Coddington, W. (1994). Environmental marketing. In R. V. Kolluru (Ed.), *Environmental strategies handbook* (pp. 643-677). New York: McGraw-Hill.

Freeman, R. E. (1984). *Strategic management: A stakeholder approach.* Boston, MA: Pitman.

Freeman, R. E., & Gilbert, D. R., Jr. (1988). *Corporate strategy and the search for ethics.* Englewood Cliffs, NJ: Prentice Hall.

Frierman, J. (1991, June 3). The big muddle in green marketing. *Fortune,* pp. 91-101.

Frosch, R. A., & Gallopoulos, N. E. (1989, September). Strategies for manufacturing. *Scientific American*, pp. 144-152.

Galbraith, J., & Kazanjian, R. (1986). *Strategy implementation: Structure, systems, and process* (2nd ed.). St. Paul, MN: West.

Gardner, G. (1995). Water tables are falling. In L. Brown, N. Lenssen, & H. Kane (Eds.), *Vital signs 1995* (pp. 122-123). New York: Norton.

Georgescu-Roegen, N. (1971). *The entropy law and the economic process.* Cambridge, MA: Harvard University Press.

Gibbons, J. H., Blair, P. D., & Gwin, H. L. (1989, September). Strategies for energy use. *Scientific American*, pp. 136-143.

Gibney, J. S. (1989, May 1). Washington diarist. *New Republic*, p. 46.

Gioia, D. A. (1986). Conclusion: The state of the art in organizational social cognition. In H. Sims & D. A. Gioia (Eds.), *The thinking organization* (pp. 336-356). San Francisco: Jossey-Bass.

Gladwin, T. (1993). The meaning of greening: A plea for organizational theory. In K. Fischer & J. Schot (Eds.), *Environmental strategies for industry* (pp. 37-61). Washington, DC: Island Press.

Gladwin, T., Kennelly, J., & Krause, T-S. (1995). Shifting paradigms for sustainable development. *Academy of Management Review, 20*(4), 874-907.

Gladwin, T., Levin, S., & Ehrenfeld, J. (1994). *Research, development, and industrial testing of a sustainability impact assessment system.* Proposal made in cooperation with AT&T, Bristol-Myers Squibb, Digital Equipment Corporation, Merck & Company, and Philips Electronics to the National Science Foundation.

Global Environmental Management Initiative (GEMI). (1992). *Environmental self-assessment program.* Washington, DC: Author.

Global Environmental Management Initiative (GEMI). (1994). *Environmental reporting in a total quality management framework.* Washington, DC: Author.

Gold, J. (1990, January 23). The pioneers. *Financial World*, pp. 56-58.

Goodland, R. (1992). The case that the world has reached its limits. In R. Goodland, *Population, technology, and lifestyle.* Washington, DC: Island Press.

Goodpaster, K. E., & Matthews, J. B., Jr. (1982). Can a corporation have a conscience? *Harvard Business Review, 60*(1), 132-141.

Gore, A. (1992). *Earth in the balance: Ecology and the human spirit.* Boston: Houghton Mifflin.

Graedel, T. E., & Crutzen, P. J. (1989, September). The changing atmosphere. *Scientific American*, pp. 58-68.

Grammas, G. W. (1985). Quantitative tools for strategic decision making. In W. Guth (Ed.), *Handbook of business strategy.* Boston, MA: Warren, Gorham & Lamont.

Green Seal. (1990). *Background on the Green Seal.* Washington, DC: Author.

Greengard, S. (1990, November). Face values. *USAir Magazine*, pp. 88-97.

Greeno, J. L. (1994). Corporate environmental excellence and stewardship. In R. V. Kolluru (Ed.), *Environmental strategies handbook* (pp. 43-64). New York: McGraw-Hill.

Gutman, J. (1982). A means-end chain model based on consumer categorization processes. *Journal of Marketing, 46*, 60-72.

Halal, W. E. (1986). *The new capitalism.* New York: John Wiley.

Hambrick, D. C., & Brandon, G. L. (1987). Executive values. In D. C. Hambrick (Ed.), *The executive effect: Concepts and methods for studying top managers.* Greenwich, CT: JAI.

Hambrick, D., & Mason, P. (1984). Upper echelons: The organization as a reflection of its top managers. *Academy of Management Review, 9,* 193-206.

Hamel, G., & Prahalad, C. (1989, May/June). Strategic intent. *Harvard Business Review,* pp. 63-76.

Handy, C. (1989). *The age of unreason.* Boston, MA: Harvard Business School Press.

Hardin, G. (1968). The tragedy of the commons. *Science, 162,* 1243-1248.

Harman, W. (1988). *Global mind change: The promises of the last years of the twentieth century.* Indianapolis, IN: Knowledge Systems.

Harman, W. (1991). 21st century business: A background for dialogue. In J. Renesch (Ed.), *New traditions in business* (pp. 19-30). San Francisco: Sterling & Stone.

Harman, W. (1990-1991, Winter). Review essay: *A cognitive theory of consciousness* by Bernard Baars. *Noetic Sciences Review,* pp. 38-40.

Harrison, E. B. (1993). *Going green: Communicate your company's environmental commitment.* Homewood, IL: Business One Erwin.

Harrison, P. (1994, Winter). Sex and the single planet. *Amicus Journal,* pp. 16-21.

Hart, S. (1994). How green production might sustain the world. *Journal of the Northwest Environment, 10,* 4-14.

Hart, S. (1995). A natural resource-based view of the firm. *Academy of Management Review, 20*(4), 966-1014.

Hart, S. L., & Ahuja, G. (1994, August). *Does it pay to be green? An empirical examination of the relationship between pollution prevention and firm performance.* Paper presented to the Academy of Management, Dallas, TX.

Hawken, P. (1993a, September/October). A declaration of sustainability. *Utne Reader,* pp. 54-61.

Hawken, P. (1993b). *The ecology of commerce: A declaration of sustainability.* New York: Harper Business.

Hayes, D. (1990). Public initiatives: The power of the green consumer: Statement of D. Hayes, Chairman, U.S. Green Seal. In *Proceedings of the Business Week Symposium, The Environment: Corporate Stewardship and Business Opportunity in the Decade of Global Awakening* (pp. 16-19). New York: Journal Graphics.

Heilpern, J. D. (1990). Principles of total quality management. In *Summary of Total Quality Environmental Workshop* (p. 5-7). Washington, DC: Global Environmental Management Initiative.

Heilpern, J. D., & Limpert, T. M. (1991). Building organizations for continuous improvement. In *Proceedings, Corporate Quality/Environmental Management: The First Conference* (pp. 11-15). Washington, DC: Global Environmental Management Initiative.

Heisenberg, W. (1985a). Science and the beautiful. In K. Wilber (Ed.), *Quantum questions* (pp. 55-68). Boston, MA: New Science Library.

Heisenberg, W. (1985b). Scientific and religious truths. In K. Wilber (Ed.), *Quantum questions* (pp. 39-44). Boston, MA: New Science Library.

Henderson, H. (1991). *Paradigms in progress: Life beyond economics.* Indianapolis, IN: Learning Systems.

Henderson, H. (1992, June). Keynote address presented at the annual conference of the Institute of Noetic Sciences, Santa Clara, CA.

Henriques, I., & Sadorsky, P. (1995). The determinants of firms that formulate environmental plans. In D. Collins & M. Starik (Eds.), *Research in corporate social performance and policy, Supplement 1* (pp. 67-97). Greenwich, CT: JAI.

Hinrichsen, D. (1991, Spring). Economists' shining lie. *Amicus Journal*, pp. 3-5.

Hoe, S. (1978). *The man who gave his company away.* London: William Heinemann.

Hoffman, A. J. (1995). An uneasy rebirth at Love Canal. *Environment, 37*(2), 3-9, 25-31.

Holdren, J. P. (1990). Energy in transition. *Scientific American*, pp. 157-163.

Hosmer, L. T. (1994). Strategic planning as if ethics mattered. *Strategic Management Journal, 15*, 17-34.

Howard, J. A. (1977). *Consumer behavior: Application and theory.* New York: McGraw-Hill.

Howard, R. (1990, September/October). Values make the company: An interview with Robert Haas. *Harvard Business Review*, pp. 133-144.

Hrebiniak, L., & Joyce, W. (1984). *Implementing strategy.* New York: Macmillan.

Hull, R. (1990). European initiatives: Where is the EC heading? In *Proceedings of the Business Week Symposium, The Environment: Corporate Stewardship and Business Opportunity in the Decade of Global Awakening* (pp. 8-10). New York: Journal Graphics.

Husted, B. W. (1994, August). *The effect of trade on environmental regulation compliance: Evidence from the Mexican case.* Paper presented to the Academy of Management, Dallas, TX.

Ilgen, D., & Feldman, J. (1983). Performance appraisal: A process focus. *Research in Organizational Behavior, 5*, 141-197.

Investor Responsibility Research Center. (1992). *Corporate environmental profiles directory: Executive summary and findings.* Washington, DC: Author.

Investor Responsibility Research Center & Global Environmental Management Initiative. (1992). *Institutional investor needs for corporate environmental information.* Washington, DC: Author.

Johannson, L. (1994). The power of IT: How can information technology support TQEM? In J. Willig (Ed.), *Environmental TQM* (pp. 331-340). New York: McGraw-Hill.

Jolly, J., Reynolds, T., & Slocum, J. (1988). Application of the means-end theoretic for understanding the cognitive bases of performance appraisal. *Organizational Behavior and Human Decision Processes, 41*, 153-179.

Jones, L. R., & Baldwin, J. H. (1994). *Corporate environmental policy and government regulation.* Greenwich, CT: JAI.

Jones, T. M. (1995). Instrumental stakeholder theory: A synthesis of ethics and economics. *Academy of Management Review, 20*(2), 404-437.

Jorling, T. (1994, October). *Economic pressures on small and large businesses: The ecological balance sheet.* Paper presented at the Environmental Ethics in Business Conference, Georgetown University School of Business and the Center for International Business Education and Research, Washington, DC.

Joseph, L. E. (1990). *Gaia: The growth of an idea.* New York: St. Martin's.

Judge, W. Q., & Krishnan, H. (1994). An empirical investigation of the scope of a firm's enterprise strategy. *Business and Society, 33*(2), 167-190.

References   253

Kane, H. (1994). Sulfur and nitrogen emissions resume rise. In L. Brown, H. Kane, & D. Roodman (Eds.), *Vital signs 1994* (pp. 64-65). New York: Norton.

Kane, H. (1995). Sulfur and nitrogen emissions fall slightly. In L. Brown, N. Lenssen, & H. Kane (Eds.), *Vital signs 1995* (pp. 94-95). New York: Norton.

Kanter, D., & Mirvis, P. (1989). *The cynical Americans: Living and working in an age of discontent and disillusion.* San Francisco, CA: Jossey-Bass.

Kelly, M. (1993). *NAFTA's environmental side agreement: A review and analysis.* Unpublished manuscript prepared for the Texas Center for Policy Studies, Austin.

Kelly, T. (1991, April). GEMI: The superhero of environmental management. *Quality Progress,* pp. 26-28.

Kendall, H., & Pimentel, D. (1994). Constraints on the expansion of the global food supply. *Ambio, 23*(3), 198-205.

Kerr, J. (1985). Diversification strategies and managerial rewards: An empirical study. *Academy of Management Journal, 28*(1), 155-179.

Kerr, J., & Slocum, J. (1987). Managing corporate culture through reward systems. *Academy of Management Executive, 1*(2), 99-108.

Kiernan, M. J. (1992). The eco-industrial revolution: Reveille or requiem for international business. *Business and the Contemporary World, 4*(4), 133-143.

King, A. (1994, August). *Improved manufacturing resulting from learning-from-waste: Causes, importance, and enabling conditions.* Paper presented to the Academy of Management, Dallas, TX.

King, A. (1995). Avoiding ecological surprise: Lessons from long-standing communities. *Academy of Management Review, 20*(4), 961-985.

Kirchgeorg, M. (1994, July). *The environmental policy concept of the Closed Substance Cycle and Waste Management Act.* Unpublished manuscript, Institut für Marketing der Westfalischen Wilhelms-Universität Münster, Münster, Germany.

Kirchner, J. W. (1991). The Gaia hypotheses: Are they testable? Are they useful? In S. H. Schneider & P. J. Boston (Eds.), *Scientists on Gaia* (pp. 38-46). Cambridge: MIT Press.

Kirkpatrick, D. (1990, February 12). Environmentalism: The new crusade. *Fortune,* pp. 50-57.

Kleiner, A. (1991a, July/August). The three faces of Dow. *Garbage,* pp. 52-58.

Kleiner, A. (1991b, July/August). What does it mean to be green. *Harvard Business Review,* pp. 38-47.

Klimisch, R. (1994). Designing the modern automobile for recycling. In B. R. Allenby & D. J. Richards (Eds.), *The greening of industrial ecosystems* (pp. 165-170). Washington, DC: National Academy Press.

Kolluru, R. V. (1994). Risk assessment and management. In R. V. Kolluru (Ed.), *Environmental strategies handbook* (pp. 377-432). New York: McGraw-Hill.

Korzybski, A. (1933). *Science and sanity: An introduction to non-Aristotelian systems and general semantics.* Lakeville, CT: Institute of General Semantics.

Kotler, P. (1990). *Principles of marketing.* Englewood Cliffs, NJ: Prentice Hall.

Kuhn, T. (1962). *The structure of scientific revolutions.* Chicago: University of Chicago Press.

Kurschner, D. (1995). So who's paid the most at Ben and Jerry's. *Business Ethics, 9*(4), 45.

Langone, J. (1989, January 2). A stinking mess. *Time*, pp. 44-47.

Lawrence, A. T., & Morell, D. (1995). Leading-edge environmental management: Motivation, opportunity, resources, and processes. In D. Collins & M. Starik (Eds.), *Research in corporate social performance and policy, Supplement 1* (pp. 99-126). Greenwich, CT: JAI.

LeBlanc, C. (1991). *The nature of growth*. Washington, DC: National Audubon Society.

Ledgerwood, G., Street, E., & Therivel, R. (1992). *The environmental audit and business strategy*. London: Pitman.

Lemonick, M. (1989, January 2). Feeling the heat. *Time*, pp. 36-39.

Lenssen, N. (1995a). Nuclear waste still accumulating. In L. Brown, N. Lenssen, & H. Kane (Eds.), *Vital signs 1995* (pp. 88-89). New York: Norton.

Lenssen, N. (1995b). Solar cell shipments expand rapidly. In L. Brown, N. Lenssen, & H. Kane (Eds.), *Vital signs 1995* (pp. 56-57). New York: Norton.

Lent, T., & Wells, R. (1994). Corporate environmental management survey shows shift from compliance to strategy. In J. Willig (Ed.), *Environmental TQM* (pp. 7-32). New York: McGraw-Hill.

Leopold, A. (1949). *A Sand County almanac*. London: Oxford University Press.

Liedtka, J. M. (1989). Value congruence: The interplay of individual and organizational value systems. *Journal of Business Ethics, 8*, 805-815.

Linden, E. (1989, January 2). The death of birth. *Time*, pp. 32-35.

Linden, E. (1994, March 14). Burned by warming. *Time*, p. 79.

Linden, H. R. (1994). Energy and industrial ecology. In B. R. Allenby & D. J. Richards (Eds.), *The greening of industrial ecosystems* (pp. 38-60). Washington DC: National Academy Press.

Lober, D., & Eisen, M. (1995). The greening of retailing: Certification and the home improvement industry. *Journal of Forestry, 93*(4), 38-41.

Logsdon, J. M. (1985). Organizational responses to environmental issues: Oil refining companies and air pollution. In L. Preston (Ed.), *Research in corporate social performance and policy* (pp. 47-71). Greenwich, CT: JAI.

Lovelock, J. (1979). *Gaia: A new look at life on Earth*. London: Oxford University Press.

Lovelock, J. (1988). *The ages of Gaia*. New York: Bantam.

Lovelock, J. (1991). Geophysiology—The science of Gaia. In S. H. Schneider & P. J. Boston (Eds.), *Scientists on Gaia* (pp. 3-10). Cambridge: MIT Press.

Lovins, A. B. (1989, February). *Energy, people, and industrialization*. Paper presented to the Conference on Human Demography and Natural Resources, The Hoover Institution, Stanford University, Stanford, CA.

Lowe, V. (1990). Whitehead's philosophy as I see it. *Alfred North Whitehead: The man and his work: Volume 2. 1919-1947*. Baltimore, MD: Johns Hopkins Press.

Luthans, F., & Kreitner, R. (1985). *Organizational behavior modification and beyond: An operant and social learning approach*. Glenview, IL: Scott, Foresman.

MacKenzie, J. J., & ElAshry, M. T. (1989, April). Ill winds: Air pollution's toll on trees and crops. *Technology Review*, pp. 65-71.

Makower, J. (1993). *The e factor*. New York: Tilden.

Makower, J. (1995). Post-mortem for green consumerism. *Business Ethics, 9*(4), 52.

Margulis, L., & Hinkle, G. (1991). The biota and Gaia: 150 years of support for environmental sciences. In S. H. Schneider & P. J. Boston (Eds.), *Scientists on Gaia* (pp. 11-18). Cambridge: MIT Press.

Martz, L. (1990, May 21). Bonfire of the S&Ls. *Newsweek*, pp. 20-25.

Maslow, A. (1962). *Toward a psychology of being*. Princeton, NJ: Van Nostrand Reinhold.

Maurits la Riviere, J. W. (1989, September). Threats to the world's water. *Scientific American*, pp. 80-94.

Mazzocchi, T. (1990, July 7). *Economics and the work environment*. Paper presented at the Other Economic Summit, Houston, TX.

McClosky, J., Smith, D., & Graves, B. (1993). Exploring the green shell: Marketing implications of the environmental movement. In D. Smith (Ed.), *Business and the environment: Implications of the new environmentalism* (pp. 84-97). Liverpool, UK: Paul Chapman.

McNeill, J. (1989, September). Strategies for sustainable economic development. *Scientific American*, pp. 155-165.

McRobie, G. (1979). Preface. In E. F. Schumacher, *Good work* (pp. vii-xi). New York: Harper & Row.

Meadows, D. H., Meadows, D. L., & Randers, J. (1992). *Beyond the limits*. Post Mills, VT: Chelsea Green.

Meffert, H., & Kirchgeorg, M. (1994). *Market-oriented environmental management: Challenges and opportunities for green marketing* (Working paper No. 43). Münster, Germany: Institut für Marketing der Westfalischen Wilhelms-Universität Münster.

Meznar, M. B., Chrisman, J. J., & Carroll, A. B. (1990, August). *Social responsibility and strategic management: Toward an enterprise strategy classification*. Paper presented at the National Academy of Management meetings, San Francisco.

Milbrath, L. W. (1989). *Envisioning a sustainable society*. Albany: State University of New York Press.

Milbrath, L. W. (1990, July 7). *Redefining prosperity on the personal level*. Paper presented at the Other Economic Summit, Houston, TX.

Mintzberg, H., Raisinghani, M., & Theoret, A. (1976). The structure of unstructured decision processes. *Administrative Science Quarterly, 21*, 246-275.

Misch, A. (1994). Assessing environmental health risks. In *State of the world 1994* (pp. 117-136). New York: Norton.

Moberg, C. L., & Cohn, Z. A. (1991, May). Rene Jules Dubos. *Scientific American*, pp. 66-74.

Montaigne, M. de. (1958a). On the education of children. In M. de Montaigne, *Michel de Montaigne essays* (J. H. Cohen, Trans.) (pp. 60-65). Middlesex, UK: Penguin. (Original work published 1580)

Montaigne, M. de. (1958b). That one man's profit is another's loss. In M. de Montaigne, *Michel de Montaigne essays* (J. H. Cohen, Trans.) (pp. 48-53). Middlesex, UK: Penguin. (Original work published 1580)

Moore, M. E. M. (1995, April). *Institutional leadership and social transformation*. Paper presented at the Conference on the New Paradigm in Business, Center for Process Studies, Claremont School of Theology, Claremont, CA.

Morgan, G. (1986). *Images of organizations*. Beverly Hills, CA: Sage.

Morgan, G. (1993). *Imaginization*. Newbury Park, CA: Sage.

Mumford, L. (1956). *The transformation of man*. New York: Harper Brothers.

Murphy, P. (1994, March/April). Coming clean: The Department of Energy, the public, and the nation's nuclear waste mess. *The National Voter*, pp. 14-19.

Naess, A. (1973). The shallow and the deep, long range ecology movements: A summary. *Inquiry, 16,* 95-100.

Naess, A. (1985, May). *Intrinsic value: Will the defenders of Nature please rise.* Keynote address presented at the Second International Conference on Conservation Biology, University of Michigan, Ann Arbor, MI.

Nash, J., Nutt, K., Maxwell, J., & Ehrenfeld, J. (1994). Polaroid's environmental accounting and reporting system: Benefits and limitations of a TQEM measurement tool. In J. Willig (Ed.), *Environmental TQM* (pp. 217-234). New York: McGraw-Hill.

Noar, J. (1977). How to motivate corporate executives to implement long-range plans. *MSU Business Topics, 25*(3), 41-42.

North, K. (1992). *Environmental business management.* Geneva, Switzerland: International Labor Office.

North Sea victory over Shell. (1995, July/August/September). *Greenpeace,* p. 1.

Odum, H. T. (1983). *Systems ecology.* New York: John Wiley.

Odum, H. T., & Odum, E. C. (1976). *Energy basis for man and nature.* New York: McGraw-Hill.

Ornstein, R., & Ehrlich, P. (1989). *New world, new mind.* New York: Touchstone.

Ottman, J. A. (1992). *Green marketing.* Lincolnwood, IL: NTC Business Books.

Page, T. (1991). Sustainability and the problem of valuation. In R. Costanza (Ed.), *Ecological economics: The science and management of sustainability* (pp. 58-74). New York: Columbia University Press.

Peters, T. J., & Waterman, R. H., Jr. (1982). *In search of excellence.* New York: Harper & Row.

Peto, R. (1985). The preventability of cancer. In M. Vessey & M. Gray (Eds.), *Cancer risk and prevention* (pp. 1-14). Oxford, UK: Oxford University Press.

Petrick, J. A., & Quinn, J. F. (1994). Deforestation in Indonesia: Policy framework for sustainable development. *Journal of Asian Business, 10*(2), 41-56.

Pirsig, R. M. (1974). *Zen and the art of motorcycle maintenance: An inquiry into values.* New York: William Morrow.

Porter, M. E. (1985). *Competitive advantage.* New York: Free Press.

Porter, M. E. (1990). *The competitive advantage of nations.* New York: Free Press.

Porter, M. E. (1991, April). America's green strategy. *Scientific American,* p. 168.

Porter, M., & van der Linde, C. (1995). Green and competitive: Ending the stalemate. *Harvard Business Review, 73*(5), 120-134.

Portney, P. R. (1993). EPA and the evolution of federal regulation. In R. Dorfman & N. Dorfman (Eds.), *Economics of the environment* (pp. 57-73). New York: Norton.

Positive energy. (1991, March/April). *Sierra,* pp. 36-47.

Post, J. E. (1991, July/August). Managing as if the Earth mattered. *Business Horizons,* pp. 32-38.

Post, J. E. (1994). Environmental approaches and strategies: Regulation, markets, and management education. In R. V. Kolluru (Ed.), *Environmental strategies handbook* (pp. 11-30). New York: McGraw-Hill.

Post, J. E., & Altman, B. W. (1992). Models for corporate greening: How corporate social policy and organizational learning inform leading-edge environmental management. In J. Post (Ed.), *Research in corporate social policy and performance* (Vol. 13, pp. 3-29). Greenwich, CT: JAI.

Post, J. E., & Altman, B. W. (1994). Managing the environmental change process: Barriers and opportunities. *Journal of Organizational Change Management, 7*(4), 64-81.

Postel, S. (1990, September/October). Toward a new "eco"-nomics. *World Watch,* pp. 20-28.

Postel, S. (1993). Facing water scarcity. In *State of the world 1993* (pp. 22-41). New York: Norton.

Postel, S. (1994). Carrying capacity: Earth's bottom line. In *State of the world 1994,* (pp. 2-21). New York: Norton.

President's Council on Sustainable Development. (1995). *Public comment survey.* Washington, DC: Author.

Progress on ISO 14,000. (1994, July). *Environmental Manager,* pp. 6-8.

Quiring, J. (1995, April). *Balancing stakeholder claims: Applied process thought and old/new paradigm dualism in business.* Paper presented at the Conference on the New Paradigm in Business, Center for Process Studies, Claremont School of Theology, Claremont, CA.

Rauber, P. (1990, July/August). The stockbroker's smile. *Sierra,* pp. 18-21.

Ravlin, E. C., & Meglino, B. M. (1987). Effect of values on perception and decision making: A study of alternative work values measures. *Journal of Applied Psychology, 72*(4), 666-673.

Ray, M. L. (1991). The emerging new paradigm in business. In J. Renesch (Ed.), *New traditions in business* (pp. 33-45). San Francisco: Sterling & Stone.

Reinhardt, F., & Vietor, R. (1996). *Business management and the natural environment.* Cincinnati, OH: South-Western.

Research alert. (1991). *Future vision.* Naperville, IL: Sourcebooks Trade.

Reynolds, T., & Jamieson, L. (1984). Image representations: An analytical framework. In J. Jacoby & J. Olson (Eds.), *Perceived qualities of products, services, and stores* (pp. 115-138). Lexington, MA: Lexington Books.

Rice, F. (1990, December 3). How to deal with tougher customers. *Fortune,* pp. 38-48.

Richards, D. J., Allenby, B. R., & Frosch, R. A. (1994). The greening of industrial ecosystems: Overview and perspective. In B. R. Allenby & D. J. Richards (Eds.), *The greening of industrial ecosystems* (pp. 1-19). Washington, DC: National Academy Press.

Robertson, J. (1990). *Future wealth: A new economics for the 21st century.* New York: Bootstrap Press.

Roddick, A. (1995, August). Distinguished executive address delivered at the Academy of Management, Vancouver, British Columbia.

Rokeach, M. J. (1968). *Beliefs, attitudes, and values.* San Francisco, CA: Jossey-Bass.

Roodman, D. M. (1995a). Carbon emissions resume rise. In L. Brown, N. Lenssen, & H. Kane (Eds.), *Vital signs 1995* (pp. 66-67). New York: Norton.

Roodman, D. M. (1995b). Compact flourescents remain strong. In L. Brown, N. Lenssen, & H. Kane (Eds.), *Vital signs 1995* (pp. 58-59). New York: Norton.

Roodman, D. M. (1995c). Global temperatures rise again. In L. Brown, N. Lenssen, & H. Kane (Eds.), *Vital signs 1995* (pp. 64-65). New York: Norton.

Roper Organization. (1992). *Environmental behavior, North America: Canada, Mexico, United States* (Report commissioned by S. C. Johnson & Son). New York: Author.

Rosch, E., & Lloyd, B. (1978). *Cognition and categorization*. Hillsdale, NJ: Lawrence Erlbaum.

Rose, R. A. (1990, September/October). Environmental investing. *Garbage*, pp. 50-53.

Rosenberg, M. (1956). Cognitive structure and attitudinal effect. *Journal of Abnormal and Social Psychology, 53*, 367-372.

Rosenthal, S. B., & Buchholz, R. A. (in press). How pragmatism is an environmental ethic. In E. Katz & A. Light (Eds.), *Environmental pragmatism*. London: Routledge.

Roussey, R. (1992). Auditing environmental liabilities. *Auditing: A Journal of Practice and Theory, 11*(1), 47-57.

Ruckelshaus, W. D. (1991). Quality in the corporation: The key to sustainable development. In *Proceedings, Corporate Quality/Environmental Management: The First Conference* (pp. 5-9). Washington, DC: Global Environmental Management Initiative.

Ruether, R. R. (1992). *Gaia and God*. San Francisco: HarperCollins.

Ryan, J. C. (1992). Conserving biological diversity. In *State of the world 1992* (pp. 9-26). New York: Norton.

Ryan, M. (1994). CFC production continues to drop. In L. Brown, H. Kane, & D. Roodman (Eds.), *Vital signs 1994* (pp. 64-65). New York: Norton.

Ryan, M. (1995). CFC production plummeting. In L. Brown, N. Lenssen, & H. Kane (Eds.), *Vital signs 1995* (pp. 62-63). New York: Norton.

Sachs, A. (1995). Population growth steady. In L. Brown, N. Lenssen, & H. Kane (Eds.), *Vital signs 1995* (pp. 94-95). New York: Norton.

Sale, K. (1985). *Dwellers in the land*. San Francisco: Sierra Club Books.

Salter, M. S. (1973). Tailor incentive compensation to strategy. *Harvard Business Review, 51*(2), 94-102.

Sarney, G. (1990). Win-win strategies for business and environment in the world market. In *Proceedings of the Business Week Symposium, The Environment: Corporate Stewardship and Business Opportunity in the Decade of Global Awakening* (pp. 59-60). New York: Journal Graphics.

Schein, E. H. (1985). *Organizational culture and leadership*. San Francisco: Jossey-Bass.

Schendel, D., & Hofer, C. (1979). Introduction. In D. Schendel & C. Hofer (Eds.), *Strategic management: A new view of business policy and planning* (pp. 1-22). Boston: Little, Brown.

Schmidheiny, S. (1992). *Changing course: A global business perspective on development and the environment*. Cambridge: MIT Press.

Schneider, S. H. (1989, September). The changing climate. *Scientific American*, pp. 70-79.

Schorsch, J. (1990, April). It's not easy being green: Can our economy come clean? *CEP research report* (pp. 1-5). New York: Council on Economic Priorities.

Schot, J., & Fischer, K. (1993). Conclusion: Research needs and policy implications. In K. Fischer & J. Schot (Eds.), *Environmental strategies for industry* (pp. 369-373). Washington, DC: Island Press.

Schumacher, E. F. (1973). *Small is beautiful: Economics as if people mattered*. New York: Harper & Row.

Schumacher, E. F. (1977). *A guide for the perplexed*. New York: Harper & Row.

Schumacher, E. F. (1979). *Good work*. New York: Harper & Row.

Schwartz, J., Springen, K., & Hager, M. (1990, November). It's not easy to be green. *Newsweek*, pp. 51-52.

Schwartz, P. (1991). *The art of the long view*. Garden City, NY: Doubleday/Currency.

Schwenk, C. R. (1984). Cognitive simplification processes in strategic decision-making. *Strategic Management Journal, 5*, 111-128.

Schwenk, C. R. (1988). *The essence of strategic decision making*. Lexington, MA: Lexington Books.

Scott, M. (1995). Inactive CERES endorsers may be sent packing. *Business Ethics, 9*(4), 13.

Sekutowski, J. (1994). Greening the telephone: A case study. In B. R. Allenby & D. J. Richards (Eds.), *The greening of industrial ecosystems* (pp. 171-177). Washington, DC: National Academy Press.

Selcraig, B. (1994, May/June). Border patrol. *Sierra*, pp. 58-64, 79-81.

Seligman, D. (1995, June 12). Keeping up: A wooden stake. *Fortune*, p. 143.

Senge, P. M. (1990). *The fifth discipline: The art and practice of the learning organization*. Garden City, NY: Doubleday/Currency.

Seventh Generation, Inc. (1991, Spring). *Seventh Generation catalog*. Colchester, VT: Author.

Sheldrake, R. (1991). *The greening of science and God*. New York: Bantam.

Shetty, Y. (1994). A point of view: Seven principles of quality leaders. In J. Willig (Ed.), *Environmental TQM* (pp. 43-49). New York: McGraw-Hill.

Shrivastava, P. (1992). Corporate self-greenewal: Strategic responses to environmentalism. *Business Strategy and the Environment, 1*(3), 9-21.

Shrivastava, P. (1994). CASTRATED environment: Greening organizational studies. *Organization Studies, 15*(5), 705-726.

Shrivastava, P. (1995a). Ecocentric management in industrial ecosystems: Management paradigm for a risk society. *Academy of Management Review, 20*(1), 118-137.

Shrivastava, P. (1995b). The role of corporations in achieving ecological sustainability. *Academy of Management Review, 20*(4), 936-960.

Shrivastava, P. (1996). *Greening business*. Cincinnati, OH: Thompson Executive Press.

Spedding, L., Jones, D., & Dering, C. (1993). *Eco-management and eco-auditing: Environmental issues in business*. London: Chancery Law Publishing.

Spretnak, C., & Capra, F. (1986). *Green politics*. Santa Fe, NM: Bear.

Starik, M. (1990). *Stakeholder management and firm performance: Reputational and financial relationships to U.S. electric utility consumer-related strategies*. Unpublished doctoral dissertation, University of Georgia.

Starik, M. (1995). Should trees have managerial standing? Toward stakeholder status for non-human nature. *Journal of Business Ethics, 14*, 207-217.

Starik, M., & Rands, G. (1995). Weaving an integrated web: Multilevel and multisystem perspectives of ecologically sustainable organizations. *Academy of Management Review, 20*(4), 908-935.

Stead, J. G., & Stead, W. E. (1986). Cancer prevention for the American worker: A never ending saga. *International Journal of Management, 3*(1), 41-49.

Stead, W. E., & Stead, J. G. (1980). Cancer in the workplace: A neglected problem. *Personnel Journal, 59*(10), 847-849.

Stead, W. E., & Stead, J. G. (1994a). Can humankind change the economic myth? Paradigm shifts necessary for ecologically sustainable business. *Journal of Organizational Change Management, 7*(4), 15-31.

Stead, W. E., & Stead, J. G. (1994b). Strategic decisions and not-so-natural disasters: Understanding the way in and the way out. *Organization, 1*(2), 369-373.

Stead, W. E., & Stead, J. G. (1995). An empirical investigation of sustainability strategy implementation in industrial organizations. In D. Collins & M. Starik (Eds.), *Research in corporate social performance and policy, Supplement 1* (pp. 43-66). Greenwich, CT: JAI.

Stead, W. E., Stead, J. G., Wilcox, A. S., & Zimmerer, T. W. (1994). An empirical investigation of industrial organizational efforts to institutionalize environmental performance. In *Proceedings, International Association of Business and Society*. Hilton Head, SC: International Association of Business and Society.

Steer, A., & Wade-Gery, W. (1994). Environmental strategies for the developing world. In R. V. Kolluru (Ed.), *Environmental strategies handbook* (pp. 851-904). New York: McGraw-Hill.

Steiner, G., Miner, J., & Gray, E. (1986). *Management policy and strategy: Text, readings, and cases* (3rd ed). New York: Macmillan.

Stipp, D. (1991a, February 28). Life-cycle analysis measures greenness, but results may not be black and white. *Wall Street Journal*, p. B1.

Stipp, D. (1991b, March 14). Lunch-box staple runs afoul of activists. *Wall Street Journal*, p. B1, B8.

Stonich, P. J. (1981). Using rewards in implementing strategy. *Strategic Management Journal*, pp. 345-348.

Stratton, B. (1991, April). Going beyond pollution control. *Quality Progress*, pp. 18-20.

Sturdivant, F. D., Ginter, J. L., & Sawyer, A. G. (1985). Managers' conservatism and corporate performance. *Strategic Management Journal, 6*, 17-38.

Sullivan, M., & Ehrenfeld, J. (1994). Reducing life-cycle environmental impacts: An industry survey of emerging tools and programs. In J. Willig (Ed.), *Environmental TQM* (pp. 43-49). New York: McGraw-Hill.

Surma, J., & Petracca, D. (1993, First Quarter). Accounting for environmental costs: What's happening in practice. *Journal of Environmental Leadership*, pp. 143-152.

Swanson, G. M. (1988). Cancer prevention in the workplace and natural environment: A review of etiology, research design, and methods of risk reduction. *Cancer, 62*(8 Suppl.), 1725-1746.

Taylor, R. J. (1994, April 18). Pollution liability climbs the corporate ladder. *National Underwriter*, pp. 10, 50.

Teets, R. W., Kuhnke, D. B., Bradley, D. B., & Bridegan, G. (1994). Applying the risk management process to environmental management. *Risk Management, 41*(2), 18-24.

Templeman, J. (1995, September 18). The Green who would be Germany's kingmaker. *Business Week*, p. 70.

Thompson, D. (1995, February 27). Congressional chain-saw massacre. *Time*, pp. 58-60.

Throop, G., Starik, M., & Rands, G. (1993). Sustainable strategy in a greening world: Integrating the natural environment into strategic management. *Advances in Strategic Management, 9*, 63-92.

Tobias, M. (1990). *Voice of the planet.* New York: Bantam.

Todd, R. (1994). Zero-loss accounting systems. In B. R. Allenby & D. J. Richards (Eds.), *The greening of industrial ecosystems* (pp. 191-200). Washington, DC: National Academy Press.

Toufexis, A. (1989, January 2). Too many mouths. *Time,* pp. 48-50.

Turcotte, M-F. (1995). Conflict and collaboration: The interfaces between environmental organizations and business firms. In D. Collins & M. Starik (Eds.), *Research in corporate social performance and policy, Supplement 1* (pp. 195-229). Greenwich, CT: JAI.

Turner, T. (1991, April). A tale of two birds: Courts move decisively to protect ancient forests. *In Brief* (publication of the Sierra Club Legal Defense Fund), pp. 1-4.

Twenty-sixth environmental quality index. (1994, February/March). *National Wildlife,* pp. 40-41.

United Nations. (1994, September 19). *Programme of action of the United Nations International Conference on Population and Development.* Cairo, Egypt: Author.

United Nations Population Fund. (1994). *The state of the world population 1994.* New York: Author.

United States v. Dean 969 F.2d 187 (6th Circuit 1992), cert. denied, 113 S.Ct. 1852 (1993).

United States v. Hoflin, 880 f.2d 1033 (9th Circuit 1989), cert. denied, 493 U.S. 1083, 110 S.Ct. 1143 (1990).

Urmson, J., & Ree, J. (1989). Whitehead. In *The concise encyclopedia of Western philosophy and philosophers.* Boston: Unwin Hyman.

Van Gigch, J. P. (1978). *Applied general system theory.* New York: Harper & Row.

Vital signs. (1991, May/June). *WorldWatch,* p. 6.

Wachtel, P. L. (1989). *The poverty of affluence.* Philadelphia: New Society.

Wade, B. (1992). Losses mount as owners seek allies in battle to clean up. *Corporate Cashflow, 13*(2), 20-22.

Walley, N., & Whitehead, B. (1994). It's not easy being green. *Harvard Business Review, 72*(3), 46-52.

Walsh, J. P., & Ungson, G. R. (1991). Organizational memory. *Academy of Management Review, 16*(1), 57-91.

Weber, P. (1990, July/August). Green seals of approval heading to market. *World Watch,* pp. 7-8.

Weber, P. (1994). Safeguarding oceans. *State of the world 1994* (pp. 41-60). New York: Norton.

Weick, K., & Bougon, M. (1986). Organizations as cognitive maps. In H. Sims & D. A. Gioia (Eds.), *The thinking organization* (pp. 102-133). San Francisco: Jossey-Bass.

Weinberg, C. J., & Williams, R. H. (1990, September). Energy from the sun. *Scientific American,* pp. 147-155.

Weiner, J. (1990). *The next hundred years: Shaping the fate of our planet.* New York: Bantam.

Welford, R., & Gouldson, A. (1993). *Environmental management and business strategy.* London: Pitman.

Westley, F., & Vredenburg, H. (1991). Strategic bridging: The collaboration between environmentalists and business in the marketing of green products. *Journal of Applied Behavioral Science, 27*(1), 65-90.

Wheatley, M. J. (1992). *Leadership and the new science: Learning about organization from an orderly universe*. San Francisco: Berrett-Koehler.

Wheelwright, P. (1935). *Aristotle*. New York: Odyssey.

White, M. (1995). The performance of environmental mutual funds in the United States and Germany: Is there economic hope for green investors? In D. Collins & M. Starik (Eds.), *Research in corporate social performance and policy, Supplement 1* (pp. 323-344). Greenwich, CT: JAI.

Whitehead, A. N. (1925). *Science and the modern world*. New York: Macmillan.

Wilber, K. (1985). *Quantum questions*. Boston: New Science Library.

Wilken, E. (1995). Soil erosion's toll continues. In L. Brown, N. Lenssen, & H. Kane (Eds.), *Vital signs 1995* (pp. 118-119). New York: Norton.

Williams, C. C. (1995, July 2). Recycling beginning to drive solid waste profits. *Birmingham News*, pp. 1D, 3D.

Williams, H. E., Medhurst, J., & Drew, K. (1993). Corporate strategies for a sustainable future. In K. Fischer & J. Schot (Eds.), *Environmental strategies for industry* (pp. 117-146). Washington, DC: Island Press.

Williams, R. M. (1960). *American society: A sociological interpretation* (2nd ed.). New York: Knopf.

Willig, J. (Ed.). (1994). *Environmental TQM*. New York: McGraw-Hill.

Wilson, E. O. (1989, September). Threats to biodiversity. *Scientific American*, pp. 108-116.

Wilson, R. (1991). *Environmental risk: Identification and management*. Chelsea, MI: Lewis.

Winn, M. (1995). Corporate leadership and policies for the natural environment. In D. Collins & M. Starik (Eds.), *Research in corporate social performance and policy, Supplement 1* (pp. 127-161). Greenwich, CT: JAI.

Wood, B. (1984). *E. F. Schumacher: His life and thought*. New York: Harper & Row.

Woodruff, D., Peterson, T., & Lowery, K. (1991, April 8). The greening of Detroit. *Business Week*, pp. 54-60.

Woodward, J. (1965). *Industrial organization theory and practice*. Oxford, UK: Oxford University Press.

World Commission on Environment and Development. (1987). *Our common future*. Oxford, UK: Oxford University Press.

Yankelovich, D. (1981). *New rules*. New York: Random House.

Young, J. Y. (1991, May/June). Tossing the throwaway habit. *WorldWatch*, pp. 26-33.

Youth, H. (1994). Birds are in decline. In L. Brown, H. Kane, & D. Roodman (Eds.), *Vital signs 1994* (pp. 128-129). New York: Norton.

Zenisek, T. J. (1979). Corporate social responsibility: A conceptualization based on organizational literature. *Academy of Management Review, 4*(2), 359-368.

Name Index

Subject Index

About the Authors

W. Edward Stead and **Jean Garner Stead** are both Professors of Management at East Tennessee State University, where they have served on the faculty since 1982. Ed earned his B.S. (1968) and M.B.A. (1972) from Auburn University, and he earned his Ph.D. in Management from Louisiana State University, Baton Rouge, in 1976. Jean earned her B.S. (1971) and M.A. (1973) from Auburn University, her M.B.A. (1979) from Western Illinois University, and she earned her Ph.D. in Business Administration from Louisiana State University, Baton Rouge in 1983. Prior to joining the faculty of East Tennessee State University, Ed served on the faculties of the University of Alabama in Birmingham and Louisiana State University, and both Ed and Jean served on the faculty at Western Illinois University.

Ed and Jean have been involved in research on various aspects of the relationship between business and the natural environment for over 15 years, focusing on topics such as cancer in the workplace, the moral implications of cost-benefit analysis, ethical behavior in organizations, managing ecological change in organizations, and implementing sustainability strategies in industrial organizations. The first edition of *Management for a Small Planet* was recognized by *Choice* magazine as one of the Outstanding Academic Books for 1992. Jean Stead received the 1995 East Tennessee State University Outstanding Teacher Award, and Ed Stead was elected as the 1996 Program Chair for the Organizations and the Natural Environment (ONE) Interest Group of the American Academy of Management.

282